MW00526579

ACHIEVING THE
IMPOSSIBLE

The Remarkable Story
of Greece's
EURO 2004 Victory

ACHIEVING THE
IMPOSSIBLE

The Remarkable Story
of Greece's
EURO 2004 Victory

GEORGE TSITSONIS

FAIRPLAY
PUBLISHING

First published in 2020 by Fair Play Publishing
PO Box 4101, Balgowlah Heights NSW 2093 Australia

www.fairplaypublishing.com.au
sales@fairplaypublishing.com.au

ISBN: 978-1-925914-08-5
ISBN: 978-1-925914-09-2 (ePub)

© George Tsitsonis 2020
The moral rights of the author have been asserted.

All rights reserved. Except as permitted under the Australian Copyright Act 1968
(for example, a fair dealing for the purposes of study, research, criticism or review),
no part of this book may be reproduced, stored in a retrieval system,
communicated or transmitted in any form or by any means without prior
written permission from the Publisher.

Design and typesetting by Leslie Priestley

Front cover image: Ben Radford, Getty Images
UEFA European Championship trophy image: Ajith Kumar
All other images via Alamy.

All inquiries should be made to the Publisher via sales@fairplaypublishing.com.au

NATIONAL
LIBRARY
OF AUSTRALIA

A catalogue record of this book is available from the National Library of Australia.

Dedication

To Sheila, Mariella and Elias. My loves.
I hope this book is always a reminder
that truly nothing is impossible.
Prepare well, work hard, be happy,
and live life chasing your dreams.

Contents

Prologue

I had attended Greece's opening match against Argentina at the 1994 FIFA World Cup with my father. I was a bright-eyed and bushy-tailed 14-year-old who had charted for months how Greece could advance to the knockout rounds in that tournament. There was no limit to my optimism or for that matter my football naiveté. My dad was different. As with so many Greek immigrants, he had experienced too much of life and seen too much in football to believe that success comes so easy. In the lead-up to the match however, I could sense a shift in his attitude.

For a brief few days, he had taken a bite of that forbidden fruit that so many football fans find so hard to avoid: hope. This rare foray of his into the belief that something potentially positive was on the verge of happening was refreshing for me. It was no longer talk of how our team would lose and lose badly as was his traditional way. Instead, his tone had changed. Hope had taken a hold of him and led him down the path of expectation. It's so easy to be enticed by the aspiration that your team can do it. That they can be the ones who achieve something special, something great. And maybe, just maybe, you will be there with a chance to cheer them on and be a part of history. For once, we were united in our feeling that something great could indeed happen.

Everything in the lead-up to the opening whistle was just magical for me. The colors, the flags and banners, the Argentines giving us smack, the Greek fans returning it, above all perhaps, the adrenaline-inducing feeling of the noise. The inevitable downpour that had been threatening the entire day could not in any way dampen my spirits and dare I say his. My dad was about as giddy as could be, his pride visible in the way he belted out the Greek national anthem.

You could tell how much it meant to him that the first game we would ever go to together was Greece's first-ever World Cup match.

Argentina scored barely two minutes in. Though disappointed, I was naive enough to think there was plenty of time to come back. I'll never forget looking at my dad's face. To him the game had finished. He was undoubtedly angry at himself for being duped into thinking that we had a chance against Argentina. His frustration was clear to see and the negativity that was restored lasted more than just the 90 minutes of the eventual 4-0 defeat. Though I was crushed that we had tickets to go to Greece's final group stage match against Nigeria my dad decided we would skip it.

For the next ten years, I too began a deep slide into sporting pessimism. Every time there looked to be an opening for Greece to qualify for a major tournament, something bad would happen. In the pre-Internet days, Greeks across the diaspora had to be quite creative to find results of the national team or clubs. My preferred way was to call the scores hotline of the biggest Greek newspaper in the United States, Ethnikos Kirikas (The National Herald). On one occasion when I inquired about the result of a home qualifier against Russia, the delightful woman on the phone said, "Unfortunately, I am going to upset you. Greece lost 3-0." To which I duly replied, "It's not the first time you have upset me and probably not the last." As the Internet came and satellite television became more prevalent, nothing really changed, the bad news just got to me faster. I was preparing myself for a long life of football heartache.

Not I, my dad or anyone else would have known that when Giorgos Karagounis' shot found the back of the net against Portugal in the Euro 2004 opener, it would be the start of the most remarkable three weeks in modern Greece's sporting history. The stunning triumph at the European Championship that summer, that magical 'Greek summer' when Athens also hosted the Olympics in the pre-crisis period for the nation, was an athletic success celebrated like no other in the country's past. It brought about a stirring show of patriotism and pride by the nation's 11 million people and those of Greek heritage everywhere. Not since the end of World War II had there been so many Greek flags hanging outside of homes and businesses.

The disappointments of the past made the shock of EURO 2004 that much greater and the taste of success that much sweeter. Millions of football-mad Greeks across the globe were finally able to experience the feeling of celebrating a championship. It was a remarkable journey that still feels like a dream. This book is the story of the team that took us on that journey. The process, the details, the individuals, and the moments that combined to create a wsporting miracle.

Above all, this is a book that emphasizes the importance of hope. With the right attitude, preparation, planning, and belief along with a dash of good fortune, anything is attainable, even achieving the impossible. If the Greek national team could do it, so can your team, so can you. Greece's de facto motto during Euro 2004 was Adidas' slogan for the tournament, 'Impossible is Nothing'. What follows is the story of a team that defied logic and one that managed to prove that indeed 'Impossible is Nothing'. Those are words we would all do well to live by.

George Tsitsonis
New Hampshire, USA

Chapter 1

History Of The Ethniki

In order to understand how big an accomplishment Greece's Euro 2004 triumph was, it is important to take a look back at the history of football in Greece and the National team. Commonly known as the *'Ethniki'* (literally translated as 'the National'), Greece had been a team that flattered to deceive more often than not in its pre-2004 history. The country has consistently been able to produce talented players throughout its football history. Names such as Mimis Domazos, Mimis Papaioannou, Giorgos Sideris, Antonis Antoniadis, Giorgos Dedes, Giorgos Delekaris, Kostas Nestoridis, Vasilis Chatzipanagis, Nikos Anastopoulos, Thomas Mavros, Dimitris Saravakos, and Vasilis Karapialis may not be well-known outside the country, but within Greece these players are legends. And if those individuals had begun playing in the last quarter century, when the borders throughout Europe have opened up for Greek players, then surely all would have been candidates for playing abroad.

Despite possessing quality individual talent, the national team's history was marked by failure after frustrating failure at the team level. Positive results against big nations are there to see, however inconsistency dogged the history of the Ethniki. The reasons for this varied. Greek football's initial lack of funding and professionalism and later on disorganisation and club disputes were the primary factors in the national team's lack of success in the post-World War II era.

Sotirios Triantafyllou is a renowned sports journalist and one of the most respected authorities on Greek football. He believes that while Greece has never had trouble producing talented players, external factors have always kept Greek football, in particular, the national team from finding real success.

"Talent has always been there and continues to be in Greek football.

That can be seen furthermore from the youth national teams and their successes over the years," states Triantafyllou. "That talent has never been fully utilised mainly due to the lack of a long-term plan as well as the relatively low level of the Greek football league, when compared to other European leagues."

The first hard evidence of football landing on Greek shores came in 1895. It was then when a British-Greek, Apostolos Vlastos, brought with him to Greece a notebook that held in it the rules of association football. Vlastos was one of the early leading figures in developing the game in Greece. Three years later, another early supporter of the sport, Ioannis Christafis, completed the job that Vlastos began by translating the rules of the game fully into Greek.

The first signs of football played in Greece could be found in the late 1800s in games played in the port cities of Piraeus and Thessaloniki. Some local accounts suggest the first time football was played in Greece occurred in Corfu in 1866, when British naval officers had a kick about in the village square. This followed the consistent story around Europe and the world that had British sailors setting up matches that attracted the interest of locals. Media reports from the time suggested that Greeks did not participate in these matches in many cases due to the 'serious risk of injury.' Newspapers characterised the sport as a 'strange phenomenon' and a 'unique spectacle.'

In any case, football began to be slowly accepted by Greeks as their exposure to it grew. The matches between the British serviceman and foreign visitors became more frequent as the new century approached with more and more Greeks taking part.

The end of the 1870s saw Greece have its first athletics clubs established. Up until then there was not a focus on sport in the everyday lives of people in the country. This was especially true with regard to football, which was initially considered a violent activity.

British pressure led to football being included in the list of events for the 1896 Olympic Games in Athens. There are records of matches being played during the first Modern Games, but all were unofficial in nature. The matches that were contested seemed to take on a sort of test-event guise.

Greeks who came to Athens from Constantinople in the aftermath of the 1896 Olympics gave a fresh dose of momentum to the growth of the game. With their command of the Greek language and the cosmopolitan style and allure they exuded, these individuals had an influence on growing local interest in the game as they played it. Further acceptance by locals during that period was also fostered by showcase football matches put on by visitors from foreign colleges.

In 1897, the Hellenic Amateur Athletic Association (SEGAS) was born. Two years later, SEGAS decided on creating an arm dedicated to the development of football. In the years to follow, the organisation held matches in Greece, keeping records of the games played, and bringing increased exposure of the sport to people in the country's bigger cities.

Interest in the game exploded with the coming of the 20th century. Even the early pioneers of the sport in Greece were shocked as to how quickly the country took to football. The influence of Greeks living or travelling abroad cannot be overstated during this era. Students returning from studies in England and other European countries brought back with them a true love of the game. High-profile Greeks living abroad hoping to help with the development and modernizing of their home country came back to Greece and one of their imports was football.

Panagiotis Vrionis was one of the most important figures in moving the game forward in Greece in the early 1900s. Born in Switzerland, Vrionis grew up in Geneva and was an accomplished player for Swiss club Servette. When he moved to Greece in 1903, he brought with him balls, cleats, and uniforms, hoping to spark an interest in the game amongst locals. In previous trips to Athens, Vrionis had noticed the passion that youngsters, in particular, were showing in football. He lamented the lack of proper equipment, however, and took action to address that matter.

1906 was a seminal year in the history of the sport in Greece. A team representing the country took part in the 1906 Intercalated Games in Athens, a sort of intermediate Olympics competition in the middle of the usual four-year cycle. Four teams featured in the football tournament of those 1906 Games. The participants included Denmark, two teams representing the Ottoman Empire, and a Greek team comprised of players from Athens, specifically from the two clubs of Ethnikos and Panellinios.

Against an Ottoman Empire side (made up of players from Smyrna along with foreign players from England and France) on April 23rd 1906, a team representing Greece played for the first time and defeated their opponents 6-0.

The next day, in what was effectively the final of the competition, Greece faced off against Denmark. The previous day's match proved to be a false dawn. Greek football was still in its infancy and the vast difference in quality and experience against the Danes was clear. Greece eventually lost 9-0. In fact, that was only the halftime score, but the Greek players, so embarrassed by the size of the deficit, decided not to take the pitch for the second half.

Also, in 1906, the first Greek national championship was played with Ethnikos defeating the likes of Peirikos and Panellinios. In the same year, the game was finally allowed to be played in schools and universities across the country. This had a massive effect on football's popularity. The game now spread across the entire nation, no longer confined to only Athens and Thessaloniki.

In the years that followed, the football boom continued, however war slowed the game's development and popularity, specifically the Balkan Wars and World War I. As the conflicts passed, the thirst for football could simply not be quenched.

A form of the Greek national team began participating unofficially in some tournaments. In Paris in 1919, a Greek side suffered heavy defeats to Italy (4-0) and France (11-0), before defeating Yugoslavia (5-1) and Romania (3-2) in an international tournament. The national team's first official match is considered by many to be at the 1920 Olympic Games (a 9-0 defeat to Sweden on 29 August 1920), but since the Hellenic Football Federation (EPO) was not yet created, the team's first official match in the history books took place in 1929. That match was played on 7 April at the Leoforos Alexandras Stadium, a ground that remains the oldest active stadium in Greece. The team was coached by Apostolos Nikolaidis, for whom the stadium would later be renamed, and subsequently lost to an Italy 'B' side, 4-1. Three months later came the national team's first away match, a 1-1 draw in Bulgaria.

The creation of a national federation occurred toward the end of 1926. It became apparent that SEGAS could not fully organize, develop, and promote the sport on its own, such was the interest football was generating. The EPO came into being, but difficulties remained. Clubs and newly formed football associations still struggled with organization. The main issues of the time had to do with a lack of funds for equipment and little football infrastructure.

The EPO succeeded in providing more organization and oversight as the 1930s came. That decade saw increased participation in football and culturally the game's importance had dramatically evolved. Football was now the preeminent sport in the country.

The first FIFA World Cup in 1930 was open to all teams who could pay to make the trip to Uruguay. There was no such luck for Greece as the EPO was in nowhere near a position to possess the funds to make that dream a reality.

Instead, the organization tried to participate in competitions closer to home such as the Balkan Cups, which for a while were the national team's only real opportunity for international matches and experience.

The Ethniki did participate in the 1934 and 1938 World Cup Qualifiers. Unfortunately, the team was paired with some of the giants of the time. In the '34 qualifiers, Italy swept aside the Greeks 4-0 in the first leg encounter. The Italians then offered the EPO money in order to skip the second leg back in Greece, which was duly accepted by the governing body as they saw no way for Greece to come back. It was a shameful moment in the history of Greek football. Legend has it that Italian dictator Benito Mussolini had agreed to the construction of a building that the EPO could use in Greece. Four years later there was more honor, but more misery in the scoreline as Hungary inflicted on Greece an 11-1 destruction, a result that remains the country's biggest-ever defeat.

War took hold in Europe shortly thereafter and like virtually everywhere else on the continent, the focus shifted to fighting and survival. Greece's denial of Axis use of military bases saw themselves thrust into World War II in October 1940. After shockingly pushing back Italian forces into Albania when Mussolini ordered the invasion of the country, the Germans overran Greek forces and occupied the country. The eventual Allied victory in 1945 did not, however, mean the fighting was over for Greece, as the country was plunged into a Civil War immediately following.

The Ethniki got back onto the pitch in 1948. Two friendly defeats by Turkey were a dent to national pride, which could have used a boost after the nation suffered through two consecutive wars. In a clear example of how poor the footballing infrastructure was in Greece, the players complained after the away defeat to Turkey citing their difficulty in playing on a grass pitch. Such were the state of football fields in Greece that very few players had ever played on grass, instead they had grown accustomed to dirt pitches.

The post-World War II era was a tremendously tough time to be a national team player in Greece. All the footballers selected for the national team were amateurs who had other jobs. That meant selection for the Ethniki forced players to be gone away from their homes and jobs for many days at a time.

The severity of these problems was highlighted in a 1953 incident on the eve of a World Cup qualifier against Israel. The players reportedly went to the EPO offices threatening to strike, demanding more money. That was the story the federation peddled, while the players insisted that they merely wanted to get away from officials who were closely watching them at the team hotel. A strike was eventually avoided, but in the aftermath the players involved were given life bans for bringing the national team into disrepute. A year later, with emotions having considerably cooled, the ban was rescinded. In that time, the banned players had only missed two matches.

In 1959, the creation of a top-flight division, known as the Alpha Ethniki, was a considerable step to improving the quality of the game in the country. The formation of a true national league brought about positive changes to football in Greece including raising the profile of the sport and improving the ability of the average Greek player. Though the league was not fully professional it nevertheless gave players increased exposure and experience in higher quality matches. The national team benefited greatly from this evolution.

The 1960s saw Greece begin to produce some of its finest players ever. Each one of the 'Big 3' clubs in the Athens area had a star on the national team. The core of the national side was formed by AEK's Mimis Papaioannou, Olympiacos' Giorgos Sideris, and Panathinaikos' Mimis Domazos. It's no surprise then that Greece nearly qualified for the 1970 World Cup with that trio in the squad.

That qualifying campaign was a tumultuous one, something that typified the politically-charged state the country found itself in when the qualifiers began in 1968. The military dictatorship that came to power a year earlier, like so many around the globe that preceded and followed it, saw football as the perfect propaganda machine. In fact, the team's journey through the qualifiers was a dramatic one, full of political intrigue and internal strife.

The team began the campaign with a 1-0 defeat to Switzerland. Kostas Karapatis, the national team manager, was sacked in the aftermath of the Swiss defeat. He had asked the wife of sports minister, Kostas Aslanidis, to leave the team bus as she was smoking with her entourage. Aslanidis, a member of the junta that had seized power in the 1967 coup, fired Karapatis with immediate effect.

Giannis 'Dan' Georgiadis, an Argentine-Greek was installed. Georgiadis seemed to instantly change the fortunes of the team. A 4-1 friendly victory over Egypt was a precursor to the best result in the Ethniki's history up to that point.

On 11 December 1968, Greece hosted Portugal in a World Cup qualifier. This particular Portuguese side had finished third at the previous World Cup in 1966 and had within its ranks one of the greatest players in football history, Eusebio. An inspired Greece, however, ran rampant against their more illustrious opponents. Greece came out 4-2 winners, sending shockwaves throughout

Europe with the result. The 2-2 draw that followed with Romania showcased the team's historical penchant to self-destruct as a pre-game bust-up between manager Georgiadis and star-man Domazos disrupted the team's preparations.

Another 2-2 draw in Portugal felt like a defeat as Greece led 2-0, but conceded twice in the final 10 minutes. Georgiadis was heavily criticized in the press due to his 'ultra-defensive attitude.' The coach was sacked a few months later after some unimpressive performances in a trio of friendly matches played in Australia.

Lakis Petropoulos succeeded Georgiadis and again there was an uptick in the team's form immediately after his appointment. A 4-1 victory over Switzerland in October 1969 set up a showdown with Romania in the group finale.

At the August 23rd Stadium in Bucharest a month later, a Greek victory would seal the country's first-ever World Cup berth. Ultimately, it was a step too far for the Ethniki, a 1-1 draw not enough to book the ticket to Mexico.

There was real disappointment at that World Cup elimination. The silver lining was that Greece had recorded some of the best results in its football history. The Ethniki had scored 13 goals against some top sides and finally became a source of pride for citizens of the country by showing it could be competitive, even against Europe's best. There appeared to be a golden age of football on the horizon for Greece. Club football was becoming stronger, culminating in Panathinaikos' run to the European Cup Final in 1971, where they lost to Ajax 2-0 at Wembley Stadium. Coached by the legendary Hungarian player Ferenc Puskas, that team remains the only Greek side to have advanced to a European final.

Unfortunately, the national team could not build on the positives of that World Cup qualifying campaign through the majority of the 1970s. Results stayed wildly inconsistent. A 0-0 draw away to Brazil in 1974 was considered a high point. The lows were very low though such as the 2-0 defeat to Malta in a 1976 European Championship qualifier. Ironically, it was during this time that the man widely considered as Greece's greatest player earned his one and only cap for Greece.

Vasilis Hatzipanagis played for Greece in a May 1976 friendly against Poland. His impressive display raised spirits around the country that he could be the superstar Greece lacked going forward. Hatzipanagis' silky smooth dribbling and fancy footwork saw him garner the nickname, 'the football Nureyev', after the famous Russian ballet dancer. Following the Poland friendly, Hatzipanagis received the news that he would no longer be eligible to play for Greece due to the fact that he had represented the Soviet Union at junior level. Hatzipanagis' parents were political refugees that fled to the USSR after the Greek Civil War following World War II. He was born in Tashkent in 1954 and grew up in the Uzbek Soviet Socialist Republic, present-day Uzbekistan. He came to Greece in 1975 and went on to play for Thessaloniki club Iraklis until 1990. Despite, being unable to play for Greece beyond that one game, his performances for Iraklis in that 15-year period saw him ranked by many as the best Greek player of all time.

Nevertheless, it wasn't all bad news during that era and the end of the decade saw Greece celebrate an unprecedented success at the national team level. In 1978, Greece set out to qualify for Euro 1980 in a group that also included Hungary, Finland, and the Soviet Union.

Two consecutive defeats to begin the campaign away to Finland and Russia suggested yet another disappointment was in the cards. A stunning result against Finland in October 1978 changed everything. The 8-1 win against the Finns gave the team belief in the quality it possessed. The renewed confidence led to an impressive 4-1 victory over Hungary in the next qualifier. A 0-0 draw away to the Hungarian side set up a decisive clash against the Russians on 12 September 1979.

Other results in the group had gone in Greece's favor, so it was known that a victory over the Soviet team would clinch a spot in the European Championship. A 9th minute goal by Takis Nikoloudis saw Greece run out 1-0 winners and make history by qualifying for their first major tournament.

The architect of this success was none other than Alketas Panagoulias. Having taken over the side in 1977, the 'American', as he was called due to his living and coaching in the United States, had become the first coach to take a Greek team to the next level.

At Euro 1980 in Italy, Greece found themselves grouped in a tough section that included West Germany, Czechoslovakia, and Holland. Greece lost their opener to the Dutch 1-0 thanks to a controversial 65th minute penalty. Despite the loss, Greece had impressed and the Naples crowd were firmly behind their Mediterranean neighbors.

Defeat to Czechoslovakia followed by a 3-1 scoreline, but there was some joy at Greece's first ever goal in a major competition scored by Nikos Anastopoulos. 'O Moustakias' (the mustached-one) as he was known would go on to become Greece's all-time leading scorer. A 0-0 draw in the Group 2 finale against West

Germany was a good result, however Greece finished fourth in the section and had been eliminated.

The team had done itself proud with its performances. The belief now was that Greece could get even better in the years to come. The same old story transpired though and it was not to be. Greece did not even come close to qualifying for the next six tournaments it attempted to in. Poor results meant less stability with respect to the managers and players in the team. The state of the domestic league surely did not help in that period. Even though the league became fully professional in the early 1980s, the antipathy between the major clubs created an environment that separated players and fans along club lines. Allegations of corruption and referee bias were hurled between the bigger teams. The national team suffered from the spiteful atmosphere that existed. Players seemed caught up in their club allegiances and the national team was relegated in its importance for many.

It would be 14 years before the country's football supporters could celebrate another major milestone. In 1992, Panagoulias was given the Greek job for the third time (he had coached his first stint between 1973-76). He was tasked with trying to lead his country to another major tournament, this time the 1994 World Cup, to be held in the United States.

The hope was that the return of the Thessaloniki-born coach would somehow spark a return to the successes of the past. Greece were placed in Group 5 for qualification for USA '94. That section included favorites Russia and Yugoslavia, along with lesser-weights Iceland, Hungary, and Luxembourg.

The six teams in the group were trimmed to five in October 1992. It was then when Yugoslavia were suspended by FIFA after having to postpone their first two qualifiers. FIFA eventually completely banned Yugoslavia from participating in the competition after United Nations' sanctions were levied against the country due to the war occurring in the Republic of Bosnia and Herzegovina.

This development opened the door for Greece to grab one of the two automatic spots to the World Cup by finishing first or second in Group 5. Panagoulias and his players kicked off their campaign with a narrow 1-0 victory over Iceland in May 1992. Indicative of the widespread apathy present amongst the public toward the national team during that time period, a miniscule crowd of 2,874 watched Greece defeat the Icelandic side. The focus of supporters was clearly on club football. There was little interest in the Ethniki after years of disappointing results and failed qualifying campaigns.

A few months later Greece won their second straight match, away to Iceland this time, again 1-0. In November 1992, Greece dominated, but could only muster a scoreless home draw against Hungary. A routine 2-0 home win over Luxembourg followed. 36,256 people watched that match in February 1993 at the Olympic Stadium in Athens. Suddenly, the expectations of a World Cup berth seemed to bring out supporters as Greece began their campaign with three wins and a draw.

Due to Yugoslavia's absence, Greece were in prime position to capitalize. And on 31 March 1993 in Budapest the chance had come to clinch a spot in the country's first-ever FIFA World Cup. It was a tight affair against Hungary with very few clear-cut chances. A handball in the box by the hosts in the 70th minute gave Greece the opening it so craved. Defender Stratos Apostolakis stepped up to convert the penalty kick, a goal that would go down in Greek football history. Greece held on for the 1-0 win as Apostolakis' goal had fired a nation to its first World Cup.

The rest of the campaign remained positive for Greece. The team managed a 1-1 draw in Russia and an easy victory followed away to Luxembourg. This set up a group finale against Russia for first place in Group 5. Greece had already qualified, but there was a desire present within the squad to dispel the notion that they had made it purely on the good fortune of Yugoslavia's absence. In front of 75,000 fans in Athens in November 1993, a splendid headed goal from young star Nikos Machlas gave Greece the 1-0 win for first place in the section. Machlas would go on to win the European Golden Boot Award in 1998 thanks to his 34 goals with Vitesse in the Dutch Eredivisie. His goalscoring exploits would lead to a switch to Ajax where he won a league title and two Dutch Cups. He would not feature for Greece at Euro 2004, playing the last of 61 caps in a friendly versus Sweden in February 2002.

In eight qualifying matches, Greece had won six, drawn two, and lost none. The team had scored ten goals and allowed only two. Long-suffering Greek fans could finally celebrate their country's participation at a World Cup. The following month saw the 1994 World Cup Draw held in Las Vegas. Greece were placed into Group D alongside powerhouse Argentina, neighbors Bulgaria, and fellow World Cup debutants Nigeria. It was considered a tough draw, but hopes were high that a focused Greek side could do well.

World Cup qualification proved to be the high point on the road to the tournament in the United States. After qualification, everything seemed to get worse. Problems with the team's preparations began to appear in the few friendlies played months before the tournament. A 0-0 draw against Poland was considered a good result and that was followed by a 5-1 thrashing of Saudi Arabia in Athens. It did not take long before the first cracks in the armor appeared. Two friendlies in Piraeus in May 1994 saw Greece lose 3-0 to Cameroon and manage only a 0-0 draw against Bolivia. The biggest pre-tournament test was set for the end of May against England at Wembley Stadium in London. England tore through the Greek team winning 5-0. It was a terrible effort by Panagoulias' men, full of shocking defensive blunders. The manager's team selection was questioned by the media as the preference seemed to be on picking older, experienced players rather than some of the exciting, young talent coming through. The media were already sounding off at the fact that creative players such as Olympiacos' Vasilis Karapialis and young AEK playmaker Vasilis Tsiartas were left home in favor of veterans well into their 30s.

Upon arrival in the United States, team morale was at an all-time low. Friendly matches followed on American soil, a 1-1 draw against the host nation and a 2-0 defeat to Colombia. The problems on the pitch were visible, but the severity of the off the pitch obstacles were truly beginning to show. Within the team, there were accusations being levied against the coaching staff and the country's football federation. Instead of the focus being on the best possible preparations for the opener against Argentina, the team were busy going to social events put on by Greek-Americans.

The Ethniki players arrived in the States to a full airport greeting them. However, in the days and weeks that followed the celebrity-style receptions began to wear on the team members. This had mostly to do with the incredible number of mandatory social functions that the players were ordered to attend. The national team members soon realized they were being exploited. Numerous individuals were trying to make money off the players' names and achievements. Elder statesman Stelios Manolas and Panagoulias clashed on one such occasion with the manager threatening to axe Manolas from the team if he did not stop complaining about the engagements the team had. It took Manolas' teammates to convince Panagoulias otherwise.

Needless to say, Greece entered their opener against Argentina in less than desirable shape. There was a negativity in the air following the team. And the preparations on the pitch seemed to be treated as an afterthought. It was no surprise then of what was about to come.

On 21 June 1994, the Greek national team played its first-ever World Cup match in Foxboro, Massachusetts. For the thousands of Greek supporters in attendance, it ended up being a disappointing experience as they watched their side get picked apart by the superior Argentines en route to a 4-0 rout for the two-time World Cup champions.

That match marked the beginning of one of the worst World Cup performances in history. A 4-0 loss to Bulgaria came next, which was followed by a 2-0 defeat to Nigeria in the Group Stage finale. Greece had lost all three matches, failed to score and conceded 10 goals in the process. The team returned back home to a hailstorm of criticism, derision, and blame. It would take years for the Ethniki to recover from the nightmare of the 1994 World Cup. The negative after-effects would be felt for nearly a decade.

Chapter 2

Aftermath Of A Disaster

Though everyone from coaches to players to fans seemed willing to completely forget the 1994 World Cup, the bitter taste of that experience remained well after the tournament was completed. The relationship between the national team players and the EPO was at an all-time low. Historically, the two sides had a tenuous relationship, but the actions of the EPO in the United States and the extra-curricular demands placed on the players meant there was a complete breakdown between the two parties.

Back in Greece an investigation was launched into the dealings of certain EPO officials who brokered deals with Greek-American groups and individuals. These agreements mainly involved exploiting the national team's popularity while they participated in the World Cup. In some cases, Greek-Americans who felt wronged by the individuals who made the agreements brought lawsuits against them.

All this did was keep the 1994 World Cup in the headlines and elongate the misery of the entire experience for those involved. This was especially true for the players. The confidence of those Ethniki members who were a part of the World Cup team was shattered. Panagoulias meanwhile did not return to Greece, at least not immediately. He stayed in the States, where he had a home, choosing to avoid the angry reception his arrival in Greece would have undoubtedly sparked. As more stories came out of what was happening in and around the Greek camp during the tournament, media and supporters became more inclined to lay the blame at the feet of Panagoulias.

It was within this environment that Greece was tasked to prepare for their qualification campaign for Euro 1996. Kostas Polychroniou was the man tabbed as Panagoulias' successor. Polychroniou had a somewhat unspectacular coaching career. He was a journeyman manager who had worked his way up to coaching the Greek U-21 side as well as Olympiacos for one season just before getting the Greek job. As a player, Polychroniou was a legend for Olympiacos, spending 15 years with the club, appearing for them over 350 times and winning six league titles and eight domestic cups. He also was capped by his country 27 times.

The EPO entrusted Polychroniou with picking up the pieces of the World Cup disaster and instilling discipline and belief into the team. The new boss also needed to make wholesale changes to the squad. This was considered the right time to bring in a new generation of players to the Ethniki. Panagoulias had been criticized well before the World Cup for his squad selection. The coach was slammed in the press and by fans for bringing older, veteran players to the tournament who many believed took their place in the squad based more for their cumulative service rather than on current form or merit.

Polychroniou was considered by most to be a stop-gap measure. It was believed that the EPO were biding their time with Polychroniou until they could entice a bigger name from abroad to take over the team. Before Greece's opening match away to the Faroe Islands in Euro 1996 qualifying, the presence of Clemens Westerhof in the team's hotel caused quite a stir. Westerhof was the former manager of Nigeria, a team whom he had just led to a successful World Cup campaign by advancing to the Second Round. His stay at the Toftir hotel fueled speculation that the EPO were after him to coach Greece. The Dutch coach insisted to the press he was there only as a tourist. In the days that followed, the rumors persisted that Westerhof was being courted to take over the Ethniki. In the end, nothing came of the entire situation, but it was the first suggestion that a well-known, foreign coach was desired for the Greek team.

Polychroniou began the Euro '96 qualifiers by refreshing the squad with a few new faces. Almost immediately, it appeared as though Greece were past the World Cup debacle. Four straight wins saw the team come flying out of the gates as the Faroe Islands, Finland, Scotland, and San Marino were all defeated. The mood surrounding the team had changed considerably. There was now talk about the real prospect of qualifying for Euro '96, hosted by England.

Any hopes of making it to a second European Championship were dashed with three consecutive defeats. Russia came to Thessaloniki in April 1995 and battered Greece en route to a 3-0 victory. Away losses to Finland to Scotland followed as Greece fell behind in the group. After an expected win over San

Marino, a crucial date with Russia in the penultimate qualifier beckoned. Only a win would do for Greece, but despite putting forward a solid fighting display, Polychroniou's men lost 2-1. The team finished off their campaign with an easy win against the Faroe Islands. Polychroniou had done a decent job of rebuilding the team. Still, it was not enough to get through and qualify.

Perhaps the lasting impact of Euro '96 qualifying were the new players that were brought into the Greek team. Six of the players called up by Polychroniou and who participated for Greece in the qualifiers would go on to be involved in Euro 2004. Theodoros Zagorakis, Vasilis Tsiartas, Nikos Dabizas, Zisis Vryzas, Demis Nikolaidis, and Georgios Georgiadis were all capped for the first time in the post-1994 World Cup period. The foundation of the team that would go on to play at Euro 2004 in Portugal was beginning to be laid.

Despite failing to qualify, the EPO kept Polychroniou on as manager of Greece heading into the qualification cycle for the 1998 FIFA World Cup. The Ethniki were drawn into Group 1 of qualifying for France '98 alongside Denmark, Croatia, Slovenia, and Bosnia-Herzegovina. Denmark and Croatia were strong sides and the favorites to claim the top two spots. Once again, Greece began their qualifying journey strongly. Wins over Slovenia and Bosnia-Herzegovina were followed by a close defeat to Denmark away, 2-1. Greece rebounded to secure point against Croatia in Zagreb. A narrow win in Sarajevo against the Bosnians followed setting up an important match with Croatia at home in April 1997. Davor Suker's goal gave the opposition a 1-0 win in Thessaloniki. Things became tougher for Greece after that result, but the Ethniki still controlled their World Cup destiny. Two wins and Greece would qualify for their second straight World Cup. A 3-0 away win at Slovenia set up an epic finale with Denmark.

The game against Denmark is one of the most famous in Greek football's recent history. While the Danes were playing for two results, the Greeks had no such luxuries. They would have to defeat Denmark in order to qualify for the 1998 World Cup. Over 60,000 fans packed into the Olympic Stadium in Athens on 11 October 1997. Greece played very well and threatened on many occasions, even managing to hit the post through a Dabizas header. A combination of Greece's inability to convert chances and goalkeeping brilliance by Peter Schmeichel kept the Greeks off the scoreboard. With two minutes left, substitute Alekos Alexandris broke free in the box and saw his goal-bound effort deflected away by Schmeichel's right knee. It was an extraordinary chance and a top-class save by one of the best goalkeepers in football history. The final whistle saw the match finish 0-0. Denmark had clinched a spot in France while Greece were out by the smallest of margins.

Failing to qualify for the World Cup was another disappointment for the Greek team and their supporters. Despite another elimination, this time there was widespread pride at how the team had battled to the end. Only three players that participated in USA '94 were part of the Greek side that took on Denmark. It was another indicator that Polychroniou had done his job by revamping the squad. Polychroniou stayed on as manager until April 1998 when he and the federation parted ways. The future seemed bright with a largely positive qualifying campaign to build on.

It was no surprise then that excitement reached fever pitch in the spring and summer of 1998. The rumors in the media stated that the EPO were, in no surprise, aiming to nail down a high-profile foreign manager to replace Polychroniou. The most popular candidate that emerged was Romanian coach Anghel Iordanescu.

Iordanescu had famously led Romania to the quarterfinals of the 1994 World Cup. The manager oversaw a side that produced superb counter-attacking football and that defeated the likes of Colombia, the United States, and Argentina along the way. In 1998, Iordanescu was still in charge of Romania having qualified the team for another World Cup. It was Romania's third straight berth in a major finals (1994 World Cup, Euro 1996, and the 1998 World Cup), but there was trouble in the camp as Romania went through qualifying for France '98. Iordanescu had fallen out with some of the veteran stars in the Romanian side meaning his influence was beginning to fade. It was announced that the successful coach would leave his position following the conclusion of the 1998 World Cup.

This was exactly the sort of manager the EPO coveted. Iordanescu had become a well-known name in the football world and he had extensive experience coaching at the national team level. Iordanescu was also a coach who was not afraid to give young talent an opportunity. It seemed like a perfect fit for a manager like that to take control of a Greek team that was youthful and ready to take the next step.

The Greek U-21 side came runners-up to Spain in the 1998 UEFA U-21 European Championship. They had defeated the likes of Germany (1-0) and the Netherlands (3-0) en route to the final. The would-be household names from Euro 2004 were just beginning their careers. Six players from that squad,

Traianos Dellas, Giorgos Karagounis, Angelos Basinas, Nikos Liberopoulos, Vasilis Lakis, and Giannis Goumas would all go on to be a part of the 2004 side. Karagounis believes the first signs of a special generation coming together could be seen as early as the mid-1990s. "We had a very good team that did not deserve to lose in 1998. A mix of bad luck and poor refereeing decisions cost us. We were also a strong side at U-18 level where we finished third at the 1995 European Championship. It could be seen then that this group was special and that there would be potential for the success to continue in the older age levels."

The EPO got their man in the spring of 1998. Iordanescu signed a lucrative deal to coach Greece through the qualifiers for Euro 2000. The Romanian became Greece's sixth foreign coach and first since Billy Bingham in the early 1970s. Greek football fans began dreaming big as soon as Iordanescu was announced as manager. He was seen as the perfect choice to bring Greece up to the level of Europe's bigger nations.

The man many hailed as the savior of the Greek team barely lasted eight months in the job. Iordanescu quit his post in March 1999 after a 2-0 defeat to Norway left Greece's Euro 2000 dreams in tatters. It was his only official defeat in the seven matches he coached Greece, but the performance against the Norwegians was the breaking point for the Romanian. The expectations that Iordanescu would repeat the success he had with Romania seemed too big to overcome. Greece's Euro 2000 qualifying group consisted of Norway, Slovenia, Georgia, Latvia, and Albania. It was considered an extremely kind group. Early draws to Slovenia and Albania put Greece off course in the section. The slow start put the pressure on Iordanescu immediately.

By the end, the tensions between the EPO and Iordanescu had become more noticeable. Details are muddy about what the exact disagreements entailed, but Iordanescu claimed he was not allowed to work in the manner he saw fit. The bad start to qualifying also caused problems between the manager and the team. Previous boss Polychroniou had been well-liked by the players. Iordanescu in turn was never fully trusted by the squad.

Iordanescu literally stormed out of Greece after the Norway defeat. He ended up in Saudi Arabia just days later, appointed as coach to club side Al-Hilal. The EPO named Vasilis Daniil as manager in the immediate aftermath of Iordanescu's departure. Daniil, like Polychroniou before him, was something of a journeyman coach in Greece. He most notably had coached Panathinaikos on three occasions, winning the double with the club in 1991. The EPO needed someone experienced with inside knowledge of the Greek game and Daniil fit the bill.

Amongst the problems confronting Daniil upon his taking over the Ethniki were issues involving the atmosphere surrounding the team. Whatever gains had been made in the Polychroniou period to creating a closer team dynamic had all been destroyed in the matter of a few months. Club rivalries in Greece had cast a shadow over the national side. Between 1996 and 2000, the derbies, specifically the ones involving Olympiacos and AEK, were particularly fierce. This led to bad blood between those groups of players when they reported for national team duty.

Daniil went about a mini-investigation of the issues affecting team unity. After a short time in charge, the new coach realized that certain players wouldn't greet one another much less look at each other. On away trips, Daniil saw the situation deteriorate even further. Cliques formed with players separated into small groups, many times among club lines.

Even though Daniil recognized the lack of team unity, it was not an easy fix. The rest of the qualifying campaign saw the issues plaguing the team persist and worsen. Several episodes occurred that showcased the extent of dislike some players had for each other. On the eve of a qualifier in Oslo against Norway, Grigoris Georgatos asked Daniil for the number 11 jersey. Days later he admitted the reason for this was so he could stick it to Demis Nikolaidis, the usual wearer of that number. Georgatos played for Olympiacos and Nikolaidis for AEK. The teams had just played out a hard-fought derby and the tensions were still high.

On another occasion, AEK and Greece goalkeeper Ilias Atmatsidis and Olympiacos and national team defender Giorgos Anatolakis nearly came to blows. The two squared up after a penalty Anatolakis conceded toward the end of a home defeat to Latvia. Atmatsidis was livid about Anatolakis' clumsy challenge on a Latvian player who was not in a goalscoring position.

It was against this backdrop that Greece had to prepare for qualification to the 2002 World Cup. The qualifying draw did Greece no favors. Germany and England were the top seeds in Group 9, which also included Finland and Albania. Widespread pessimism greeted the news of Germany and England's presence in the group. Even a Greece firing on all cylinders would find it tough against sides of that caliber, let alone this Greek team whose current state was one of such turmoil. The fractious nature of the team was evidenced by the decision of three key players to declare themselves unavailable for selection.

AEK players Ilias Atmatsidis, Michalis Kasapis, and Demis Nikolaidis had all been national team starters in the previous qualifying cycle. However, the trio announced they would not play for Greece as a form of protest due to problems in the domestic league. The issues at hand specifically concerned alleged favoritism by officials toward Olympiacos in the Greek league.

Daniil had his work cut out for him. His main goal was not necessarily qualifying his side for the upcoming World Cup to be co-hosted by Japan and South Korea. Instead, the needs were more immediate in nature. Greece needed a manager who could put out a competitive side, but who mainly would improve the hostile atmosphere that existed between members of the squad. Daniil's solution to this was to draft in a whole host of new players and drop those individuals he had identified as causing problems within the group.

In theory this made sense. The problem was that against the likes of Germany and England, trying out so many new players was always going to be extremely risky. In the opener of Greece's 2002 World Cup qualifying campaign, Daniil made six changes to the starting line-up compared to Greece's last qualifier, 10 months before, for Euro 2000. Out of the fourteen total players used by Daniil in the first match, a 2-0 away defeat to Germany, there were eight new faces as compared to Greece's last competitive fixture. The Germany loss was expected and the team bounced back for a 1-0 win over Norway in the next match. The storm clouds began to form though in the third qualifier, a 2-0 loss away to Albania. Daniil and the players faced heavy criticism after that result.

Next up was Germany at home and Greece's last opportunity to stay alive in the group. A 4-2 defeat spelled the end of another World Cup dream. This second loss to Germany cut deeply. Greece fought to a 2-2 halftime score. But, Germany, down a player for the last half-hour, scored twice in the last 10 minutes to seal the win. Daniil was absolutely slammed in the press. The team had reached its lowest ebb since the 1994 World Cup. The absence of any sort of team chemistry, the complete loss of confidence by the players, and the loss of belief in yet another manager meant the team had hit rock-bottom. Daniil was essentially a lame-duck coach by this point. The rumors were already starting about whom Greece could appoint next. Two matches followed, a victory over Albania at home and a loss to England. On 7 June, the EPO decided the time was right after the defeat to England to relieve Daniil of his duties. Greece had nearly three months until their next qualifier and only two matches left in their campaign.

Daniil's reign was considered by many to be a mediocre one. Initially there was some hope he could improve the team after Iordanescu's disastrous spell. Some credit the Greek coach for bringing in new players and weeding out some individuals who were responsible for the creation of a poor team unity. Results, especially in the big qualification matches, were the main reason for his removal. Daniil did not help himself with his relationship with the media. He had a tendency to shoot from the hip, releasing odd soundbites that the Greek press would latch on to. At one point, Daniil told journalists he was "100 years ahead of them" in terms of football knowledge. In a quote that is still famous in Greek football to this day, he also stated that it worked against his team when Germany went down to 10 men in the 2002 World Cup qualifier between the two sides in Athens. These sorts of comments did not endear him to the media and what resulted was an antagonistic relationship between the two parties.

The immediate favorite to emerge for the national team job in the days after Daniil was sacked was Dusan Bajevic. The Bosnian manager had loads of experience in the Greek game having played for AEK from 1997 to 1981 and then coaching the likes of AEK, Olympiacos, and PAOK since returning to Greece in 1988. Bajevic's spell at PAOK was not going so well when the Greece job became vacant and thus was deemed by many as the natural choice.

Eventually, Bajevic was considered to be too close to the matters of Greek football. An outsider who could not be influenced was preferred to motivate a group of talented, but under-achieving players. The EPO decided to look elsewhere. Amazingly enough, the decision was made to place an advertisement on the EPO's website. What began as a joke by a Federation official eventually turned into reality. In order to fill the role of Greek national team coach, essentially a help wanted ad was placed on the Federation website. "Truly after Daniil, I thought long and hard. It was hard for me to trust anyone so I wanted the actual resumes of those who actually wanted the job," said Vasilis Gagatsis, the EPO President at the time. The list of managers to express interest in this included well-known coaches such as Javier Clemente, Marco Tardelli, Terry Venables, Nevio Scala, and Otto Rehhagel.

The EPO narrowed down the list to three, Venables, Scala and Rehhagel. Eventually, Venables would rule himself out of the job. That left Scala and Rehhagel as the remaining possibilities. Scala had established himself as a manager by bringing Parma up from Serie B in Italy to win four cups, three of them in European competition. The Italian also had stints in Germany with

Borussia Dortmund and Besiktas in Turkey. Rehhagel meanwhile had spent his entire career in Germany, winning the league with the likes of Werder Bremen and Kaiserslautern. The two managers had a history of leading unfancied sides to glory.

Both men were invited to Athens for interviews. The two coaches were eventually separated not by the strength of their career bio, their footballing philosophy or their ideas for improving the national team. The final decision came down, in part, to money. "It was an easy choice because I wanted Rehhagel after Iordanescu left. However, he was unavailable then. Even before I headed the EPO, Rehhagel was a manager who clicked for me considering what he did at Kaiserslautern. That showed he was a big manager. He was also asking for half the money that Scala had requested. It was an easy decision for us," stated Gagatsis.

On 9 August 2001, Rehhagel was unveiled as the new manager of Greece. He had been out of work for nearly a year and this was the first job he had taken outside his country. Rehhagel's appointment was greeted with mixed reviews. Some saw him as a respected manager who had worked wonders in Germany, while others viewed him as an uninspiring choice who wouldn't change the team's fortunes.

Chapter 3

Rehhagel - The Man Who Would Be King

Well before he achieved footballing immortality, Otto Rehhagel was known simply as 'the firefighter.' This was a nickname garnered by the coach during his early days coaching in the Bundesliga and 2. Bundesliga, Germany's first and second divisions. Whether it was for six months or even six weeks, he gained a reputation as a specialist, a manager who was able to transform a struggling side into one that could grab the results necessary to avoid the drop into a lower division.

His success in reviving the fortunes of teams in trouble in order to avoid relegation worked against him for a period of time. Rehhagel was typecast as a manager who could provide an initial spark to save a club from dropping down a division, but little else. This eventually frustrated a proud man who possessed great self-belief and had faith in his ability to manage at the highest level. For the first part of his career, he fought hard to change this perception. Eventually, with a long reign at Werder Bremen he not only rid himself of the 'firefighter' label, but also found success at the top level of professional football.

The odds were stacked against Rehhagel from the start. Born in Essen, Germany on 9 August 1938, Rehhagel grew up in an extremely difficult period of time in his country's history. At the age of 5, he experienced the bombings of Essen by Allied forces toward the tail end of World War II. The city was a key industrial center which included the Krupp family armament factory and thus became a prime target for the Allies. Rehhagel's family went without much food in the weeks following some of the heaviest raids in March 1944. For a time period, the young Rehhagel was also left homeless alongside over 50,000 others in the city due to the destruction caused by the bombing campaign of the Royal Air Force. Living in temporary housing along with ten other families had a profound impact on Rehhagel. "I said to myself, this can't go on like this. I have to do something to get away from the destruction, the hunger, and the misery," remembers Rehhagel.*

Jean Julien Beer reported on Bundesliga matches for over 20 years and was a long-time editor of the famed sports magazine *kicker*, the largest football publication in Germany. Beer followed Rehhagel closely toward the latter stages of the manager's career in Germany. He believes that Rehhagel's experiences as a child made him unflappable as a manager later in life. "The difficult beginnings of his life, especially the war, shaped him. As a coach, he has often cited that example. Even during his last coaching job at Hertha where the team was relegated and there was tumult on the field, Rehhagel later said, 'I was not afraid, I sat in a cellar in Essen in 1943 when the Americans bombarded us.'"

Rehhagel grew up in Altenessen, one of the city districts in Essen. His father worked in the Helene coal mine which was run by the Krupp family and named after Helene Krupp, co-founder of the family's industrial empire. The mine facilitated a real bond between the families that worked at it. It was difficult work, but there was widespread gratitude amongst the community that it existed, especially in the years following World War II.

Rehhagel's experiences as a young boy shaped his character and worldview, but also his ambition. His father passed away at only 39, Rehhagel himself just 14 years old at the time. Living through the war and its aftermath and then the death of his father convinced Rehhagel that he wanted to make it out of Essen. According to those closest to Rehhagel he never talked about his father's death much, but he often mentioned how his father worked for the mine for nearly 25 years and never once set foot outside of Germany. Rehhagel wanted more than what Essen could offer him.

The young Rehhagel felt there was only one way out for him and that way was through football. From an early age it was apparent that the game was his greatest passion. As a young boy, Rehhagel played football in the streets of Altenessen using balls made from rags in many cases. At the age of 10, he signed up for his first club, TuS Helene 28. The local team, Altenessen 06, was closer, but Rehhagel wanted to show loyalty to TuS Helene, which was the official club of the mine his father had worked for.

Rehhagel spent his teen years with the same club moving up through the age groups. He began to gain a reputation as a tough-as-nails individual whose game occasionally bordered on being dirty. Even against teammates he showed an unwillingness to hold back. During one training session he tackled a teammate so hard that it caused him to miss the next two months through injury. Rehhagel did bring that same friend to the hospital though on his bicycle following the tackle. His commitment on the pitch could not be questioned, nor could his desire to make it as a professional footballer. In order to bring in additional income to his mother and two sisters, Rehhagel worked as a painter for the mine households. His infatuation with football, however, ensured that he would continue on the path of wanting to make it as a pro. "Football was his stage, he always believed this. Here he was a great man, in real life just a craftsman," says Beer.

In 1957, after nine years with the youth teams of TuS Helene, he signed his first professional contract with the same club. Rehhagel played for the first team for three seasons as a hard-working attacker. In 1960, he made his first big professional move to Rot-Weiss Essen. In that same year, he picked up his only caps for his country with two appearances for the West Germany amateur national team.

At Rot-Weiss, Rehhagel's reputation continued to grow. He was moved further back on the field and began to become established as a defender. His playing style, one based on intensity and tireless effort, was more suited to being a defender and he would spend the majority of his career at the back. "At the end of his career, Rehhagel became a big figure in football. He made more of his life than what was foreseen in his childhood. As a player, he was not an artist, but a worker, a very uncompromising defender," confirms Beer. That willingness to work would help him rise through the ranks as a player, and later as a coach.

After three years at Rot-Weiss, Rehhagel moved to Hertha Berlin in 1963. It was the first time he had been out of Essen for an extended period of time. His transition was helped by the fact that he married his long-time sweetheart Beate ahead of the move. Beate would not only go on to impact Rehhagel's personal life, but she would influence his professional one as well. "Otto always had a lot of ambition with regard to football in his life and he was always accompanied closely by his wife Beate," says Beer. Beate was outspoken in her support of her husband in difficult periods of his coaching career. She also acted as a liaison of sorts in welcoming new players to Rehhagel's clubs. From organizing dinners to figuring out living arrangements for players and their families, Beate was ever-present and most willing to help in matters that often went over-looked during that era.

At Hertha, Rehhagel became an established professional and participated in the inaugural season of the Bundesliga. To this day he is one of only two individuals (the other being Jupp Heynckes) who has played and coached in over 1,000 Bundesliga matches. His long-standing career in Germany's top-flight earned him the nickname, 'the child of the Bundesliga.'

Rehhagel spent just two seasons in Berlin before moving to Kaiserslautern ahead of the 1965-66 season. It is there where he spent the majority of his career at the top level. He did not find much success with the club in his six seasons there as the team bounced between midtable and just above the relegation places. What he did come across was a treasure trove of coaching knowledge and contrasting styles. Kaiserslautern's mediocrity during Rehhagel's time there as a player meant a regular changing of managers. Thus, Rehhagel had six different head coaches during his playing days for the club. He was exposed to varying coaching philosophies ranging from tactics to interactions with players.

Rehhagel's playing days were eventually cut short by injury. A hard tackle seven matches into the 1971/72 season against Duisburg saw him sustain a knee injury requiring surgery. It was the last time he ever appeared on a football pitch. After 201 Bundesliga matches and countless battles on the pitch, Rehhagel had to face the facts that his career was over. The German's preparation, however, for his next experience in football had already begun. In 1970, Rehhagel had received his coaching license from the Athletics Academy of Cologne. His view on what the future held was clear, he had to remain in football. While other teammates pursued careers in business or the retail and marketing side of the sport, Rehhagel knew he wanted to become a coach. One of his former managers, Dietrich Weise had tabbed Rehhagel as a successful manager stating that he had the right mindset and cleverness to stand as a coach.

Whilst still playing, Rehhagel spent a short time coaching at the amateur level for FV Rockenhausen. The experience left him wanting more. 18 months after stepping off the field for the last time as a player, Rehhagel was appointed to his first head coaching position. He took over FC Saarbrucken ahead of the 1972/73 season.

Rehhagel's first taste as a head coach was a bittersweet one. The new boss had hoped to build on Saarbrucken's 13th place finish from the previous season. It was a topsy-turvy campaign where Rehhagel at one point had his team near the promotion places. A tough run-in saw Saarbrucken fall away and finish 13th once again. The experience left Rehhagel disappointed and he left after just one season.

Rehhagel was off to the Bundesliga the following season. This time the position was at Kickers Offenbach as an assistant coach to one of his former managers at Kaiserslautern, Gyula Lorant. A member of the Hungarian national team of the 1950s who were known as the Mighty Magyars, Lorant played in the 1954 World Cup Final for that stunning team, one which would eventually go down as one of football's best-ever sides. Lorant was a manager who spent most of his coaching career in Germany. In 1975 he joined PAOK in Greece after doctors told him he needed more sun due to a skin disorder. He led PAOK to the league title, becoming a hero in Thessaloniki for his exploits. That championship was PAOK's first in Greek league history and the only title Lorant won in a coaching career spanning two decades. Lorant returned to Germany after falling out with PAOK's owner and eventually went on to coach Bayern Munich. He returned to PAOK in 1980. This time he defied doctor's orders and the advice to find a less stressful line of work due to a heart condition. In May 1981, Lorant died on the bench during a league match between PAOK and Olympiacos. The medical report stated that he suffered a heart attack due to an elevated, emotional state.

Rehhagel's coaching style would eventually be characterized, in part, as one where order and discipline ruled. Serving as an assistant under Lorant surely influenced this. The Hungarian manager expected full adherence to team rules. He was known as a hardline coach who could strike fear into the heart of his players. Stories were passed on that told of a man who would check on players by telephone or by spying on them to ensure they were not out partying before matches.

Offenbach had finished 7th in Lorant's first season in charge and were considered an up-and-coming side in the Bundesliga. They could not build on that success and by the spring of 1974 the club had fallen to 12th in the table. A 4-0 defeat to VfB Stuttgart saw Lorant get sacked. Rehhagel was selected to finish the season out with the club and save them from a relegation battle. In his Bundesliga coaching debut, Rehhagel picked up a 2-2 draw at home to VfL Bochum. Another draw followed away to Hamburg before the manager picked up his first win in the German top-flight with a 3-0 home victory over Fortuna Dusseldorf.

It was a positive finish to the season for the new manager as Offenbach climbed up to 10th, finishing well clear of the relegation zone. Rehhagel had loosened the vice-like grip Lorant had on the players. He created a more positive atmosphere and the players responded in kind. He showed interest in individual players by trying to motivate them and just talking to them about their lives. It was a characteristic that would define his coaching career. Behind the rough exterior that journalists and opponents saw during matches there was a human touch that Rehhagel had with his players. "There was never any psychological support when I was a player. I felt alone. I promised myself if I ever became a manager I would talk to my players about whatever bothered them, even the smallest problem," explains Rehhagel.

Offenbach were happy with Rehhagel's impact and decided to sign him to a one-year contract. The ensuing season started off in perfect fashion. The team, buoyed by its strong form to end the previous campaign, exploded out of the blocks. Rehhagel led his side to an astonishing 6-0 defeat of Bayern Munich on the opening day of the season. He made headlines across Germany for the first time as a coach. Offenbach continued their strong play in the opening weeks of that season. They were top of the table in November and carried on that form until the mid-season mark where they dropped slightly to second. Rehhagel's men were playing superb, attacking football and scoring goals for fun. Unfortunately, it wouldn't last. A leaky defense saw a capitulation in the second half of the season and Offenbach fell all the way down to eighth. It was a disappointing placing considering how the season had begun. Sadly for Rehhagel, the downward spiral continued into the following campaign.

A slow start to the 1975/76 season was not the only trouble the manager would encounter. Some heavy, early defeats in the league meant the pressure was on for the derby against Eintracht Frankfurt. After a controversial penalty was awarded to Eintracht, Rehhagel accused the referee of taking a bribe and verbally abused the linesman as well. The man in the middle, Walter Eschweiler, gave the German Football Federation (DFB) his match report. Within it, he detailed Rehhagel's accusations. Rehhagel was beginning to gain a reputation as a temperamental coach. He was a fascinating watch for many who loved his histrionics on the touchline and explosive passion. However, to some his actions were deemed excessive and frowned upon. The season before he had been widely condemned after it was revealed that he had said to one of his defenders to tackle an opposing player. Rehhagel maintained that he was not talking about anything malicious, but the damage had been done. He was becoming known as a good coach, but one who could become unhinged at a moment's notice on the bench.

Eschweiler's report was damning and the DFB banned Rehhagel for one month and fined him 3,000 Deutsche Marks. It was the beginning of the end of the manager's stint in Offenbach. The initial one-month ban turned to three upon a review and with Offenbach slipping down to last place in the table, the board took action to sack Rehhagel.

Rehhagel landed at Werder Bremen three months later in February 1976. The situation there was in need of a firefighter if there ever was one. The club were at the wrong end of the table. To make matters worse for Rehhagel, the previous manager, Herbert Burdenski, was well liked by the players and one of those, the goalkeeper, was his son, Dieter.

As the season wound down relegation looked like a real possibility. Rehhagel eventually managed to do just enough. His impact on the team began to show as the final matches came. In one of the last games of the season, Bremen defeated Duisburg 2-0 to avoid the drop. After the final whistle, the players hoisted Rehhagel on their shoulders. It was a game that would forever be talked about in Bremen.

Rehhagel had turned a team dangerously low on belief into a group of players who were confident they could be winners. His tactical adjustments were a big part of Bremen's push toward safety. He employed a man-to-man system of defense and found success with it, just as he would with Greece nearly 30 years later.

Bremen saw the quality of Rehhagel's work and wanted to sign the coach to a new contract. That may have seemed like a natural course of action, but Rehhagel was keeping tabs on the situation at Borussia Dortmund. It was Rehhagel's great dream from a young age to go to Dortmund. The club had been relegated to the second division and were pushing for promotion to the Bundesliga. When the position opened at Dortmund and the club called upon Rehhagel, it was obvious what his decision would be.

The manager wouldn't have much time to prepare for life in his new job. He joined Dortmund at the end of the 1975/76 season, the same season in which he had just led Bremen to safety. He was successful in leading his new charges through the promotion playoffs and back into the Bundesliga. And in his first full season with Dortmund, Rehhagel had his side playing some exceptional football. The club finished eighth, scoring a whopping 74 goals for the season. The problem was that Dortmund also conceded 64 times.

It was at Bremen and Dortmund that Rehhagel's coaching philosophy really began to take hold. Always a lover of Brazilian football, Rehhagel preferred to have his sides play attacking football. This may come as a surprise to those who followed the latter stages of his career, especially his time as Greece boss, which was characterized by his steadfast approach to defensive solidity. Rehhagel was a pragmatist, however, and remained so throughout his career. He saw what he had for personnel and tried to devise a system that would work. At Dortmund especially, he first displayed an affinity for working with older players. The purchases of players such as Erwin Kostedde, Willi Lippens, and Siegfried Held were evidence of that, all three in their 30's when they signed for Dortmund.

In veteran footballers, Rehhagel saw the importance of experience. In addition to that, he truly believed that older players were more settled in their personal life and that could only have a positive impact on their football. It was also in Dortmund where Rehhagel began to display signs of difficulty in working with star names, a problem that would pop up again later in his career. "Yes, dealing with stars was his big problem. He was not a moderator as a coach, he was a dictator. And of course, big stars did not like that," explains Beer. When Rehhagel arrived, there was talk of the club chasing German international Gunter Netzer, who was then playing for Real Madrid. Rehhagel was unequivocally against the purchase of the big-name midfielder, citing that the player didn't fit in with how he envisioned the team.

The team's play in Rehhagel's first full season gave rise to increased hopes from the Dortmund supporters going forward. Ultimately, the club were unable to push on, weighed down by the growing expectations. A midtable finish was the best they could muster the following season. However, the final match of that 1977/78 season was one that would inflict years of pain on Rehhagel and lead to the end of his stay at Borussia.

On 29 April 1978, the Bundesliga's last round of the season was scheduled. Dortmund were indifferent having secured their top-flight status with a few matches remaining. Their opponents however, Borussia Monchengladbach, had all to play for. They were tied on 46 points with Koln atop the league. Koln held the advantage going into the final day of the season with a plus ten goal difference over their title rivals. Monchengladbach were hoping that Koln would slip up in their final game, an away match at St. Pauli.

The match that ensued at the Rheinstadion in Dusseldorf between Monchengladbach and Dortmund would go down in German football history. Monchengladbach's Jupp Heynckes scored within the first minute in a sign of things to come. After an incredible first half display, the hosts had raced out to an unfathomable 6-0 lead. Dortmund were shell-shocked. Goalkeeper Peter Andrulat, the team's usual back-up, was even asked by Rehhagel at halftime if he wanted to come off the pitch. He declined, a decision he would later say he regretted. The second half was more of the same. Dortmund could not come to grips with the match. The goals continued to come for Monchengladbach and suddenly the massive goal difference gap had been closed considerably. Koln were winning at St. Pauli, but their big goal advantage was being wiped away.

Monchengladbach eventually finished with a 12-0 win. Koln managed to win 5-0 and thus took the Bundesliga title on goal difference, by a narrow plus three. The 12-0 scoreline just about eclipsed Koln's achievement. The talk in Germany was about Monchengladbach's amazing victory and Dortmund's spectacular capitulation. The result became the Bundesliga's largest ever margin of victory and remains so to this day. Rehhagel expressed to those close to him that his time as Dortmund manager would end with this defeat. And he was right. The next day, the club sacked the manager. The supporters would continue to blame the players in the aftermath, but the board saw Rehhagel as the man responsible or perhaps the one person they could make a scapegoat out of.

That loss saw Rehhagel lose a good degree of credibility in an instant. Before that match, his work at Dortmund and Bremen had seen his stock rise. He was then considered one of the most sought-after managers in Germany. His role in the 12-0 destruction of a side he coached saw him suffer a serious downgrade. He was a firefighter. Nothing more than that. That might have been harsh, but that was the prevailing notion by those in the media and those working within the German game. "That defeat saw him receive much criticism", says Beer. "At the time, the media reported on this match very critically and asked lots of questions. Otto became even more closed off with them after that."

As was consistent with his career, Rehhagel did not have to wait long to find work again. He decided to accept Arminia Bielefeld's offer in October 1978. The club were in tough shape and Rehhagel appeared to be the perfect man for the job. Initially, things went well. Rehhagel successfully organized the players and achieved some fine results. It was clear to see that there was a distinct lack of quality in the squad. An avoidance of relegation would have been a big success for a side like this. Bielefeld played Borussia Dortmund in the last match of the 1978/79 season and a 2-0 defeat saw them relegated to the second tier. It was ironic that Dortmund would be the side to send Rehhagel's team down. In many ways, the manager had not yet overcome the embarrassment brought about by the 12-0 defeat a year before. It was a match that dogged not just the coach, but the man. He became known as 'Torhagel', literally a storm of goals, a reference to his role in that game. The historic loss to Monchengladbach weighed heavily on him and his coaching suffered because of it. It was not as though he performed poorly at Bielefeld with an under-strength side, but for Rehhagel the joy and passion derived from coaching seemed to have slipped away.

He remained with the team in the second division for the start of the 1979/80 season. It was a difficult start to the campaign and Rehhagel's mind seemed elsewhere. In October, it was he who stepped away. The relations between the club and Rehhagel were good, but this proud man wanted to rebuild his reputation and find the success he craved in his career. He firmly believed this could not be done at Bielefeld.

Rehhagel's relationship with the media during his career was in most cases tense and it certainly impacted how he was portrayed. This was especially true in the early stages of his career before his successes began to pile up. The media branded him as a loose cannon. His demonstrative nature on the sidelines coupled with his straight-talking style in press conferences and interviews gave reporters ample evidence to support their claims. "The media in Germany were not necessarily unfair with him on the whole. One has to say honestly that Rehhagel was often arrogant in dealing with reporters," explains Beer. The journalist believes that Rehhagel's stinging attacks against some individuals, which at times included "severely hurting or ridiculing them with his arrogant words", were a response by the manager when he felt he was being treated too unfairly. This began to develop a vicious cycle where the more Rehhagel would attack, the more critical some members of the press would become. One press conference at Kaiserslautern later in his career typified this. "Rehhagel said to reporters at the press conference he only wanted to answer technical questions that day. One fed up television reporter then asked, 'Mr. Rehhagel, a technical question. I would like to paint my house which color can you recommend?' It was a clear shot at his previous profession as a painter. Of course, Otto raged upon hearing that," Beer points out.

Despite, the ever-present battles with the press, the most damning indictment of the coach was that by the time he left Bielefeld in 1979, he was still considered a short-term specialist. There was the two-year stint at Dortmund, but other than that he was in jobs for a year or less. Rehhagel hated that he had been typecast as this sort of manager, one who was only capable of the quick fix. There was also not yet any titles to speak of.

After undergoing early struggles in the 1979/80 season, Fortuna Dusseldorf sought out Rehhagel's services. Rehhagel took the role which brought him back to the Bundesliga. He had to win over a group of players, who on the whole, were none too excited about the new manager coming in. The perception from the players was that their new boss was a demanding character who would not be in the job very long. Rehhagel started his reign with an emphatic 6-2 win against VfB Stuttgart. This helped sway the doubters in the squad about his ability. It was a trick Rehhagel pulled off quite often in his career. He was a master of achieving very good results, very quickly. This bought him the time needed to implement his ideas and win over the players.

Dusseldorf did well enough to finish 11th under Rehhagel in that first season. However, the real story for Rehhagel and the club was in the DFB-Pokal, the German Cup. Dusseldorf had won the competition the previous season, defeating Hertha Berlin in the final 1-0 in extra-time. Before Rehhagel took over in October 1979, Dusseldorf had gone through the first two rounds of the competition, easily defeating the likes of Borussia Neunkirchen and Wacker 04 Berlin.

In the 3rd round, Rehhagel oversaw his side beat SV Goppingen before disposing of Karlsruhe 5-2 in the Round of 16. Next up was a quarter-final date against his former side Kickers Offenbach. Dusseldorf scored three times in extra-time to win the match 5-2. In the semi-finals, it was another of Rehhagel's former clubs who stood in the way in the form of Borussia Dortmund. A 3-1 win for Dusseldorf sent them to the final for a second consecutive season. Rehhagel would finally have a crack at the first trophy of his managerial career. The final was played at the Parkstadion in Gelsenkirchen on 4 June 1980. The opponent was FC Koln, who struck first blood after 26 minutes thanks to Bernhard Cullman's goal. Dusseldorf fought back and turned the match on its head in a five-minute span in the second half. Rudiger Wenzel equalizing after an hour and in the 65th minute, Thomas Allofs scoring the eventual game-winner. After eight years as a coach, Rehhagel celebrated the achievement of his first trophy.

That cup success did not lead to better days for Rehhagel in Dusseldorf.

Genuine excitement led to increased and rather unrealistic expectations for the mid-size club. The following season saw the team begin in terrible form and matters went from bad to worse. They dropped to 16th before a big match against 1860 Munich. Dusseldorf looked good having raced out to a 3-0 lead. However, a Rudi Voeller-inspired 1860 side battled back, eventually winning 4-3. Rehhagel was sacked. Dusseldorf's poor form led to him losing his job, but in all reality the club had reached its ceiling. There was a chasm between what the club wanted Rehhagel to achieve and what was possible. The firing did not bother the coach too much, as his aspirations were growing once again. Just like Essen as a young boy, Dusseldorf was no longer big enough for Rehhagel. His reputation had been restored thanks in large part to the DFB-Pokal victory and he could now set his sights on his next move.

It was eventually a car accident that did not involve him at all that changed the course of Otto Rehhagel's career. Having been without a job for five months, Rehhagel received a call from Werder Bremen in March 1981. The team were performing well in the 2. Bundesliga. They were chasing promotion from the North Division. This was the last season the German second division was split into northern and southern tiers, beginning from the 1981/82 season those two sections became consolidated into one sole second division.

All was going to plan for Bremen as they topped the table well into February. It was then when head coach Kuno Klotzer suffered a car accident. He only suffered minor injuries from the crash, but after six weeks he began complaining more often about terrible headaches. Bremen needed to find a manager for the final set of matches that season. Though his previous stint at Bremen was only for four months, Rehhagel was highly regarded there and ultimately was the man selected by the club. It seemed like the perfect fit for Bremen and Rehhagel. A short-term deal, should promotion be achieved then Bremen would win, Klotzer would come back, and Rehhagel would further enhance his reputation.

Things did not work out exactly how they were drawn up. In fact, they worked out better than any of the involved parties could have possibly imagined, with the exception of Klotzer. Rehhagel ended up staying on as manager of Werder Bremen for 14 years, not leaving until the end of the 1994/95 season. In that time he led the club to two Bundesliga titles, two DFB Pokal victories, 3 German Super Cups, and one UEFA Cup Winners' Cup success. He took the small, regional side from Northern Germany and turned them into a domestic force, into a team that competed season after season in the upper echelons of the Bundesliga standings. Not only that, but Rehhagel brought European football to Bremen, qualifying for Europe in the majority of his seasons at the club and winning a continental trophy in the 1991/92 Cup Winners' Cup.

Rehhagel's belief in himself to find success at the top level and the experience of his previous coaching stints had all come together at Bremen. What also played a major role was the relationship he had with Willi Lemke. Bremen's business manager joined Werder a few months after Rehhagel came to the club. Lemke believed in Rehhagel's ability and rated him very highly. It was perhaps the first time someone in such a high position at a club showed Rehhagel that sort of commitment and devotion. The success in that 14-year spell speaks for itself, it was undoubtedly the club's golden age. "Rehhagel is a very selective person, he trusts few people. In Bremen, Kaiserslautern, and then Greece, the presidents all understood how Rehhagel worked. He was not someone who wanted to be overridden. He always thought he was the one who should decide when it came to football matters," says Beer.

Rehhagel early results convinced the Bremen higher-ups that he was the man that should stay regardless of the Klotzer situation. With only six matches remaining in that 1980/81 season, Rehhagel did what he was brought in to do, oversee Bremen's promotion to the Bundesliga. In doing so he managed to persuade the club in that time that he should replace the previous boss. Klotzer had a meeting with the club's hierarchy at the end of the season and it was clear that the club wanted to move in a different direction. "You can say that Rehhagel was looking for his luck during his first years as a coach, but never finding it. A difficult character like Rehhagel does not fit in with every club. He found the right fit in 1981, with Bremen, in the province. Here he could be the strong man, here he could be left to work in peace," states Beer.

A master of quick starts, Rehhagel's first full season with the club was extremely good as Bremen finished fifth, clinching an UEFA Cup berth. That season was not without its difficulties however. In just the second match of the Bundesliga season, Werder were playing their home opener against one of Rehhagel's old clubs, Arminia Bielefeld. At one point, Bremen defender Norbert Siegmann came through with a late tackle on Bielefeld's Ewald Lienen. The challenge saw a yellow card produced, but the aftermath revealed the horror of what happened. Lienen had suffered a 25-centimeter long and 5-centimeter wide flesh wound from the tackle. After initially getting up, Lienen looked back down at the side of his leg and collapsed to the ground from the shock of seeing his exposed bone.

A terrible tackle soon exploded into something much more. Lienen not only went directly to the Bremen bench, but he pointed the finger right at Rehhagel, insisting it was the Bremen manager who had ordered the tackle. To this day, Rehhagel maintains that while he wanted his players to tackle Lienen, it was only in order to win the ball, not in a way to purposely injure. Lienen eventually pressed charges against Rehhagel and Siegmann. The manager and his player suffered death threats in the days and weeks following the match. Rehhagel had to have his family stay with friends, such was his fear that something would happen to them as a result of the fallout. An athletics tribune eventually saw the charges dropped, but once again the damage had been done and Rehhagel and Lienen never resolved their differences.

Unlike at Dortmund when he had his legal troubles there, Bremen backed Rehhagel and supported him through the ordeal. He felt comfortable at the club and saw this as his big opportunity to find a home and build a team over the course of time. The following campaign, the 1982/83 season, Bremen came within goal difference of the league title. They were tied on 52 points with nearby rivals Hamburg, but lost out as their goal difference was +38, compared to Hamburg's of +46.

The disappointment of missing out on the league title by the narrowest of margins was massive. However, Rehhagel kept on challenging with Bremen, always keeping them near the top of the table for the next few seasons. Thanks to his exploits with Bremen, he had become one of Germany's top managers. By the time the 1985/86 season had come, the firefighter label had worn off. In that campaign, Bremen were playing some superb football and entered the penultimate match of the season against Bayern Munich knowing that a victory would guarantee them their first league title since 1965.

With the score 0-0, Bremen received a late penalty-kick. If regular taker Michael Kutzop scored, then the league title would be Bremen's. Kutzop had scored on all 28 penalties he had taken in his professional career up until that point. The Polish-born defender struck the outside of the right post with his shot and the match finished 0-0. Kutzop played nearly 275 matches in a 12-year career in football, and out of 40 penalty kicks that he took, the one against Bayern that day was the only one he ever missed. The penalty miss would become one of the most memorable in Bundesliga history. Bremen lost the title again on goal difference the next weekend to Bayern as the Bavarians defeated

Borussia Monchengladbach 6-0 while Bremen lost to VfB Stuttgart 2-1, the same side they had beaten 6-0 earlier in the season. It was another agonizing finish to a season for Rehhagel, his players, and for Bremen supporters.

Despite a dip to 5th place the following season, Rehhagel managed to keep the bulk of the side together. Finally, in 1988, Rehhagel celebrated the first league title of his career. Bayern's three-year grip on the Bundesliga had been ended. That Bremen side had at its heart a truly defensive mentality and conceded only 22 goals over 34 matches. Winning the league not only cemented Rehhagel's legacy at Werder Bremen, it also ensured he would now be viewed as a winner.

In the seasons that followed there was something of a drop off with 7th and 9th place finishes in 1989/90 and 1991/92, respectively. However, there were successes either side of those campaigns. A DFB-Pokal cup was lifted in the 1990/91 season with a win over Koln on penalty-kicks. And then in 1992, Rehhagel conquered Europe for the first time.

The DFB-Pokal win in the spring of 1991 gave Bremen a ticket to the 1991/92 UEFA Cup Winners' Cup competition. After easily thrashing Romanian side Bacau 11-0 in the 1st Round, Bremen defeated Ferencvaros in the 2nd Round, 4-2 on aggregate. In the quarter-finals against Galatasaray, a 0-0 draw in the second leg ensured Bremen would go through to the semi-final after a 2-1 first leg win at home. Against Club Brugge in the semis, Bremen lost the first leg 1-0 in Belgium. Back in Germany, a 2-0 win thanks to goals from Marco Bode and Manfred Bockenfeld sealed the comeback and sent Bremen to their first ever European final. Bremen would take on Monaco in the final to be held in Lisbon, Portugal at the Estadio da Luz. Little did he know that 12 years on, Rehhagel would contest another final in that very same stadium. Klaus Allofs gave Bremen a 40th minute lead before Wynton Rufer doubled the advantage ten minutes after halftime. Bremen won 2-0 and the club had claimed a European trophy for the first time. Rehhagel's star was continuing to rise.

The following year saw Bremen win the Bundesliga again, beating out Bayern to the title, this time by a single point. Another trophy, a second DFB-Pokal with the club was won in the next year. By this point, Rehhagel had achieved legendary status in Bremen. By the time Rehhagel finished the 1993/94 season, where the team finished 8th, he began to think about leaving Bremen. He had achieved all he thought he could with the club and was keen on a new challenge. He remained one final season and in that campaign (1994/95) nearly claimed another league title, only to miss out once again in agonizing fashion by a single point.

Rehhagel's time at Bremen was without question the most successful in the club's history. "In Bremen, Rehhagel could build something with his eye for good players. It is no coincidence that he was successful in smaller environments, where he could be the absolute boss like in Bremen and later Kaiserslautern and Greece," says Beer.

Perhaps Rehhagel's greatest achievement, besides all the trophies won, was the way he transformed Bremen from a mediocre side to a team that could consistently challenge Germany's best for honors. No other side battled Bayern Munich for domestic supremacy on a consistent basis during that era than Bremen during Rehhagel's 14-year stay.

Then that is perhaps the reason why in 1995, Bayern reached out to Rehhagel. After a poor campaign by Bayern's lofty standards where they finished 5th in the 1994/95 season, Bayern set out to bring Rehhagel to Munich. Having achieved all that he could with Bremen, Rehhagel agreed to join Germany's biggest and most successful club. This appeared like it would be the culmination of his career. Having been branded by some as country boy, merely, capable of coaching smaller, provincial teams, Rehhagel had always gone to great pains to show his sophistication, both as a coach and an individual. "Rehhagel had sophistication, the question was always whether his character and stubbornness would fit in a big club with world stars. And with club presidents who like to give interviews," suggests Beer. "Rehhagel himself has always made great efforts not to act like a man from the province. He was very fond of quoting great poets and of pointing out his achievements and the extent of his knowledge."

Rehhagel had a point to prove. He wanted badly to succeed at the top with Bayern. It eventually ended up being one of the bleakest chapters of his managerial career. Ironically, everything began so well. With Rehhagel at the helm, Bayern were unstoppable in the early stages of the 1995/96 season. Seven wins in a row suggested Rehhagel and Bayern had both made the right choice. However, trouble began to brew in October and November. Internal problems between some of the bigger personalities in the squad, such as Lothar Mattheus and Jurgen Klinsmann, were the first signs of trouble. That season was one that helped give birth to Bayern's nickname of 'FC Hollywood.' Bayern were at a stage where following the club was like watching a soap opera. Players freely spoke against teammates in the tabloids and squad morale was extremely low.

Rehhagel would not see out the season at Bayern. He was sacked on 27 April 1996, despite the fact that he had his team in second place in the league and through to the final of the UEFA Cup. It was not a disastrous position to be in by any stretch, but Rehhagel could not survive the off-the-field chaos surrounding him. From the start, there were murmurs of discontent from the players about Rehhagel's training methods. Those turned into full-fledged attacks as the season progressed with players slamming the manager in post-match interviews or by secretly going to the media. Rehhagel could not control the situation.

There could be fault laid at his feet as well. Known as a disciplinarian, Rehhagel changed his style once he joined Bayern. He gave his players more freedom than usual and this backfired spectacularly. Dressing room talks were leaked to the media and it was apparent he had no control. "Rehhagel was not used to the fact that at Bayern the stars liked to talk to the media or complained to the president if they did not like the training. Munich was a whole new world for him, but it was not his world," says Beer. Once again, he showed a difficulty in working with star names. The bigger the ego, the tougher it appeared it was for Rehhagel to manage that sort of player, especially individuals who expected special treatment. "At Bremen and Kaiserslautern, Rehhagel worked in the same pattern. He was looking for players with special character, real men who were already married and had a quiet family life. From these men he believed he could form a team with one hundred percent character and team spirit," says Beer.

After the fantastic long-term spell at Bremen, the Bayern experience was a real knock to Rehhagel's aspirations of coaching a huge club. For someone who had dreamt of managing Real Madrid one day, the stint at Bayern was a major setback. Besides a short spell at Hertha Berlin in 2012, where he failed to save the team from being relegated in the dying weeks of the season, Rehhagel took on his final club coaching post in the summer of 1996 when he agreed to take over Kaiserslautern.

For some it was a prime example of how far Rehhagel had fallen due to the Munich debacle that he was taking over a side that had been relegated to the 2. Bundesliga. Rehhagel was returning to the team he once played for after 24 years. The club from southwestern Germany had recently fallen on hard times, dropping down to the second division after 30 years in the Bundesliga. The only target was immediate promotion to the top-flight. The job had a do-or-die feel to it. Failure to get Kaiserslautern back up would be a fresh blow to the veteran manager.

From the get-go Rehhagel received a confidence boost from the people running the club. Those individuals were convinced that Rehhagel could do with Kaiserslautern what he did with Bremen, take a second division side up and then have them feature in the Bundesliga. There were many similarities between this new position and when Rehhagel took over at Bremen. In both cases, a decent-sized club had lost its way and was seeking someone to bring back the glory days.

The people of Kaiserslautern saw in Rehhagel an individual who could make the improvements needed, happen very quickly. And that is exactly what occurred. Drawing heavily upon a group of experienced players, Rehhagel rediscovered his coaching touch at Kaiserslautern. It was not so much less pressure than at Bayern as it was a different sort of pressure. In the 2. Bundesliga, it was all about results and football. The Bayern job had spiraled into something more than that and despite his own vast experience Rehhagel was completely unprepared for it.

That first season at Kaiserslautern for Rehhagel was about reclaiming himself as a manager. He went back to square one and focused on what had made him so good at his job rather than trying to be someone else. Kaiserslautern did not exactly light it up on the pitch through the 1996/97 season, but they were consistent, and as the season wore on showed they had the quality and the spirit to achieve promotion. At times there was some friction between the supporters and Rehhagel about the attractiveness of the football on display. Rehhagel shrugged that off by stating, "They called me to come here to help. If the people don't like that then I can leave again." The bullish response was indicative of a man steadfast in his beliefs and true to his style.

Kaiserslautern achieved promotion in the spring of 1997, easily outpacing the likes of Wolfsburg and Mainz by ten points. It was the quick return to the Bundesliga everyone had wanted. Rehhagel had been planning for the team's return to the top division well before promotion had been achieved. "At Bremen, they still use a Rehhagel phrase as law, 'There are no young or old players, there are only good or bad players'. That was always his philosophy," says Beer. While he entrusted veteran players to carry the load in the 2. Bundesliga, he was convinced that the squad needed refreshing in order to compete in the Bundesliga. Though the bulk of the roster was the same, Rehhagel bolstered the midfield with the likes of the Bulgarian Marian Hristov, long-time VfB Stuttgart midfielder Andreas Buck, a young Michael Ballack, and Ciriaco Sforza, the supremely talented Swiss playmaker. Sforza and Rehhagel rarely saw eye to eye during their time together at Kaiserslautern, but during that first season their relationship was strong. Sforza needed to find form after a difficult season at Inter Milan where could not find a regular place in the team. Rehhagel meanwhile, saw in Sforza the missing link that Kaiserslautern needed to break down opposing defenses.

The fixture simulator tossed out the appetizing opening day match between defending champions Bayern Munich and newly promoted 2. Bundesliga champions Kaiserslautern. This offered Rehhagel an opportunity to go up against his former employers immediately. Away to Munich, Rehhagel exacted a measure of revenge on Bayern with a 1-0 victory thanks to Michael Schjonberg's goal ten minutes from time. The result was considered by many observers as a fluke, the type of early-season surprise that occurs from time to time.

In all actuality, that victory was the start of one of the most historic campaigns in Bundesliga history. That win in the opening round gave Kaiserslautern a big shot of momentum going forward. Rehhagel had molded together a very good squad, one comprised of the right mix of warriors and artists. *Die Reuten Teufel* (The Red Devils) won three of their first four matches to start the season as they climbed to the top of the table. It was a lead they would never relinquish. Rehhagel had struck the perfect balance. Strong and tough in defense, speed and goalscoring ability up front, Rehhagel built up the midfield with his offseason moves and masterfully put together a squad capable of winning.

The penultimate day of the season saw Kaiserslautern come up against Wolfsburg at home. A victory coupled with Bayern dropping the points would seal an unlikely title for Rehhagel and his side. Kaiserslautern ripped their opponents apart in a 4-0 victory and Bayern could not find the breakthrough in a 0-0 draw at Duisburg. Kaiserslautern had won the Bundesliga for the second time in their history and became the only side to ever win the championship in their first season since promotion.

Rehhagel had undoubtedly been the architect of this shocking success. His personnel moves in the summer had given him the squad depth needed to sustain a title challenge. Tactically, Rehhagel had been spot on all season with his team selection and formation. His use of Czech defender Miroslav Kadlec as a libero was a brilliant move. The 33-year-old Kadlec was an introvert and thrived with the belief that Rehhagel placed in him. Kaiserslautern's style of play bore Rehhagel's trademark as well. All eleven players on the pitch were committed to winning the ball and fighting for each other, even the strikers. Though he demanded hard work, commitment, and discipline, Rehhagel allowed the players a good deal of freedom on the field. He did not over coach and knew that he had enough leaders to ensure the right decisions would be made. He had provided the structure, but did not restrict the creativity his attacking players possessed.

It was perhaps off the pitch where the manager did his best work. In 1996, Rehhagel inherited a Kaiserslautern squad filled with players who were low in morale and belief. He succeeded in turning them into a tight-knit group whose distinguishing traits were teamwork and confidence. There was an absence of star power in the team, but as Rehhagel preferred, the team was the star. The all for one, one for all mentality perfectly encapsulated that Kaiserslautern side. Also of great benefit was the union Rehhagel had helped create between coaches, players, and supporters. The atmosphere around the club during his first two seasons there was positive in all aspects. The victory over Bayern to start the championship season brought about great enthusiasm and the team rode that wave of emotion through the entire campaign.

Rehhagel was unable to sustain that feel-good factor in the years that followed. The next two seasons saw Kaiserslautern pick up consecutive fifth-place finishes. There was even a run to the Champions' League quarter-finals in the 1998/99 season. Despite, consistently challenging near the top of the Bundesliga, Rehhagel's initial success had brought about disappointment that Kaiserslautern were no longer winning titles. He began losing the trust of the players and after a rough start to the 2000/01 season he left the club by mutual consent. His difficult relationship with Sforza had a lot to do with that as the players began to side with their teammate rather than their coach. By the end, it had all broken down between the manager, the players, and the club hierarchy. Many suggested Rehhagel had been the victim of a smear campaign.

Regardless, Rehhagel was out of a job again. There would undoubtedly be suitors vying for his services, but leaving Kaiserslautern had brought the man to a crossroads. He had played and managed in Germany for his entire professional career. There was a yearning for something different. At 62, Rehhagel knew that his career was edging closer to the end. It had also taken up so much of his life, the endless days, weeks, and months of being on the training pitch, the club headquarters, or travelling to and from matches. The daily grind, year after year, was taking its toll. Thus, he began to consider international management. He had been the subject of rumors to take over the German national side after their disastrous Euro 2000 campaign. The DFB decided on going with Rudi Voeller instead, one of his former players. In fact, several of Rehhagel's players went on to coach professionally. Some, such as Thomas Schaaf, found success at the highest level and many publicly spoke about the impact Rehhagel had on their own coaching styles.

Coaching a national team had a certain appeal for Rehhagel. He decided to take the risk of moving outside his comfort zone in Germany and seek a new challenge. He applied for the vacant managerial position of the Greek national team in the summer of 2001. "He was tempted to work on the world stage," believes Beer. "In Germany, that was not possible for him after the disaster in Munich. That experience left him very angry and motivated. As a national team coach, playing in a big tournament would be the culmination of his career." Before applying for that job, he suggested at that stage of his career he could afford to be picky about where he next worked. "I am open to any interest," Rehhagel claimed, "It's very nice to be in a position to say, I don't have to do it, I will do it only if I like it." On his 63rd birthday, Otto Rehhagel was unveiled as the new head coach of the Greek national team. A manager, who had coached and played at the professional level for over 40 years solely in Germany, would now go abroad for the first time.

Chapter 4

Rising From The Ashes

"With Germany, Rehhagel would have never been able to have the success he had with Greece," believes Beer. "In Germany there were too many stars, too much media, and too many people who want to have a say and decide. Greece was the perfect environment for him as a coach, but also as a person. Rehhagel was always very interested in culture."

Despite claiming he knew a lot about Greek history and culture, but very little about Greek football, Rehhagel seemed to have his finger on the pulse at his first press conference. The Ethniki's new coach spoke about the problems between the big clubs in Greece and the effect that had on the national team. There were already hints as to the changes that Rehhagel wanted to make with regard to off-the-pitch matters. He described the national team's training facilities as 'third-world' and then spoke about the lack of motivation he saw in the players.

While acknowledging the negatives, the German sought to strike an optimistic tone. He was complementary of the technical skill of Greek players and while he immediately ruled out any talk of Greece still having a chance to qualify for the 2002 World Cup, he did show his belief in the team looking forward. Rehhagel told the media at his presentation as Greek boss about his first mission. "Qualifying for the 2002 World Cup is not an option, but I wouldn't have taken over if I didn't think I could lead Greece to Euro 2004," said Rehhagel, only to continue with, "The national team until now has had no incentive. It's then an incentive for me to work with a team that isn't good, so they can improve. With hard work, however, will come successes."

Greece had a friendly with Russia in Moscow scheduled before Rehhagel was appointed. It was decided by the new coach and the EPO that it would be better if Rehhagel just observed this friendly and not take the reins of the team yet. Instead, Nikos Christidis would take over as interim manager for this one match. Christidis was a former Greek international goalkeeper with 29 caps to his name. He spent the majority of his 21-year career with his first club, Aris. He was able to celebrate a Greek Cup victory in 1970 with the Thessaloniki club. For the final six years of his career, Christidis moved to AEK. There he also found success winning the domestic double in the 1977/78 season and another league title the following campaign. For AEK supporters he gained legendary status in AEK's run to the UEFA Cup semi-finals in 1977. In the quarter-final against Queens' Park Rangers, AEK found themselves going back to Greece with a 3-0 deficit from the first leg defeat in England. The team brought the tie back to level terms in the second leg and eventually into a shoot-out. Christidis had been on the bench for the most of the match, but in the 117th minute he came on so as to be the team's goalkeeper in the shoot-out. Christidis made two penalty saves helping AEK famously advance as he cemented his place in the club's folklore.

As Rehhagel watched from the stands, Greece were impressive as they battled out a 0-0 draw against the Russians. The players showed their individual quality and did well to grab a result against a decent side. Traditionally, the Ethniki have been notorious for below-par performances in August friendlies. Perhaps Rehhagel's influence had already been felt, even at that early stage as the players put forth a display full of commitment. Rehhagel had also taken a look at the U-21 side in his first few days as Greek coach and had spoken highly of young Panathinaikos defender, Giourkas Seitaridis, a player who would end playing a big role in the coming years for the Ethniki.

Greece were set to play Finland on 5 September in what would be Rehhagel's first match in charge. Four days earlier, Finland had a qualifier away to Albania. Rehhagel decided he wanted to take a look at Greece's opponents in person and thus travelled to Tirana. He came back to Greece with a good account of the Finnish team telling the media that Finland were a strong and committed side and reminding many that they were undefeated in their own stadium.

Up until the match against Finland, Rehhagel had held only a couple of training sessions with the team. There were early murmurs of criticism from the media about the manager's decision to go back to Germany after being announced as Greek coach. As soon as Rehhagel did run a couple practices with the players, it did not take long for conflicts to arise. As Greece held their final training session on the eve of their match in Helsinki, a substantial bust-up took place between Rehhagel and Greece's left-back Grigoris Georgatos. The 29-year-old was arguably the most recognizable Greek player in Europe at the time. Georgatos started his playing career at Panachaiki as a teenager. At the age of 22, he was signed by Olympiacos. His development in Piraeus continued as he established himself as a dynamic defender who could attack with pace on the flanks and whip in extremely dangerous crosses with his lethal left foot. After winning three straight league titles with Olympiacos, Inter Milan came calling in 1999. The Italian giants snapped up Georgatos for a fee of €7 million. It was amongst the most high-profile transfers of a player in the history of the Greek game. Inter Milan's squad possessed unbelievable world-class quality. Names such as Ronaldo, Roberto Baggio, Christian Vieri, Alvaro Recoba, Ivan Zamorano, Clarence Seedorf, Laurent Blanc, and Javier Zanetti were all top players of their generation. For Georgatos to have made the switch to such a star-studded squad was a source of pride for Greeks. In his first season in Italy, Georgatos was ever-present, featuring in 34 matches total, including 24 starts. His performances won over the Inter faithful as well as the Italian press. Due to the club's below-par defensive record, changes were needed in the following season so Georgatos found himself back at Olympiacos on loan. By the 2001/02 season he returned to Inter for one more season.

Without a translator yet, Rehhagel used defender Kostas Konstantinidis as his way to speak to the players. Konstantinidis was born in Germany and played for Hertha Berlin when Rehhagel took over Greece. As Rehhagel instructed his players on how they would set up against Finland, Konstantinidis took the lead role in translating from German to Greek to the rest of the squad. Rehhagel explained that he wanted Georgatos to play as an attacking wing-back against the Finnish team. No sooner had Konstantinidis relayed Rehhagel's directives to Georgatos, had the player fired back with a stinging rebuttal. Georgatos made clear in no uncertain terms that he was not interested in playing in that position. When pressed by Rehhagel about what Georgatos said, Konstantinidis could not bring himself to translate in an exact manner due to the profanity used by his teammate. Even if Rehhagel could not understand Greek, the way in which Georgatos responded was enough to tell him everything about what the player thought of his request.

Rehhagel appeared to allow the issue to pass as Georgatos was included in the starting eleven as the day of the game arrived. For his debut, Rehhagel selected a very attacking line-up which included three strikers in Charisteas, Machlas, and Zisis Vryzas. A crowd of 27,000 provided a good atmosphere at the Olympic Stadium in Helsinki as Otto Rehhagel took his seat on the Greek bench for the first time. In Greece, a deal could not be struck to show the match and thus back home supporters had no television coverage. It might well have been a blessing in disguise.

Over the next 90 minutes, the Ethniki put forth one of the most shambolic displays in its history. Rehhagel surely could not have envisaged such a nightmare for his first match. Finland took control of proceedings from the start and had taken the lead after just 14 minutes. That was when striker Mikael Forssell was allowed to dribble into the box untouched to score from a very tough angle after being put through by Teemu Tainio. Eight minutes later it was 2-0 as an unmarked Aki Riihilahti headed past Dimitris Eleftheropoulos in the Greek goal.

Greece were shell-shocked, but the manner in which they conceded the first two goals highlighted a team that looked undisciplined and frankly uninterested. At the back, Eleftheropoulos looked out of sorts, and defensively players were out of position and committing wild challenges. The general body language of the players was downright awful. Despite, Karagounis' long-range effort which pulled Greece back to 2-1 on the half-hour, there was never the suggestion that a comeback was possible. That goal was merely a footnote in an otherwise woeful performance.

Finland used the remaining fifteen minutes of the first-half to inflict even more damage. Wingers Mika Nurmela and Joonas Kolkka, who at that time was playing for Panathinaikos, were running rampant and looking unstoppable. Kolkka scored the hosts' third goal in the 39th minute with a splendid shot. The effort was from such a tight angle that Eleftheropoulos again should have done better. The Finnish team sliced and diced through the Greek midfield at will. Time and time again they were finding loads of space behind the opposition defense. On the stroke of halftime, a terrible giveaway from Georgatos saw another lightning-quick Finnish counter-attack that resulted in Nurmela finding Kolkka on the left, he evaded Eleftheropoulos and cut the ball back for Forssell. The striker saw his initial shot blocked, but was quickest to the rebound to score his second and make it 4-1.

The second half began in a similar manner as Finland added to their haul of goals eight minutes after the break. Jari Litmanen, the team's captain and perhaps the greatest Finnish player of all-time, made it 5-1 from the penalty spot after being fouled in the box. Greece were lucky that the scoreline finished in that way, because Finland could have added more in the second half as the visitors offered no response.

That Finland side included some of the best players the country had ever produced. In addition to Litmanen, there were the likes of Sami Hyppia, Antti Niemi, Tainio, Forssell, and Kolkka, all players who left an indelible mark in their nation's football history. The evident individual quality of that Finland side could still not mask how bad the defeat was for Greece. This was a loss of epic proportions, an indicator as to how far the national team had fallen. Not purely in a competitive sense, more so with regard to the atmosphere surrounding the team. The environment seemed poisoned by the problems that had long afflicted Greek football. It seemed clear that the players did not place great importance in playing for their country.

Despite the match not being televised in Greece, there was widespread condemnation due to the heavy nature of the defeat and the ensuing reports of the performance. Rehhagel was not given a free pass by the media despite that being his first match. Headlines slammed the Ethniki and their new manager. Newspaper Sportime led with "Pou Pas Re-hhagel?" ("Where are you going, Re-hhagel?"), a play on Rehhagel's name with a common slang interjection. The new manager was heavily criticized for his tactics and personnel choices. The players were severely attacked, everything from their abilities to their commitment questioned.

In speaking to the press after the match, Rehhagel spoke clearly about what he saw on the pitch. "My players did not battle at all and did not try out on the pitch," said the coach. He would go on to rate that performance as one of the worst he ever saw from one of his teams. Rehhagel did attempt to accept part of the blame by stating, "I might only be here a little while on the bench, but I would like to share in the responsibility of the defeat." He was repeatedly asked about his decision to play with three recognized forwards. He explained by simply saying, "We wanted to chase the match and the win."

There was only one qualifier remaining for Greece in their World Cup qualifying campaign. That would come against England at Old Trafford in October. Rehhagel made it immediately clear to those in power in the EPO, that he expected the changes he desired to be carried out immediately. While better training facilities were something that the manager knew would take time,

Rehhagel was clear on other conditions he wanted met. There was a request by Rehhagel that on away trips the travelling group would be trimmed down. He saw too many hangers-on and unnecessary distractions for the players as a real issue when playing away from home.

Mainly, Rehhagel began making changes to the personnel. This was a team that needed rehabilitation on and off the pitch. The Finland match would be the last time Georgatos played for the Ethniki. The player himself announced he was retiring after the match, lamenting the fact that he always bore the brunt of the blame when the national team lost. Either way, Rehhagel wanted to instill discipline into a side sorely lacking it. After his training ground outburst, it was always likely that Georgatos would never be called up by Rehhagel again. As he showed throughout his coaching career, Rehhagel would always choose to work with players he deemed as having the right character rather than only talent. For the German, Georgatos simply did not fit the bill.

Journalist Sotirios Triantafyllou points to the match versus Finland as being the key to Rehhagel establishing control. "The defeat to Finland was a very strong warning bell for Otto Rehhagel, who at that point had not been able to convey his philosophy being in the job just a short time. He slowly implemented his ideas and his iron-clad discipline and he believed that certain footballers had characters that were not in line with what he expected, such as Georgatos."

It was not only about chopping players he saw as difficult to build a team with, Rehhagel also desired to heal the wounds of the past. One of his first great masterstrokes was to convince Demis Nikolaidis to come out of international retirement.

* * * *

In 1993, a 20-year-old Nikolaidis found himself in Athens negotiating a move between his boyhood club, Ethnikos Alexandroupoulis, and first division side, Apollon Athinon. When he studied the contract he was about to sign he realized there was no salary written on the agreement. He called his father who told him to sign it regardless. The advice for that leap of faith was so Nikolaidis could make the big jump with the reasoning that no matter what happened at Apollon, the promising youngster would quickly show that he had what it took to make it at the top level. Giorgos Nikolaidis could not have possibly known his son better.

Nikolaidis signed for Apollon and hit the ground running in the Greek top-flight. His first full season at the Rizoupouli Stadium saw Nikolaidis quickly establish himself as one of the top strikers in Greece. He formed a formidable partnership with Bosnian-born forward Bernard Barnjak and Nikolaidis' 17 goals in 33 matches helped Apollon to a surprise fourth-place finish. While he succeeded in punishing weaker sides with his deadly finishing, energy, and work ethic, it was his goals against the top teams that saw him really garner attention. During that first season he scored against the likes of Olympiacos, Panathinaikos, and PAOK, whilst also winning a penalty against AEK. He never scored against the latter, not for want of trying. AEK was the team Nikolaidis supported. He wanted to score against them more than anyone, so that they would become more interested in purchasing him.

It was his performances for Apollon that gave him the exposure necessary to be called up to the Ethniki. Apollon were traditionally a smaller club with modest resources, though during that period they were punching well above their weight, even managing to play in the preliminary round of the 1995/96 UEFA Cup. Nikolaidis first played for Greece in April 1995 against Russia. An indicator of how unique it was to have a player called up to the national team from such a small club, no player has since been called up to the senior side while playing for Apollon. His first goal for his country came in only his second cap, the opener in a 2-1 defeat to Finland. Until he stepped away from the team in 1999, Nikolaidis had scored eleven times for Greece and along with Nikos Machlas was the team's biggest goalscoring threat at the end of the millennium.

After two-and-a-half seasons with Apollon with nearly 50 goals in all competitions, the race to sign Greek football's hottest talent had intensified. Panathinaikos and Olympiacos looked closest to snapping up the striker ahead of the 1996/97 season. An agreement was finally reached with Olympiacos, with only personal terms between Nikolaidis and the Piraeus club needed to close the deal. Nikolaidis eventually could not go through with the move. He balked at the switch and waited until AEK came in with an offer.

The player got his wish and in July 1996 became an AEK player. Nikolaidis spent seven seasons with the Kitrinomavri, winning three Greek Cups and one Greek Super Cup. On an individual level, he thrived, becoming Greek League top scorer in 1998/99 and winning the Greek Footballer of the Year award three times. At one point, Belgian side Anderlecht came in with an incredibly lucrative offer, but the player stayed loyal to the club of his heart. Eventually, his time at AEK ended in 2003 after his relationship with the club's President, Makis Psomiadis, had broken down completely. After a period of tension between the two men, the breaking point came when Psomiadis visited Nikolaidis at his house one evening. Nikolaidis alleged in a statement to police at the time that Psomiadis had brought several bodyguards to threaten him, reportedly saying, "I'm going to break your ribs and legs and you will never play football again." He went to Atletico Madrid for the final season of his career, where he was fantastic in the early stages of the 2003/04 season, forming an explosive duo with a young Fernando Torres. Injuries took their toll and though Atletico were interested in extending the player's contract, Nikolaidis took the decision to stop his playing career.

* * * *

After seeking a meeting with the player, Rehhagel expressed to Nikolaidis his belief that this team needed him. Nikolaidis, seeing the opportunity for a fresh start with the Ethniki, was immediately convinced by the new boss. He declared himself available for selection for the match against England. Nikolaidis' teammate at AEK, Michalis Kasapis, also took hold of the olive branch Rehhagel offered.

While Greece had been eliminated from contention for qualification to the 2002 World Cup, England were on the cusp of booking their spot in the finals. Sven Goran Erikson's side would qualify if they could match or better Germany's result. While Greece were limping into the final qualifier having just lost 5-1, England were full of confidence having defeated Germany away by the same scoreline in September. It was a historic result for England, underlining the quality of the team at that time.

Seemingly out of nowhere however, England began to develop problems going into the Greece match, both on-and-off the pitch. Frank Lampard, Chelsea's new signing from West Ham, was omitted from the squad for the qualifier due to his drunken actions in a Heathrow hotel along with a few other Chelsea teammates. Eriksson had warned players at the beginning of 2001 that he would take a hard-line on any lack of professionalism from his players. Lampard and his teammates were reportedly loud and accused of vomiting on the occasion, which was made much worse due to the fact that the incident occurred a day after the 11 September terrorist attacks in the United States and the hotel in question was full of stranded Americans.

A highly-publicized outing by Steven Gerrard on the eve of joining up with the England squad only added to England's woes. Gerrard was pictured out at a bar until 2 am, and the English media were quick to make the situation a big headline. The fact that Gerrard was not drunk probably aided his cause to not be axed from the side, though Eriksson by that point probably did not want to cause more upheaval to the squad.

England's selection headaches made Gerrard's participation in the match even more vital. The team were already missing a trio of starting players including Michael Owen, Sol Campbell, and David Seaman. Squad players such as Alan Smith and Nicky Butt were also unavailable.

For Greece, besides the absence of Georgatos, there were further defensive issues as the Ethniki's number one goalkeeper during the time, Olympiacos' Eleftheropoulos, withdrew from the squad citing family reasons. Eleftheropoulos had been recently criticized for his performance against Finland as well as an error-strewn display for his club against Lille in the Champions' League. The goalkeeper was superb against Russia in the 0-0 draw that began the Rehhagel era. After getting the nod against Finland, it looked as though Rehhagel had put his confidence in 'Ele' to be Greece's starter.

Eleftheropoulos was one of the top goalkeepers in Greece during the end of the 1990's and beginning of the new millennium. As a 20-year-old he burst onto the scene at Olympiacos, playing an important role in the team winning the Greek title in 1997, their first championship in a decade. He went on to win seven titles with the Erythrolefki, finally departing in 2004 to make the move abroad. He spent five seasons in Italy, beginning with a stint at Messina. He impressed enough to earn a move to Italian giants AC Milan, but there he was unable to make the grade. A short spell at Roma was the segway to one season at Ascoli and two at Siena, before Eleftheropoulos moved back to Greece to end his career with time at PAS Giannina, Iraklis, and Panionios. To suggest the player's decision to pull himself out of the Greek squad for the England match deeply hurt his career might be too simplistic. The fact remains that Rehhagel never selected him for the national team again and the Finland defeat was the last of his twelve international caps.

Rehhagel was keen on bringing new blood into the squad. Nikopolidis would take Eleftheropoulos' spot in goal against England and there were the returns of Nikolaidis and Kasapis into the national team fold. Young full-back Giourkas Seitaridis was also brought into the Ethniki squad for the first time. The Finland defeat had cast a dark cloud over the players, but also the new manager.

Just a couple months into the job and it was clear that Rehhagel was already under immense pressure. The media were having a field day with the 'Germano'. Some of the criticisms spewed out were unfair and way off the mark. Despite his proven record as a club manager in Germany, there were many in the media and in Greece that questioned the wisdom of his appointment. The tired line was that this was another manager coming to Greece to retire with one last paycheck.

This ignored the simple fact that Rehhagel's asking price for a salary was a fraction of the one that Scala had requested. Still, Rehhagel's actions brought upon a certain degree of questioning as to whether he was indeed serious about the job. Rehhagel lamented the fact he did not have more time to prepare his team against England, when in truth it was his decision to travel from Germany to Greece with only time for one training session before departing for that final qualifying match. After the Finland loss, Rehhagel returned to Germany. He was lambasted for that as the media pointed out that he had not attended a single Greek league match up until that point. Rehhagel frequently stated he watched all the big derbies and all of the games that Greek clubs played in European competitions. His belief was that only in those type of big matches with all the pressure that comes with them can you truly tell if a player was suited to the demands of the national team.

Regardless of this philosophy, he was beginning to be seen as a coach in exile, one with a hands-off approach who could not be bothered to come to Greece until just before a match. It was not a view without some merit. Since being announced as Greek manager in August, Rehhagel had held only three training sessions with his team ahead of the flight to England.

It was not only the media and a cautious public that were having trouble warming up to Rehhagel. The players too were slow in embracing their new boss. The Finland defeat surely did not help matters, nor did Rehhagel's brief time on the training ground with the team. The relationship between players and manager ahead of the England game could be described as tenuous at best. While they were not outspoken against Rehhagel, the pre-England comments from squad members revealed an underlying uneasiness about the coach. Nikopolidis, in speaking to the English press, clearly stated the players really didn't know much about Rehhagel yet. "We haven't got past the getting-to-know you stage with the coach," said the Panathinaikos goalkeeper, "It's far from ideal having had only one training session before we depart for the match." Fellow teammate Giorgos Georgiadis was even more blunt when he told assembled journalists, "We've yet to see what he is going to bring to the job."

Rehhagel did himself no favors in the lead-up to the match at Old Trafford by consistently talking about how he hoped to help Germany secure a place in the World Cup by getting a result against England. Rehhagel, working as an analyst on German television a week before the match, told German national team coach and his former player Rudi Voeller he would be doing his utmost to win the game so Germany would go through. Statements such as "my heart still beats for Germany" did not go down well in Greece for a manager that was already being questioned with regard to his commitment and loyalty to the job. The backdrop to this was that Rehhagel had not yet signed a contract. Essentially, Rehhagel and the EPO were working on a handshake agreement as the paperwork had not been fully signed.

Having dropped Eleftheropoulos and defender Giorgos Amanatidis from the squad, Rehhagel then had to deal with claims of bias against Olympiacos because he had selected only two of the club's players, Christos Patsatzoglou and Stelios Venetidis, for the England game. There were seemingly few people happy with anything that Rehhagel was doing.

As the opening whistle approached against England, many pundits feared Greece would suffer a similar defeat to that in Helsinki, or worse. The last trip to England the Ethniki took ended in a 5-0 drubbing in that friendly just prior to the 1994 World Cup. With all the recent problems of the national team, including poor form and the bad atmosphere within the team, coupled with the questions surrounding Rehhagel, the worry was that the national team had not hit rock-bottom yet.

Legendary BBC commentator John Motson was very confident of England's chances for victory as he began his broadcast on English television. That was the prevailing mood across the spectrum. England would win and do so comfortably.

From the start, Eriksson's side blasted out of the gates, immediately confirming their status as clear favorites. Greece looked shaky in the opening stages, but to the surprise of just about everyone they settled quickly. England captain, David Beckham, tested Nikopolidis early with a 35-yard curling free-kick that the Greek keeper did well to save diving to his right. It was a battle that would continue to be waged throughout the afternoon between those two players.

Rehhagel had an uncanny ability to frustrate sides better equipped with talent than his own. This was the first match he showed this characteristic as

Greek manager. The German went about with a change in formation, playing a 5-4-1. The defensive set-up saw Greece play with the center-back tandem of Leonidas Vokolos and Nikos Dabizas, with Kostas Konstantinidis playing behind them in a sweeper role. Takis Fyssas and Christos Patsatzoglou played as wing-backs with Theo Zagorakis and Giorgos Karagounis as the central midfielders. Rehhagel would often make an unorthodox move with his team selection, in this case it was to put Michalis Kasapis, normally a left-back, as essentially a left winger. The other flank saw young attacker Angelos Charisteas moved out wide, while Demis Nikolaidis played as the team's lone forward.

Karagounis' driving run from midfield and long-range effort that was saved by Nigel Martyn in the England goal was a chance that was quite symbolic of the game's early exchanges. Greece were playing very well and looking to counter-attack when possible. Further Greek chances came inside twenty minutes as Nikolaidis half-volleyed just over the bar after a terrific long ball by Karagounis and Charisteas also shot high after a neat turn saw him create his own chance.

By the time Zagorakis' long-range shot was saved by Martyn at the half-hour mark, it was clear that Greece were controlling the match. The Ethniki were superb in possession, sturdy at the back, and looking very dangerous on the counter-attack. England, though they possessed the likes of Gerrard, Beckham, Paul Scholes, and Robbie Fowler in attack, looked noticeably puzzled at how to break Greece down. Their only real opportunities were coming from Beckham free-kicks.

On 36 minutes, Greece found themselves ahead. Patsatzoglou's run saw him pass Ashley Cole down the right and whip in a cross that was cut out by Rio Ferdinand. The ball fell into the path of Charisteas whose low left-footed shot flew past Martyn into the goal. It was no less than Greece deserved after such a fine first half display. Only a last-ditch tackle by Ferdinand on Nikolaidis prevented Greece going up by two goals as halftime came. England went back to the locker-room amidst a deafening silence at an Old Trafford that had undergone a transformation from expectation to anxiety.

* * * *

Angelos Charisteas had a habit of scoring goals in big matches. On his debut for Greece against Russia in February 2001, he struck a brace. The goal against England continued a trend that would see him score many of his 25 international goals against football powers such as Germany, France, Spain, Portugal, and Ukraine.

His tendency to produce when it mattered should not have been surprising. The lanky striker joined Aris after playing amateur football for his hometown club Strymoniko Serron. In his debut for Aris as a 19-year-old, he scored twice in a 4-1 win over city rivals PAOK. His career trajectory took a knock when he was loaned out to Athinaikos in 1999 for six months. He returned to Aris focused on becoming a mainstay in the team. He managed to do so, making 74 appearances in the next three seasons for the *Kitrinomavri*. While his goal return during that time period (17 goals) would not be described as prolific, his work rate and performance as a target man was promising. So much so that clubs around the continent were beginning to take notice. When Werder Bremen asked Rehhagel about the player he gave a glowing recommendation. He moved to Bremen in 2002 and was a hit at the Weserstadion. In three seasons, he was an integral part of the team, helping the club to a league and cup double in 2003/04.

That period of time was the best of Charisteas' career with Euro 2004 the undeniable pinnacle. He struggled later to recapture that form. There were solid spells with Ajax (2005-2007) and Nurnberg (2007-2009) , but later stints at Feyenoord, Bayer Leverkusen (on loan), Schalke, Arles-Avignon, Panetolikos, and Al-Nassr were all short-term moves that never quite worked out. The early achievements with Greece and in Germany with Werder Bremen outweighed the later disappointments in his career, such were the magnitude of those successes.

Rehhagel cherished Charisteas' energy, hunger, and clutch play. Charisteas was an ever-present in the Greece squad throughout Rehhagel's time in charge. He represented Greece 88 times, the bulk of those coming under Rehhagel, and participated in Euro 2008 and the 2010 World Cup. From 2001 to 2004 he was arguably the most important player for the Ethniki. At Euro 2004, his crucial goals led Greece. His header in the final not only locked down his place in Greek football history, it also ensured he achieved footballing immortality.

* * * *

Charisteas was the best player on the pitch, but his teammates were not far behind. The belief in Greece's game belied the fact they had experienced a smack down of embarrassing proportions just a month before in Finland.

The second half saw England not only change personnel (Andy Cole on for Nick Barmby), but also ramp up their intensity. Beckham threatened from a free-kick again before Cole forced Nikopolidis into a great double-save. Despite England playing with more purpose and energy, Greece did not crumble. Karagounis found himself clean through on goal following a counter-attack and shot straight at Martyn. Karagounis' ability on the ball and his play between the England lines was giving Greece's opponents headaches all match long.

An injury to Greek captain Zagorakis, saw him come off just shy of the hour mark. England twice came close to equalizing through Scholes. Karagounis then forced Martyn into another save after he dribbled 30 yards, played a give-and-go with Nikolaidis, and found himself with only the England goalkeeper to beat. Eriksson brought on Teddy Sheringham in the 68th minute and within seconds England were level. Sheringham's first-touch of the game being a clever back-flick header from a Beckham free-kick that looped over Nikopolidis. It was the quickest ever goal by an England substitute.

With the momentum of that goal, England looked poised to go on and win. The following minute though saw Greece retake the lead in a match that was quickly becoming a classic. Basinas received the ball back from Charisteas and sent a ball into the heart of the box, Dabizas flicked across for Nikolaidis. The AEK striker settled the ball quickly and fired into the bottom left-corner of the goal from close range. 2-1 to Greece.

The final 20 minutes were played out mostly in Greece's half as England looked to find a precious equalizer. That would be enough if Germany and Finland remained a scoreless draw. Rehhagel made his two remaining changes with a more orthodox winger in Vasilis Lakis coming on for Charisteas and Nikos Machlas replacing Nikolaidis up front.

Greece looked close to a historic win as Beckham's eleventh free-kick of the night was deflected wide in the final minute. Then deep into injury time, Konstantinidis was called for a foul on Sheringham. Beckham lined up from 25 yards and unleashed an unstoppable curling effort past the stranded Nikopolidis to make it 2-2. Old Trafford erupted as Beckham celebrated in what has now become iconic fashion. It was perhaps his greatest game as an England player, there is no doubt it was the most dramatic.

The disappointment on the faces of the Greek side was visible as the full whistle came. That match will always be remembered in England for Beckham's riveting display, capped off by the free-kick that led to qualification for the 2002 World Cup. For Greece, it was not a victory, but a crucial moment in the nation's modern football history. One era of the national team died with the humiliating defeat to Finland a month earlier. At Old Trafford on 6 October 2001, a new team was born, and the Rehhagel era had truly begun.

Chapter 5

Two Right-Hand Men

Rehhagel's appointment as Greece manager was facilitated by a change in leadership in the EPO. Shortly before the German was selected as Greek boss, Vasilis Gagatsis was elected as President of the Federation, taking over from Kostas Alexandridis. Gagatsis' ascension to the presidency was the culmination of a long career in the game. Born in Lagkada, northeast of Thessaloniki, Gagatsis had to endure the loss of his father when he was just six years old. In football, he found solace and was captivated by the game growing up. "It's a fact that my biggest passion was football. My house growing up was right next to the old stadium of Makedonikos Thessalonikis and that meant I was on the pitch everyday", recalls Gagatsis. He played at the amateur and semi-professional level before putting all his energies into becoming a lawyer. He graduated from the Aristotle University of Thessaloniki and settled in as a lawyer in Greece's second largest city.

While he entered the legal world and eventually the political one as a local representative for the PASOK party, Gagatsis always wanted to be involved in football. He did this initially by providing his services as a legal counsel to both boyhood club PAOK and Iraklis. He then went on to become the general secretary of the Union of Football Clubs in Macedonia from 1984 to 1987. Gagatsis moved to Athens in 1988 and ended up working for Olympiacos and Athinaikos, once again as a lawyer for the clubs.

Toward the end of the 1990s, he rose to prominence in football circles and eventually accepted a role as the general secretary of the EPO. It was a position he held for nearly four years. His greatest achievement in that time was helping to bring Anghel Iordanescu to Greece as manager of the Ethniki. Iordanescu's time as coach was brief and deemed a complete failure by many. However, the

Romanian's views on how a national team should be run had a lasting impact on Gagatsis as the two forged a close friendship during their time together.

Gagatsis greatly respected Iordanescu's work with Romania and that was the main reason he lobbied so hard to bring him to Greece. Eventually he found it eye-opening the way Iordanescu spoke about how players must be cared for. "In our hours-long conversations, Iordanescu would explain to me the proper way for a national team to function. So, when I was elected president I put into place that which he taught me along with what I saw first-hand when visiting the Royal Spanish Football Federation (RFEF) and my interactions with President Angel Maria Villar," says Gagatsis.

Iordanescu was of the belief that national team players must be treated as stars. They were the main characters and should be handled as such. Players being flown in for national team duty in Business Class was just one of the seemingly small details that Iordanescu deemed crucial. The Romanian manager's assertion was that proper, top class transport and accommodation, such as staying in the best hotels, was key to keeping players happy. Particularly in Greece, Iordanescu was adamant that the Ethniki needed its own training ground. It was unacceptable he stated that the team had to use club facilities. In general, there had to be a more organized effort to look after the players and have them feel that their needs were being looked after.

Gagatsis took on these ideas and planned to implement them should he ever become president of the EPO. That finally occurred in July 2001. Traditionally the number two in most of the positions he held in football, Gagatsis was now the leading man overseeing the sport in Greece. His job could not have been more difficult at the start. Greek football was at an extremely low ebb at the time. It was not just the Ethniki's recent troubles, but also a poisonous atmosphere surrounding club football where allegations of corruption and club favoritism were rampant. Gagatsis' first order of business was to find a coach for the Ethniki.

So much of the reason in eventually selecting Rehhagel over Scala came down to money. Scala wanted €1 million per year, while Rehhagel requested only €400,000 per year. The EPO was in no place to spend anywhere near Scala's amount, thus Rehhagel was picked. While financial considerations were at the heart of Rehhagel getting the nod, Gagatsis was a big fan of Rehhagel's work, primarily what he had achieved at Kaiserslautern just a few years earlier. In meeting Rehhagel, Gagatsis was also convinced by the German's temperament, which he believed was similar to that of a Greek.

When Rehhagel was unveiled as new manager of Greece in August 2001, he was essentially beginning work with a gentleman's agreement. There was an instant mutual trust that formed between Rehhagel and Gagatsis that saw the German manager work for nearly three months before officially signing a contract. Rehhagel laid out a few conditions he wanted to be met in order to take over the Ethniki. Besides the agreed upon salary, the only other personal requests from Rehhagel were a car and a house for when he stayed in Greece. With regard to the actual job itself, Rehhagel, like Iordanescu before him, believed it was a necessity for the team to have its own training facilities. The other major request was the hiring of an assistant coach, one he would approve of and would have the ability to change if he so desired.

The relationship between Gagatsis and Rehhagel was positive from the start. "From the first moment with Rehhagel I felt very easy. Specifically, after the 5-1 defeat to Finland when there was also the episode with Georgatos. I asked Rehhagel why he did not retaliate. He responded by saying that it was not proper to rush and everything would happen as it should. Georgatos was never picked again. I said to myself after that he was on the right road," says Gagatsis.

The result against England was the only remaining piece of evidence Gagatsis needed to be convinced he made the right choice in selecting the German coach. "It was confirmed that Rehhagel was the man for the job with that 2-2 draw in England where we truly put forth a fantastic performance. Everything started to change after that. Steadily and methodically the work done by the manager and the players and federation I believed would at some point bring about even greater success."

Rehhagel's other major request was the hiring of an assistant coach, one he would approve of and would have the ability to change if he so desired. Since Rehhagel did not speak Greek and was fluent only in his native tongue, one of the main qualifications of the assistant coach had to be that he spoke German and Greek. While Rehhagel was not in a hurry at first to find a number two, the embarrassing defeat to Finland certainly changed the timetable. Rehhagel realized that he needed a translator and could not rely purely on a player like Konstantinidis to relay his instructions to the rest of the group. The episode with Georgatos was a clear indicator that being able to properly communicate with his players was going to be vital.

Reports in Greece suggested that Makis Katsavakis was the favorite to be announced as the new assistant manager of the Ethniki. A graduate of the German Sport University of Cologne, Katsavakis seemed to tick all the boxes that Rehhagel required. He spoke German, had lengthy coaching experience in the Greek top-flight, and was also a former national team player having represented Greece.

It was nothing short of a major surprise then when Rehhagel settled on Ioannis Topalidis. It was as obscure an appointment as the new manager could have made. Topalidis was the son of Greek parents who had immigrated to Germany. His family kept close ties to Greece so Topalidis learned both German and Greek. He grew up in in Southwest Germany near Stuttgart and was an avid footballer from an early age. He began his playing career in the youth set-up at SpVgg Ludwigsburg at the age of nine and remained there until he was fifteen before moving to VfR Burstadt. There he played for seven seasons in the third and fourth tier of the German football league pyramid. A central midfielder with good technical ability, the hallmark of Topalidis' game was his non-stop running. He realized that the semi-professional level was his ceiling as a player and ended his career with Starkenburgia Heppenheim in 1987 after a three-year stint. Having come to the end of his playing days, Topalidis was fully dedicated to continuing in football and trying his hand at coaching. In his early 30s he began the process of getting his coaching licenses. As a player and a coach just getting his feet wet, Topalidis worked various jobs outside football in order to make a living. His desire though was to fully dedicate himself to being a manager.

He began his coaching career at Eintracht Esslingen as a player/manager for three seasons. In 1993, Topalidis took over SC Geislingen in the third tier of German football. Geislingen was a well-known club, who at one point, counted Jurgen Klinsmann amongst their youth products. TSC Backnang was his final coaching destination between 1996-98 before his big break came.

Having had modest success in the German lower divisions, Topalidis got his shot at the top level in 1998. Not in the form of a first-team head coach, rather as a scout. Topalidis' friendship with Jurgen Rober was the catalyst for the move. Rober had taken over Hertha Berlin in January 1996 and promptly led the team to promotion to the Bundesliga. Topalidis was approached about the scouting position and agreed terms. 'Topa' relished the opportunity to work at that level. His three-year stay coincided with one of the best spells in the club's post-war history. Hertha finished third, sixth, and fifth during Topalidis' time there, complete with qualification to the Champions' League and the UEFA Cup.

"It was a wonderful experience for me at Hertha. It was my goal to work at the highest level and at Hertha I accomplished that. I would go to many matches everywhere scouting opponents. I went to Bundesliga fixtures and Champions' League matches to analyze the opposition. I always wanted to make it to the highest level and that was it," Topalidis remembers fondly.

Topalidis' three seasons in the German capital could well have been more as his relationship with his manager and friend Rober was superb. However, a unique and fascinating opportunity had begun to take shape. In the summer of 2001, Topalidis was well aware of the fact that Rehhagel had become manager of Greece.

"Of course, I was interested. Many of my colleagues were telling me that I would be the perfect assistant to Rehhagel. For a while I thought about what I should do as surely there were others who would want the job too," said Topalidis.

Topalidis made a phone call to a colleague from Hertha asking if they knew Rehhagel. They did not, but the individual said he had a friend that did. Soon after, Topalidis received a call indicating that he should send over his CV as the mutual friend would pass on his information to Rehhagel.

Topalidis describes in detail how it all happened so fast. "Greece played Finland and lost heavily. Two days later, I received a call from Rehhagel. I thought it was someone playing a joke at first. Luckily, I didn't hang up. He asked if we could meet in Berlin in two days. When we met he told me he looked over my materials and that Greece were playing against England at Old Trafford and that he wanted me to be there on the bench with him. He went on to say that he couldn't promise me anything after that."

For Topalidis, the opportunity to represent his ancestral country was the achievement of a lifelong ambition. During the 1994 World Cup, Topalidis was working toward his coaching license in Poland. He was the butt of jokes from his fellow coaches as Greece's performances went from one embarrassment to another. He vividly recalled a feeling then that turned out to be prophetic, "There, everyone, including all the Germans, were making fun of me. When I was doing my license I promised myself and believed that one day I would be with the national team and that we would do very well. I had that in my head. And it happened!"

In the beginning, the relationship between Rehhagel and Topalidis began as very cautious. In many ways, going into the England match, the feeling between manager and assistant and manager and players was very similar. There appeared to be a willingness to all work together, but there was an uneasiness to start. The trust that would eventually develop between all parties had not yet been cultivated.

The performance against England helped to bring the players closer to Rehhagel and vice-versa. The same effect was had on the manager and his interim assistant. A bond began to be forged as Topalidis explained, "In the beginning we were very cautious as we did not know each other very well. But, as time went on and the team played friendlies and improved so did our relationship grow."

Though he did not know whether he would be kept on, Topalidis was happy to merely sit on the bench for one match for Greece, even if nothing else materialized. "The result was very important and it was a very big result against England at Old Trafford. Rehhagel was very happy, as was I. It was something unreal for me to be a part of that. I could have been fine if I didn't continue on as assistant after that. At least, I was able to have the experience of being on the bench for that game," Topalidis admits.

Topalidis, of course, did stay on. For nearly nine years he was Rehhagel's lieutenant and close confidant. The two formed a cohesive partnership as well as a lasting friendship. Topalidis was clear on what Rehhagel saw in him, "I believe he saw in me someone who was very trustworthy and someone who worked extremely hard for the team. He saw that and felt that. Then there developed a blind trust between us."

That 'blind trust' was shaped initially by constant communication between the two after the England game. The longer the two men talked about football, the more they realized that their views on the game were very similar. "Rehhagel was always open to everything I said, but above all it worked between us because we were both realists. We tried to figure out how we could match up against opponents. We knew we couldn't play like Barcelona or reproduce Ajax's 'Total Football.' We knew what we had to do in order to have success and so our philosophies were in line with one another."

One of Topalidis' major roles with the Ethniki was the scouting of opponents. This was a similar job he performed during his time with Hertha. Topalidis would watch matches of the opposition and sometimes travel to see games. He would then put together a DVD that Rehhagel and him would analyze and devise tactics for upcoming games. On the football side, there was plenty of worth in what Topalidis brought to the table. It was the assistant's communication with the players however that really saw Topalidis become such an important individual for the Ethniki, especially in the pre-Euro 2004 period.

Topalidis translated Rehhagel's words and thereby his ideas and motivation to the players. It would have been wrong to call him a translator. What Topalidis did more so was interpret what Rehhagel said and explain it to the players in a style he thought they could accept. "It's true that I said things in a more 'Greek' way. That happened over and over again. I knew how the players wanted to hear something so I explained it in that way," admitted Topalidis.

One small example of this was Topalidis choosing to change certain key words when Rehhagel spoke. When the manager would say 'gentlemen', Topalidis would change it to 'paidia' (Greek for 'boys'). It may have seemed like a very small detail, however the players felt closer to Rehhagel with this type of interpretation. Topalidis insisted this was vital, "You cannot translate every German word into Greek. But, more importantly, in Germany things are said in a different way. I knew I had to say things in Greek in a more delicate tone, to go about it with a softer touch so the players would take on the message."

In a relatively short period of time, Ioannis Topalidis became a vital part of the Ethniki set-up. Rehhagel would later call him his "most important employee." Indeed, Topalidis contributed so much on the pitch and off. It's worth noting that from the time Topalidis was hired until the end of Euro 2004, the Ethniki coaching staff was comprised of only two coaches; Rehhagel and Topalidis. "In that time, Rehhagel and I developed such a partnership and trust that you have to realize at the national team it was only us two coaches. No conditioning coach, no goalkeeper coach, not even an analyst or a scout. We did it all by ourselves," said Topalidis, "No one did anything for us."

Rehhagel was a well-known name in European football when he became Greece manager. Topalidis knew that most people, even close observers of Greek football, had no idea who he was. Topalidis described how this made him enjoy the experience even more, "When we defeated Northern Ireland and we qualified I was so happy. You have to understand that Rehhagel was a big manager and all of our players were from major clubs and well-known. The only person that was a 'no-name' was me. So for me to be a part of something so special, like qualification for the European Championship, filled me with pride."

Gagatsis' route to the head of Greek football was much more direct and followed a traditional path. Topalidis and his journey to the assistant coach post of the Ethniki was not as straightforward. Yet, despite the ways in which they came to those positions, the fact remained that they became Rehhagel's closest colleagues. Rehhagel had two right-hand men in order to move forward with. The two relationships differed, but they were both strongly based on one main trait; trust.

Rehhagel felt immense trust from Gagatsis, who always gave Rehhagel carte blanche to decide on all matters concerning the team and on many occasions consulted with him on off-the-pitch affairs. Perhaps of greater importance was Rehhagel felt how strongly Gagatsis believed in him and his work. This was not a trigger-happy president ready to fire him at the first sign of trouble. The bond that was forged was not unlike what Rehhagel found at Werder Bremen with Willi Lemke. "We had a good relationship with Gagatsis. He was the President and we did put him under some pressure for many matters. He came through for us. In the beginning, when we lost the first couple qualifiers he was under a lot of pressure to fire Rehhagel. After those losses, you know how it is in Greece, everyone gets involved and it's not easy. But, he kept him on and put trust in him," says Topalidis about Gagatsis.

And Rehhagel trusted Topalidis' knowledge of football, his work on scouting opponents, and the strength of the assistant's communication with the players.

Rehhagel received praise of the highest order for his success with Greece and deservedly so. He was undoubtedly the central figure and the one who made the final decision on all footballing issues. However, the triumph at Euro 2004 came from the foundations laid in 2001, specifically the appointments of Gagatsis and Topalidis to their respective positions. With those two, Rehhagel had the support and trust to be able to calmly go about building a team that would shock the football world.

Chapter 6

The Real Work Begins

The one player best placed to gauge the importance of the draw away to England was Nikos Dabizas. Having spent the previous three seasons with Newcastle United, Dabizas was the sole Greek national team member with experience in the English Premier League. "We were wounded in a mental and emotional sense from what happened in the previous match against Finland and wanted to restore our pride," said Dabizas reflecting on that time. "After the draw against England, when I went back to Newcastle it was a big topic of conversation. It was stated by many in England how well we played against their team and I believe it did a world of good for our image as a national team in general."

Dabizas was not the first Greek player to compete in the English Premier League, that honor went to Giorgos Donis, who signed for Blackburn Rovers in 1996. However, Donis, capped 24 times by Greece between 1991 and 1997, lasted only a season at Ewood Park. Dabizas then was the first Greek player to stay in England for an extended period as he eventually played in the Premier League for seven seasons after moving from Olympiacos to Newcastle in 1998.

* * * *

Born in the Macedonian region of Greece in the town of Amyntaio, Dabizas did not appear to be destined for a career in football. In fact, he was a late bloomer, not really taking up the sport in any serious sort of manner until the age of 17. His plan was always to end up working for his father's milk factory, a family business that produced a variety of milk-related products. As he began playing for his local club, fourth division outfit Pontioi Veria, it was quickly determined that Dabizas indeed had a knack for the game. After three seasons in the fourth tier, word had spread with regard to the young defender's abilities and Olympiacos signed the player in 1994 after closely following his progress. He was a leading figure in the side that saw the Piraeus club end a decade-long title drought, winning league titles in his last two full seasons with the team. Midway through the 1997/98 season, amidst rumors that clubs from England were interested in the physical center-back, Newcastle snapped up the player for £2 million. Over the next five and a half seasons, Dabizas became a fan-favorite at St. James' Park for his committed and robust displays. He made 130 appearances for the Magpies, especially endearing himself to supporters for his ability to score goals. He achieved legendary status in February 2002 when his headed goal gave Newcastle a 1-0 away to rivals Sunderland in the Tyne-Wear derby. He finished his time in England with a spell at Leicester City, joining the East Midlands club in 2003 and remaining there until 2005.

Dabizas made his debut for Greece in a Euro '96 qualifier against Finland in 1994. He quickly became a stalwart with the Ethniki, his rise to prominence mirroring his ascent into the Olympiacos first team at club level. Until qualification for Euro 2004, Dabizas had not yet experienced much joy at the national team level, his words a reminder as to the difficulties of the post-1994 World Cup period. "My participation with the Ethniki was the most important thing I could do for my country and my career. But, it was very difficult in the pre-Rehhagel years. There were tough times with few fans, little support, and no successes. The only exception being almost making the 1998 World Cup when we barely lost out to Denmark."

Injuries at inopportune time periods took the gloss off of Greece's Euro 2004 win for Dabizas on a personal level. Despite being a regular starter for his country before and after Rehhagel took the helm, Dabizas did not play a single minute for Greece during the tournament itself. A car accident in June 2003 saw the player lucky to survive as he was thrown out of the front window of his Aston Martin DB7 when it crashed. The car caught on fire immediately after as Dabizas literally came within seconds of being killed. That accident left him with a badly broken arm that delayed his return to preseason at Newcastle. He ended up losing his place for club and country due to a long recovery. When he came back he eventually reclaimed his place in the Greece starting eleven.

As Euro 2004 approached, he looked like a shoo-in for one of the center-back positions. Ten days before the opener against Portugal, Dabizas incurred a groin injury in a warm-up friendly against Poland. He was ruled out of the

Portugal game, but was forecasted to recover for the rest of the Group Stage matches. He was never picked however. The Greek defense began well and became stronger as the tournament progressed. Rehhagel could not change the team in those circumstances and Dabizas was the odd man out at the back. "It was a terrible feeling to have given ten years of service to the national team, to go through all those difficult times, and to be finally on the verge of playing at the European Championship and ten days before to be ruled out of the opening match due to injury", Dabizas painfully described. "It's a terrible feeling on a personal level. But, there you put the team and the country above the 'I'. You try to be a member of the team and be able to help in your own way off the pitch those players who are playing by supporting them."

Dabizas was one of the more experienced squad members when Rehhagel came to Greece in 2001. He recalls being in the hotel with Rehhagel after the 5-1 loss to Finland and seeing his new manager appear "very upset", but reassuring him that he and the rest of the players were behind him. "It was simply a bad start. It was the first match with a new manager and you cannot say he is good if he wins and bad if he loses. Us, older and more experienced players, tried to support him," said Dabizas, "telling him it was one bad result and that we were going to get better."

The support Rehhagel received from those players following the defeat to the Finns may have been the first sign of a bond forged not only between the Greek players themselves, but also with their new coach. Such a disastrous start might have led previous Greece sides to separate into factions, split between those who supported the new boss and those who did not. This time it was different. Perhaps tired of the infighting and drama of past teams, the players seemed to collectively be united in giving Rehhagel a firm backing.

As the months passed it was Rehhagel who began to repay that faith toward his new players. According to Dabizas, there was no magic performed by Rehhagel as he began rebuilding the team. It was mostly down to trust. "Under Rehhagel we began to build a strong foundation as he developed a core of players he trusted and played them consistently together," said Dabizas. "The trust we received from the coach, we tried to give back to him with strong performances."

One such performance was undoubtedly the one against England. As Dabizas and other team members would go on to suggest, there was no big shock at the quality of the display against the English. There was instead affirmation of the talent in the team and confirmation that an organized and united Greek side could be successful.

Dabizas believes one massive influence on the team was the experience many Ethniki players had while playing abroad. From the late 1990s to early parts of the new millennium, the borders seemed to open up around Europe for Greek players. Footballers from Greece were beginning to be looked at as a good investment. On the one hand, they were battle-tested in some high-pressure environments in the domestic game. They were also cheap. Selling players to European clubs was a fairly new revenue stream for clubs in Greece so on most occasions a player would be sold if the offer was suitable.

"We started to get more players playing abroad in very competitive leagues," Dabizas explained. "That was very important in Greece becoming more competitive as the quality of those leagues was higher than the Greek league. Every weekend in the bigger leagues you go up against top teams and players. That higher level of competitiveness you find in say, the Premier League, helps bring you to a different level as a player."

Nearly half of the Greek Euro 2004 squad were either plying their trade abroad when the tournament began in Portugal or had played outside of Greece during their career. Contrast that with the last tournament Greece had qualified for. That team's 1994 World Cup squad did not possess a single player with any experience abroad.

Rehhagel emerged from the England match with newfound credibility. At the very least, his commitment and seriousness for the job were both under intense scrutiny after the Finland match. The more aggressive pundits and football fans had questioned the entire wisdom of his appointment, openly ridiculing him in the lead-up to the game against England. The players though had bought in. Something had changed from Helsinki to Manchester. The match at Old Trafford was a turning point. "We saw when he began that he wanted to place order in the team. He threw out some top-class players because he was interested not in what any individual could do, but rather what the team could do together. That affected the rest of the group considerably seeing that. It made us realize we had to become a team. He showed he was able to make strong decisions early on and ultimately that helped the team. We realized only if we were together could we achieve anything," says Karagounis.

The English game has always been especially revered by Greeks. So, such a display and result against a nation held in such high football esteem was given extra weight by the Greek public. The uncertainty concerning Rehhagel's appointment and management of the team eased considerably after that 2-2 draw. What also aided was the fact that Rehhagel finally put pen to paper on a contract in late October 2001. Rehhagel was heavily criticized in the first two months of his reign for not yet signing a deal. Many in the media took that as the German coach not being entirely convinced of wanting to stay in the job. Rehhagel maintained throughout that he had every intention of signing and that any delay was down to legal matters and finally getting his lawyer to come to Greece to finalize everything in person. The agreement signed was a two-year contract with an option for another year pending Greece's performance in the qualifiers for Euro 2004. The salary agreed upon was for $360,000 per year.

Rehhagel did request two key conditions to be met in order to put his signature to the contract. The Ethniki received one million Drachmas as a bonus for the draw in Manchester. Rehhagel saw bonuses as necessary and demanded that they be a regular occurrence for the national team rather than special one-offs. Rehhagel also asked that he be given leeway in finding a new assistant in case he decided that he was not happy with Topalidis. Rehhagel put great importance in the position of the assistant coach. In the early days of his relationship with Topalidis, he remained unsure of whether Topalidis would be a long-term appointment or not. This became a non-issue in a relatively short period of time as the two men developed a fine partnership. Eventually in Topalidis, Rehhagel found exactly who he needed to fulfill the role of his assistant.

Drawing against England away and Rehhagel finally signing a contract helped go a long way in changing the mood surrounding the manager and the team in general. There was not exactly a free pass allotted to Rehhagel and the players, but it did feel as though there was a general acceptance to allow the new manager time to work. The dark atmosphere following the Helsinki humiliation had gone. One performance and a signature had combined to ease the pressure on the manager and players.

Greece had two matches remaining as 2001 was coming to a close, a pair of November friendlies at home against Estonia and Cyprus. These games would provide a good opportunity to build upon the core group of players Rehhagel was trying to find. The low-key nature of these matches would also allow new blood to be drafted into the squad.

Eventually, seven players who hadn't featured against Finland or England were tried out by Rehhagel in the two games. Greece defeated Estonia 4-2 at AEK's old Nea Philadelphia ground. That result represented Rehhagel's first win as manager of Greece. The Ethniki put together a terrific first half display against an overwhelmed Estonian side, racing to a 4-1 halftime lead. The visitors managed to pull another goal back in the second half before a raft of changes saw the match peter out. A few days later neighboring Cyprus came to Athens to play a friendly at the Stadio Kaisarianis, the stadium of then first division club Ethnikos Asteras. The momentum put together against England and Estonia came to a halt as Cyprus prevailed 2-1 thanks to a late winner by Cypriot defender Ioakim Ioakim.

Rehhagel was unhappy with the team's defensive reaction over the two matches, especially on set pieces, lamenting to the media, "The last Cyprus goal was the fifth goal we have given up from a free-kick since I've been here. We are a little slow back there."

After Giannakis Okkas had given Cyprus a 40th minute lead (Machlas had missed a penalty for Greece midway through the first half), Greece's Nikos Liberopoulos equalized four minutes from time before Ioakim's intervention in injury time. Liberopoulos' case was a peculiar one. The Peloponnesian-born striker was one of the top talents in Greece and at the time, the reigning Greek Footballer of the Year. An ankle injury had kept him out of Rehhagel's first two squad selections. However, neither the goal against Cyprus nor his overall good form could convince Rehhagel to try to fit him into future teams. That Cyprus cap was only one of three Liberopoulos was given in the pre-Euro 2004 period. The manager instead preferred attackers such as Nikolaidis, Machlas, Charisteas, and later on Vryzas. After Euro 2004, Liberopoulos was someone who Rehhagel did rely on and he included the player in Greece's Euro 2008 squad. The technically-adept Liberopoulos was a proven goalscorer, bagging more than 250 goals in his club career as well as 13 goals in 76 appearances for his country.

Another player who never made it to Euro 2004 despite being considered one of Greece's top players was Akis Zikos. An episode toward the end of the Cyprus friendly was the catalyst for Zikos to never be called up to the Greek team again. After having played the final 25 minutes against Estonia, Zikos was also on the bench in the match against Cyprus until late on. Five minutes from time, Rehhagel called for the player to replace Greek captain Theodoros Zagorakis. Zikos displayed an unwillingness to enter the game, reportedly asking what the point was of going in with such little time remaining. After a short discussion between manager and player, Zikos eventually went on in the 87th minute. Those three minutes and resultant injury time were the final moments of Zikos' international career.

Zikos began his career at Xanthi as a 19-year-old who quickly became a stalwart of that team. After five seasons there he made the move to AEK. He continued to flourish with the *Kitrinomavri* in four years with the Athens' giants. Monaco approached him in 2002 and he made the move to the French principality. The defensive midfielder played the best football of his career in France as a part of a very good Monaco side. He made 42 appearances in all competitions in the 2003/04 campaign, helping Monaco reach the Champions' League final. Though Monaco suffered a 3-0 defeat to Jose Mourinho's Porto in the final, Zikos was widely considered one of the best players on the pitch. His participation in that game saw him become the first Greek player to ever compete in a Champions' League final.

Due to his impressive displays for Monaco and superb form at the time, there was widespread clamor for Zikos to be included in Greece's Euro 2004 squad. Rehhagel, though tempted, refused. The manager was accused of not treating Zikos fairly and of handling the situation poorly. Topalidis urged Rehhagel to go and watch player, and while Rehhagel did, he ultimately decided against bringing Zikos back into the fold. Topalidis said that Rehhagel was convinced he did not need the player, "I maintained that he should go and see Zikos. After doing so, Rehhagel stated that while a good player, Zikos was not special. He truly believed that Zikos was not better than the midfielders we already had".

Rehhagel's ruthlessness was condemned by some sections of the media, many expressing bewilderment as to how such a player could not be selected in a 23-man squad for Greece. Rehhagel saw all that he needed to see in Zikos' reaction at the end of the Cyprus friendly. In the way Zikos had acted, Rehhagel possibly saw a glimpse of the old Greek sides, where players did as they wished, where they said whatever they wanted to say, lacking discipline and seriousness. In order to build a side where unity and togetherness were at the forefront, where each player took pride and responsibility of wearing their nation's shirt, Rehhagel saw it impossible to bring players in or keep them in the team if they were not committed to the cause. Rehhagel took a hardline with Zikos, just as he did with Georgatos, but for him it was the only decision he could make. The manner in which he handled those situations matched what he did in similar circumstances as a club manager in Germany. He was a manager willing to change his strategy or make tactical tweaks. When it came to his philosophy of no one individual being more important than the team, Rehhagel was not flexible at all.

Besides personnel issues that he sought to sort out, Rehhagel quickly encountered another major problem after coaching the team on Greek soil for the first time. Though Rehhagel had known that the public was in an apathetic mood toward the Ethniki, the friendlies against Estonia and Cyprus made him realize the situation was much worse than he had feared.

A tiny crowd of barely 1,000 supporters came out to see the victory over Estonia at the Nea Philadelphia Stadium. The stands had a few more souls in them against Cyprus, but 3,000 people in attendance was still considered incredibly small. The top Greek clubs at the time were drawing many times those figures for league matches. For the European games those teams played, the stadiums were full on a regular basis. Even Greece's U-21 side was playing in front of more fans. In a crucial match against Turkey in November 2001, the 'Elpides' defeated their rivals in front of 7,000 in Ioannina. That match may have sparked interest as Greece were trying to book a ticket to the European Championship the following year and many may have wanted to come watch their side beat the Turks, Greece's historical foes. Regardless of the reason, it was clear to see the lack of interest on behalf of the public toward the senior national team.

One of Rehhagel's first directives with regard to Euro 2004 qualifying was that the national team needed a suitable stadium to play their home matches. The cavernous Olympic Stadium was deemed too big. Smaller stadiums in Athens were checked out while cities from outside the capital were also considered. Ultimately, it was Panathinaikos' Apostolos Nikolaidis Stadium which the German gave the okay to. Commonly referred to as the Stadio Leoforos Alexandras due to the street on which it is located, the 16,000 capacity ground underwent a €7 million renovation in 2001 as Panathinaikos returned to their traditional home after playing at the Olympic Stadium since 1984.

Rehhagel was a fan of the narrow gap between the pitch and stands at the Leoforos. There was a belief that even smaller crowds would provide the national team with a home advantage in this stadium. A crowd of 15,000 would just about fill it as opposed to the same size attendance in the 75,000 seat Olympic Stadium which would still feel remarkably empty.

Chapter 7

The Building Of A New Team

Three countries contested the rights to host the 12th edition of the European Championship or Euros as they began to be called. The final vote took place on 12 October 1999 in Aachen, Germany. The UEFA Executive Committee met to decide between Spain, Portugal, and a joint bid from Austria and Hungary. Spain were the clear favorites, possessing an unrivalled set of facilities already in place, a thriving football culture along with a superb track record of hosting big competitions. Add to this strong transportation, telecommunications, and security links and the Spanish bid was considered a shoo-in to win the vote. Austria and Hungary based much of their focus on the political and historical connections between the two countries. That bid seemed to be particularly attractive as co-hosting was en vogue during that time period (Belgium/Holland had been awarded Euro 2000 and Japan/South Korea were selected as co-hosts for the 2002 FIFA World Cup). Tom Kundert has been a well-established journalist covering the Portuguese game for a quarter century. Kundert is the Portugal correspondent for World Soccer magazine and has co-authored two books about the Portuguese game, including *A Journey Through Portuguese Football* and *The Thirteenth Chapter*. Kundert tells the story of how, at first, Portugal wanted to co-host the tournament with Spain. "Ironically, the initial idea of the Portuguese Football Federation (FPF) was to have a joint bid with Spain, but the Spanish refused so Portugal had to go it alone," details Kundert.

Portugal then were the rank outsiders. The day before the final vote, a straw poll saw Spain garner 11 of the 16 votes on offer. A landslide was expected. So when Portugal were unanimously declared winners to stage the tournament 24 hours later it was a shock of epic proportions within the European football community. Though it was considered a giant upset, the Portuguese bid had gained momentum in the months leading up to the decision. The interest within Portugal to host Euro 2004 was palpable as evidenced by the 34,000 football supporters who packed into the national stadium in Lisbon the previous July to recreate the country's proposed logo for the competition. The Portuguese slogan was "We Love Football", a simple, but effective message, conveying the deep affinity the country had for the sport.

While Portugal's facilities were nowhere near the caliber of those of Spain, the Executive Committee were won over by the detailed development plans that had been laid out. This included the construction of several new stadiums across the country as well as the renovation of existing arenas. The proposed $580 million for this construction to take place was considered suitable by UEFA, the European governing body seemingly swept away by the romantic thought of developing Portuguese football. This was the hope of many involved in the Portuguese government and FPF, two sides that had cooperated very closely in the bid process. "When the decision was made to make a bid to host the tournament by itself, Portugal was going through a rare moment of economic growth and the FPF got the full backing of the government to fund the significant investment in ambitious plans to sell the bid to UEFA," says Kundert.

Ahead of the vote, Portugal Sports Minister, Jose Socrates, a man who later become the nation's Prime Minister, suggested to the press that UEFA should see this decision as a way to develop the game in other countries. "UEFA could simply hand the final stage of Euro 2004 to a country that already meets all the conditions," Socrates stated, "but I believe it has a duty to help promote football across Europe."

Ultimately, the emotion and excitement surrounding Portugal's bid coupled with the positive working relationship between the government and FPF and the desire of UEFA to bring the competition to a new country saw the rights to stage Euro 2004 go to the underdog. Kundert describes what that meant to the country. "It was a tremendous moment of pride for the Portuguese people, who took the advantage to show the best of themselves as naturally hospitable and welcoming people."

In early 2002, with the construction process of the new stadiums well underway, though not without delays and increasing costs, Portugal's first test as host was about to occur. On 25 January, the draw for the Euro 2004 qualification groups was set to take place at the Europarque Congress Centre in

Santa Maria da Feira, a city some 25 kilometers south of Porto. The UEFA delegation were welcomed to the city amidst much fanfare complete with a fireworks celebration as Portugal tried to make a good first impression with their hosting credentials.

The draw would see ten groups of five teams drawn. The group winners would qualify automatically for Euro 2004, while the runners-up would go into play-off pairings to determine the remaining five teams. Portugal automatically qualified as hosts. In November 2001, UEFA announced the teams that would be seeded for the draw based on the UEFA's National Team Ranking Table. Countries would be ranked by how they performed in Euro 2000 qualifying and the 2002 World Cup qualifiers.

Greece were in 29th place in the rankings, good enough for a place in Pot C. The draw would begin with the selection of teams in Pot E, the weakest sides, and proceed to Pot A, which included the top ranked teams. Portuguese football legend Eusebio was the star of the show and conducted the draw with UEFA Chief Executive Gerhard Aigner.

As the draw reached the stage for the Pot C countries, Greece were pulled out and placed into Group 6 alongside Northern Ireland and Armenia. It was already a bad start for the Ethniki as Armenia were the strongest side in the weakest section and Northern Ireland were amongst the better teams from Pot D. From Pot B, Ukraine found their way into Group 6. Greece had avoided the bigger names such as England and Holland, but Ukraine were certainly no pushovers. The biggest anticipation was going to which team were drawn from Pot A. Spain were eventually pulled out as the group became fully formed.

The qualifying draw brought about mixed reaction back in Greece. Qualification seemed doable, but Spain and Ukraine were clearly the teams to beat. Speaking after the draw was made to the assembled media, Rehhagel appeared to concede first place to Spain, indicating Greece's target was to finish second. "It's a very interesting and difficult group. I have already developed an initial view of our opponents. Definitely, Spain is the favorite for first place, but we have a good side with chances to fight for second place." He continued by saying that the hard work was about to begin, "We will begin a very strong preparation with upcoming friendlies so that we are ready when we need to be."

Vasilis Tsiartas spoke to the Greek media on behalf of the players and also suggested that Greece needed to be serious about their preparations. "If we exclude Spain, all the other teams are unknown to us, because we have not played them, even at club level. From our end we need to have a good preparation and a low profile." Tsiartas then sent out a warning to his own team by saying, "The key for us are the matches against the smaller teams. We cannot repeat the mistakes of the past." He finished by asking for the support of not only the public in this new phase, but also the EPO to provide the proper organization and preparation.

Spain manager Jose Antonio Camacho outlined the fact that it was not going to be an easy section. "It is a really competitive group and we know that Ukraine will be the most difficult opponents", said the coach of the team ranked third overall in Europe. Camacho expressed his belief that Greece and Northern Ireland would also provide "tough opposition", something similar to the remarks of Spain captain Fernando Hierro. He expressed confidence that Spain were the group favorites, but cited the difficulties in facing Ukraine's quality individuals, Northern Ireland's long-ball game, and the stadium atmospheres in Greece.

The comments from the Northern Ireland and Armenia camps mirrored what the other coaches were saying. All were in agreement that Spain were the big favorites to win Group 6, while Ukraine seemed to be the team most would be fighting against for second spot.

The Group 6 sides needed to meet to come up with an agreed upon fixture list before a deadline at the end of March. The meeting was set for Athens on 11 March 2002. Failure to come up with a schedule for the matches would mean that a draw to compile the fixtures would be held at UEFA Headquarters in Nyon, Switzerland. The gathering in Athens was basically over before it began. This was a group where four out of the five teams genuinely saw an opportunity of claiming second place. Thus, there was a belief that a favorable schedule could open up the path toward qualification.

Outsiders Northern Ireland and Armenia wanted to play their opening matches at home while the Irish did not want to play two matches during the June 2003 dates as their domestic league would be ending a month earlier. The main sticking points though came between Ukraine and Greece. On their part, Greece wanted to open the campaign with two consecutive home matches, first against Armenia and then Spain. They would then travel away to Northern Ireland in October 2002 and Ukraine in March 2003. Ukraine did not want to play Greece during that time because their league would be in its first weeks of a new season. Their contingent also had a demand for Ukraine to play three matches in 2002 as the end of that year would see their players in prime form. With five teams in the group there would always be one side who would not play on every matchday.

Failure to come to an agreement meant the team representatives would head to Nyon. Lars-Ake Lagrell, chairman of the UEFA National Teams' Committee, conducted the draw for Groups 2, 3, 6, and 7. The fixture list that came about seemed to leave most teams happy. Ukraine got their three matches in 2002, Northern Ireland received one June 2003 date instead of two, while Armenia's wish of a first game at home was granted.

Greece received a home opener, but not against a preferred team like Armenia. Instead they would begin qualifying at home against Spain and then make the trip to Kiev to face off against Ukraine. It was a mighty challenging start to a campaign that would follow with a home match to Armenia before consecutive away trips to Northern Ireland and Spain. The best news for Greek fans was the fact that the Ethniki would finish qualifying with two of their final three matches at home (Ukraine home, Armenia away, and the final match against Northern Ireland at home).

In the days following the draw, Rehhagel was scheduled to name his first squad in 2002 for the friendly match against Sweden. The German manager was probably unaware of the intense blowback that his selections would cause. Rehhagel was accused of bias as only one player from reigning champions Olympiacos was named to the squad. The media had a field day with this as only defender Christos Patsatzoglou had made the cut from the Piraeus club. Reports from Turkish media received widespread coverage suggesting that Olympiacos players did not want to play for the national team. This was the beginning of a longstanding accusation by some sections of the media and certain supporters that Rehhagel preferred Panathinaikos players in his team.

When questioned by the press, Rehhagel attempted to clear up any confusion clearly outlining his selection process, "It was never said officially from the Olympiacos players' lips that they did not want to play for Greece. I did not call up a certain number of players from specific clubs and I do not rate the players by the club they play for. I put into effect that which happens across Europe, inviting players from clubs doing well in European competitions." Rehhagel went to great pains to explain his decision for the squad. He drew parallels to other national teams as well as specifically citing how things were done in Spain, England, and Germany, where in some cases he said the squads generally come from just two clubs. "90% of my squads come from four teams, all of whom are at the top of the standings and in Europe," Rehhagel said, driving his point home further.

As Rehhagel tried to play the role of firefighter once again in his career, he inadvertently caused a firestorm on the eve of the Sweden friendly. At that press conference, while trying to explain his squad selection, he told reporters that "I'm German, I cannot be bribed when it comes to call-ups." The comment was latched on to by the papers who took those words as meaning that Rehhagel believed other managers, namely Greek ones, could be bought. After the Sweden match, Rehhagel once again went on the defensive as he aimed to clarify his statement, "I was talking about myself and no one else. I did not have the intent to insult anyone. I highly regard Greek managers and all those who have worked for the national team. Whoever was at the press conference understood that I used that particular phrase relating solely about myself."

Whatever goodwill Rehhagel had received from the England game, did not appear to be enough to counterbalance the prevailing atmosphere in Greek football at that time. The animosity between the big clubs and all of their respective supporters remained a prodigious barrier to progress for the Ethniki. These problems were magnified in the friendly against Sweden.

The match took place at Charilaou Stadium in Thessaloniki, the home ground of Aris. Even though the EPO gave 5,000 tickets to schoolchildren, the total crowd of 15,000 was a welcome sight for a national team match. There appeared to be a measure of truth to those who had long claimed that the Ethniki would be better served by playing home matches in other cities besides Athens. Unfortunately, it did not take long for trouble to start as the game kicked off. For much of the 90 minutes, some segments of the crowd not only chanted derogatory songs against rival clubs, but in many instances certain players were jeered and booed when they received the ball. It was a clear indication that fans were not anywhere close to putting club loyalties aside for the sake of the national team. Midfielder Giorgos Karagounis criticized the atmosphere in his post-match interview, "We need supporters, not club supporters. Hearing the team slogans aimed at some of our players was sad. It mustn't be repeated." Tsiartas echoed his teammate's sentiments in front of the Greek press, "The Ethniki does not want fans like these."

On the pitch, there was a much more positive feeling. Rehhagel called the Sweden friendly the start of the team's Euro 2004 qualifying preparation. And the manager would have been content with what he saw against a Sweden side ranked 16th in the FIFA Rankings and who had qualified for the 2002 FIFA World Cup. Though they were without the likes of star players Henrik Larsson and Freddie Ljungberg, Sweden did feature a young Zlatan Ibrahimovic leading the line and were a very well-balanced side. The match finished in a 2-2 draw, Greece receiving goals from Takis Fyssas and Karagounis, the latter providing the equalizer with six minutes remaining.

Though Sweden took the lead on two occasions and were probably more in control overall, it was a display by Greece that offered hope for the future. The Ethniki showed they were a side still prone to defensive lapses, however the positives outweighed the negatives. Greece looked decent going forward as they created some good opportunities throughout. Also present was a growing spirit within the team. There appeared to be a collective desire to grab a result. Whilst only a friendly, the eventual late goal came about from a team fully committed to chasing the game, not one that was indifferent to the final score.

Perhaps the brightest spot of the night was the international debut of young right-back Giourkas Seitaridis. The 21-year-old had just been crowned the Young Greek Footballer of the Year for 2001 and after some superb performances for the U-21 side and his club Panathinaikos, Rehhagel had decided to bring the player into the fold for the senior team.

* * * *

Seitaridis had been born into a football family. His grandfather was a forward in the post-World War II period playing for Proodeftiki and Panathinaikos. He went on to coach after that, a career path his sons Dimitris and Miltos (Giourkas' father and uncle, respectively), both followed.

Giourkas Seitaridis began his professional career in 1998 at PAS Giannina. The 17-year-old began to arouse interest with his displays for the club known as the 'Ajax of the Epirus'. He would not stay in Giannina for long though, only a season and a half before Panathinaikos would snap up the player. An agreement had been in place between the two clubs for Seitaridis to make the move to Athens ahead of the 2001/02 season. An injury crisis at Panathinaikos meant that the switch would occur six months earlier. So upset was Giannina boss Giorgos Paraschos that Seitaridis had been allowed to leave early that he ended up resigning shortly after the player departed.

At Panathinaikos, Seitaridis would work with Ioannis Kyrastas, a manager who would play an important role in his development. Kyrastas saw great potential in Seitaridis and expected a lot from his young defender. After a league match against Panachaiki where Seitaridis nearly received a second yellow card which would have deemed him unavailable for an upcoming derby against AEK, Kyrastas confronted the player in the dressing room. He ended up slapping Seitaridis as he reprimanded him. It was a shocking way to get the player's attention. Kyrastas later called Seitaridis to his office and apologized for his actions. The irony was that Kyrastas went on to explain to Seitaridis that he needed to better control his emotions and responses toward opponents. He proceeded to tell Seitaridis that someday when he left Panathinaikos and played for Manchester United or Real Madrid, he would remember him.

Seitaridis never played for Real Madrid, but only just. His growth as a player continued at a torrid pace, perhaps somewhat understandable for a person who had an intense love for Ferraris and speed. At Panathinaikos, he celebrated a league and cup double in the 2003/04 season as he swiftly became a right-back of enviable quality, not only in Greece, but in Europe as well.

Seitaridis entered Euro 2004 in good form and was magnificent throughout the competition. After his display in the opening match against Portugal, he attracted interest from many European clubs including Inter Milan and Valencia, with an actual offer tabled by VfB Stuttgart. It was Porto though who came in the strongest and Seitaridis was swayed by Jose Mourinho's desire to bring the player to the reigning Champions' League winners as a replacement for Chelsea-bound full-back Paolo Ferreira. A deal was signed between the two parties in record time. It would be announced soon after that Mourinho would also be heading to Stamford Bridge. Seitaridis still believed he made the right move. That is until a couple of weeks later. The player's performances at Euro 2004, where he would eventually earn a spot on UEFA's team of the tournament, had convinced Real Madrid of his worth. A representative from the club met with Seitaridis at the Ethniki's hotel in Portugal ahead of the semifinal against the Czech Republic. The official produced a briefcase with a contract ready to be signed along with Madrid boss Jose Antonio Camacho on the phone, who explained his thoughts on making Seitaridis the team's starting right-back. This was a dream come true for the 23-year-old defender. However, he had to alert Real of his agreement with Porto. Seitaridis refused to renege on the deal with the Portuguese giants and thus missed out on his chance to play for Real.

After a season in Portugal and then in Russia for Dinamo Moscow, he eventually made it to Madrid, but this time to sign for Atletico for €6 million in time for the 2006/07 season. He played three seasons at the Estadio Vicente Calderon, an Achilles tendon injury limiting him to about 70 appearances over that stretch. He moved back to Greece and finished off his playing career at Panathinaikos.

* * * *

In the period between March-May 2002, Greece played four friendlies. In March they came from two goals behind to defeat Belgium (3-2), proceeded to draw 0-0 against the Czech Republic the following month before winning both games against Romania (3-2) and Cyprus (3-1) in May. All four games were played in various parts of Greece in front of packed, albeit smaller, stadiums. If the results did not matter as much, the attitude of the team certainly did. Rehhagel had begun to construct a different sort of Greek team. While there was not yet a truly recognizable style of play, what could be seen was a fresh approach taken by the players. The mid-May friendlies against Romania and Cyprus were evidence of this. The media offered glowing reports of the way the players performed in matches coming right at the end of the club season and just before the players' summer holidays. There was no apathy or indifference to be found. This may have seemed like a small step, but for a public that had become accustomed to a team who consistently lacked the requisite drive and effort, it was very important. Rehhagel declared following the Romania victory that the team performed well during such a difficult period.

Against the Czech Republic, 13 of the players who took part in that 0-0 draw, six Greeks and seven Czechs, would find themselves on the pitch again when the two teams in the Euro 2004 semifinal. It was the first of those quartet of friendlies though, against Belgium on 27 March 2002, that was arguably the most important in the development of Rehhagel's team.

The lead up to the Belgium match was marred by the chaos that erupted in a derby between Panathinaikos and Olympiacos just a few days earlier. The fiery league encounter between Greek football's 'eternal enemies', saw referee Makis Efthimiadis whistle for an injury-time penalty after Olympiacos and national team left-back Stelios Venetidis was brought down in the box by Cypriot striker Michalis Konstantinou, a player who would later make the switch to Piraeus.

The penalty was converted by Olympiacos' Predrag Djordjevic and it gave his side a crucial 1-1 draw in a close title race. The final whistle saw Efthimiadis confronted by Panathinaikos staff and players. Some staff appeared to strike the referee. Worse yet was the fan invasion that followed. Soon scores of people surrounded Efthimiadis and he could be seen bleeding from the head. The 2,000 strong police force tasked with providing adequate security at the ground struggled to control the melee. The images of the bloodied and downright fearful Efthimiadis quickly made the rounds on news outlets around the world. The normally unflappable Rehhagel remarked, "It's the first time in my life I have seen such behavior on the football pitch." To make matters worse, all this occurred at the Leoforos Stadium, the location that Rehhagel had selected for Greece's Euro 2004 qualifiers to be played.

Stadium bans would be issued to a couple members of the Panathinaikos staff, including head coach Sergio Markarian, along with an assistant from Olympiacos, former national team player Tasos Mitropoulos. The air was tense as the Greek players met up for the Belgium friendly. This time, three Olympiacos players had been called into the squad, so there was widespread interest to see how they would interact with their Panathinaikos counterparts. Those expecting drama or episodes between the players were to be disappointed. Rehhagel was in no mood to discuss the situation at the press conference before the match insisting only that, "The atmosphere here is good. The players have accepted the new start. Our performances in the past few games have been good. We continue step-by-step and we improve." And it was as the manager indicated. Two defensive lapses saw Greece go down 2-0 by the 55th minute in the Ethniko Stadio in Patra. What followed though was the biggest indicator yet that there was something new, something different about this team.

Instead of accepting defeat and the surefire criticism that would have followed it, the Greek players fought back. The introduction of Perugia striker Zisis Vryzas at halftime helped to change the complexion of the match. The 28-year-old attacker won the penalty that was converted by Tsiartas in the 58th minute. Then Vryzas pulled Greece level less than ten minutes from the end with a fantastic glancing backwards header from a Angelos Basinas free-kick. 10,000 fans had shown up for this match and the stadium was absolutely rocking by the time Vryzas' goal tied the game. With three minutes left, the comeback was complete as a pinpoint long ball from Basinas found the probing run of Vasilis Lakis. His stabbed pass reached Vryzas whose first-time effort beat from just inside the box found the net to make it 3-2. There was delirium inside the ground. Rehhagel celebrated with his hands raised and then immediately turned around on the bench and began blowing kisses to the crowd. It was a clear sign of his gratitude for the atmosphere that the public had created.

Greece's comeback victory was impressive. More so than the fact that they had turned the game around though was the way in which they approached those final 20 minutes. Buoyed by a crowd who was willing them on, the players on the pitch wanted to change the narrative they had been a part of for so long. They seemed to want to shed their reputation as individuals who could not be bothered when it came to the Ethniki. The 'new start' that Rehhagel had mentioned was embraced by the fans in Patra, but also by the players. Despite, the poisonous climate that was affecting Greek football at the time, on that night the players were keen to distance themselves from that. To show that they were prepared to rise above that. To show that once and for all the Ethniki could be a team that Greeks could be proud of.

Chapter 8

The Road To Portugal Begins

An August 2002 friendly away to Romania in Constanta was the final warm-up match ahead of the start of Euro 2004 qualification. Injuries meant Greece would be without the likes of Karagounis and Patsatzoglou. Dabizas meanwhile had asked for an exemption due to a full schedule with Newcastle United. Rehhagel called 20 players into the squad. The big news was the omission of Machlas, who was having issues with club boss Ronald Koeman at Ajax. Without any first-team football for months, this period would signal the end of Machlas' international career.

An early Stelios Giannakopoulos goal at the Gheorghe Hagi Stadium gave Greece a 1-0 victory. The Ethniki were especially impressive in the first half against Romania, leading Rehhagel to indicate after the game that "the first half performance is a compass for the Spain game." That win made it four in a row as Greece headed into the first qualifier on the back of some real momentum.

Rehhagel had been in charge barely a year and the atmosphere surrounding everything the team was doing had improved considerably. The players were taking results in the friendlies seriously as they sought to build a stable foundation. Rehhagel was overjoyed at how the majority of matches in 2002 had gone. Since the German took over the team, Greece had won five matches, drawn three, and lost only two. The record was decent, yet there were still a number of matters that needed addressing. The defense, surprisingly, was one. Over that stretch of ten matches, 19 goals were conceded. That statistic shows that the rock-solid defense displayed at Euro 2004 did indeed take time to construct. Rehhagel gave caps to 35 different players during that time period. Of those players called up, 20 would eventually go on to be part of the Euro 2004 squad. Only Michalis Kapsis, Kostas Katsouranis, and Dimitris Papadopoulos had not yet featured for Greece under Rehhagel. The consistency of his team selections surely gave rise to a core group of players he could trust. Some sections of the media criticized the coach, saying he was making the Ethniki 'a closed club'. There was probably some truth to that, but Rehhagel made his decisions quickly. Some players would be assessed based on only a single appearance or two. If they did not fit into Rehhagel's plans then he had no reservations about continuing on without them. This might have seemed like a harsh approach. For Rehhagel, it was simply what had to be done in order to build the team with the vision that he had.

A journalist asked about the possibility of recalling Grigoris Georgatos in the press conference following the friendly victory over Romania. Rehhagel responded firmly, "From what I understand, Mr. Georgatos said goodbye himself to the national team." It was a question that reminded how much resilience the German had shown since he had been appointed. Rehhagel had navigated his way through a series of difficult situations. From his humiliating debut versus Finland, to his banishment of a star player like Georgatos from the team, to convincing club supporters he was not playing favorites to trying to mold together a competitive side, it was a year full of problems that had to be solved. The scale of his accomplishment grew if one also counted his ability to get his players to begin playing together and caring about the national team again. The ill-disciplined environment of previous sides was banished, already feeling like something from a different era altogether.

Rehhagel's call-ups for Spain saw Dabizas and Patsatzoglou return to the side, however Karagounis did not make the cut as he lacked match practice from an injury suffered against Barcelona in the Champions' League quarter-finals the previous April. Despite that absence, Rehhagel could choose from a fully-fit pool of players.

In order to be properly prepared to open up qualification, Rehhagel had expressed the necessity for the Greek league to begin earlier. The starting date of 24 August was found to be adequate as the majority of team members would have the benefit of two club matches before reporting for international duty. An extra bonus for the team was the opening of their own training center ahead of the Spain game. The facility at Agios Kosmas that Rehhagel had said from his first days in charge was mandatory, was finally able to host the Ethniki.

Everything seemed to be falling into space as 7 September and the visit of Spain approached. *La Furia Roja* were third in the FIFA Rankings at the time.

The caliber of Greece's opponents was not in question. They possessed a collection of elite players, such as Iker Casillas, Raul, and Xavi, stars who went on to be considered amongst the best to play in the modern game. Before the start of a historic run in 2008 that saw the country win three major international tournaments in a row, Spain had a reputation of underachieving at major tournaments. Months earlier at the 2002 World Cup, the Spanish side looked extremely good. Jose Antonio Camacho's men winning three straight Group Stage matches, scoring nine times in the process. They survived a hard-fought battle against Ireland in the Round of 16, winning on penalties, before they met co-hosts South Korea in the quarters. There, they eventually succumbed in penalty-kicks, but not after a controversial match where Spain saw two goals disallowed. Conspiracy theories were rampant at the time as many believed Spain were robbed of a berth in the semis. Spain then had extra motivation heading into Euro 2004 qualifying.

Despite the obvious quality they were up against, the hope remained that a battling performance by Greece could bring about a positive result to start qualification. The renewed optimism regarding the Ethniki had spread to the fans. A weary public began to warm to the team and the match at the Stadio Leoforos had sold out days in advance.

As Greece's first qualifier kicked off, the atmosphere inside the stadium was electric. The decision to use the Leoforos already seemed like a masterstroke, even at that early stage. Unfortunately, things went sour quite early against Spain. Nikos Dabizas' errant pass just outside the Greek penalty area was picked off by Juan Carlos Valeron. The Deportivo La Coruna playmaker slipped a pass to Raul whose first-time low drive evaded Nikopolidis' dive and found the back of the net. Eight minutes in and Greece had already conceded. The early deficit was a shock to a team that had entered the match expecting a special night. Indeed, Spain's midfield pressing disrupted any rhythm Rehhagel's men attempted to find. Nikolaidis' diving header from a Tsiartas free-kick was all Greece had to show for their efforts in an underwhelming first half.

Rehhagel decided to start gambling early, detecting his team's inability to win the midfield. Injury forced Kostas Konstantinidis off after 40 minutes. The Hannover defender had been converted to a central midfielder by Rehhagel for this match. Karagounis was put in his place. Though he was not part of the initial squad announcement, Rehhagel recalled Karagounis after a spot opened up. At the half, Konstantinidis' midfield partner, Theo Zagorakis, was also substituted in favor of Angelos Basinas. The double move worked quickly. The better mobility and ball control of Karagounis and Basinas forced the midfield to open up. Greece looked like a rejuvenated side and nearly equalized in the 56th minute after Basinas hit the upright after some beautiful build-up play by the Ethniki. Nikolaidis then missed two big chances, a diving header that went just wide and a deflected shot as he drove into the box. Spain were on the back foot by this point with Greece looking lively and dangerous whenever they went forward.

Just as the crowd's roar was reaching a crescendo, sensing an equalizer was on the verge of happening, Spain made it 2-0 on 77 minutes. Slack defending by Greece allowed Spanish winger Vicente to put in a cross. Raul and Valeron switched roles this time as the former teed up the latter for an uncontested finish from just inside the box to double Spain's advantage. Substitute Zisis Vryzas' late header was cleared off the line by Garcia Calvo. The second goal was a fatal blow in Greek efforts to get back into the match. The scoreline held and Greece had fallen at the first hurdle in qualifying for Euro 2004.

Rehhagel lamented the early goal Greece conceded saying, "Effectively, it was an own goal. You do not expect a mistake like from experienced players, but it happened. We had to attack more and risk and against a team like Spain you can be caught out."

The backlash was muted from the media, recognizing the strength of the Spanish side. Rehhagel was not immune to criticism though and his team selection and tactics were questioned. The starting midfield duo of Konstantinidis and Zagorakis was considered a big mistake as was going to a three-defender system in the latter stages of the game. Fear that the qualifiers were already in danger of getting away from the team was present. EPO President Gagatsis had to field questions on a radio program about whether Rehhagel's position was secure. Gagatsis laughed off the notion, insisting he was happy with Rehhagel and of the way the crowd supported the team. The players seemed to take the loss in stride, Traianos Dellas, the Roma center-back who was becoming an increasingly influential player for Rehhagel, asked for patience from the public, "I keep the belief we have and the enthusiasm for us to do well. This game is now behind us and I send a message to the people that we won't be disappointed. We will go for the win in Ukraine next month and that is the mindset we will have for all the remaining matches."

Already, the Ethniki's next match, away to Ukraine in October, was deemed a critical one for qualification hopes. The good news for Greece was that their next opponents opened up their campaign with a draw away to Armenia. After racing out to an early 2-0 lead, Ukraine took their foot off the gas and paid for it as Albert Sarkisyan's injury-time penalty saw Armenia equalize and claim a point in the 2-2 draw.

Greece's preparations for that showdown in Kiev were rocked by the collapse of Alpha Digital TV. The bubble that had burst across Europe with regard to digital pay-tv subscribers reached Greece in September 2002. Ridiculously high payouts to clubs for rights to their matches by Alpha Digital was not met with an adequate amount of subscribers within Greece, thus forcing the channel to go under. The shutdown of the Greek League's main broadcaster saw top-flight matches postponed for a month, including the two weeks before Greece's next qualifier in Ukraine.

Unsurprisingly, Rehhagel did not go about many changes to the squad for the Ukraine match. The only absentees were Pantelis Konstantinidis, out through injury, and Kostas Konstantinidis. It could be said that Greece were playing their next opponents at the perfect time. Ukraine had thrown away a two-goal lead in their first qualifier and had a rash of injury concerns going into the match against the Ethniki. Star striker Andriy Shevchenko was a real doubt and also ruled out were the duo of Yuriy Dmtrulin, and Andriy Nesmachniy.

The Olimpiskiy Stadium or Olympic National Sports Complex as it was officially known was not expected to fill for the upcoming qualifier. Regardless, nearly 60,000 supporters were still expected and Rehhagel had warned his players of the difficult environment. He particularly expressed the need to focus early on and not lose their coolness. In the press conference on the eve of the match, the German had specifically asked his players to perform with "passion, desire, and organization."

It was a rainy Saturday night in Kiev as the two teams prepared to line-up, the weather keeping the crowd size down to 50,000. The wet pitch seemed to work in Greece's favor to start the match as the Ethniki began brightly. Ukraine appeared affected by their key absences and matters were made worse for the hosts when two of their starters, Sergiy Serebrennikov and Genndiy Moroz, were both forced off through injury within the opening 25 minutes. Ukraine were a solid counter-attacking side and always posed danger on the break, but Greece looked more likely to make the breakthrough in the opening half. Tsiartas was running the show for Rehhagel's men, everything good Greece created coming from his left foot. A beautiful, 40-yard ball to Nikolaidis ended with the striker seeing his vicious drive batted away by Ukrainian goalkeeper Vitaliy Reva. A driving run by Karagounis that ended in a foul just outside the box also started with a clever ball by Tsiartas that had found a huge hole in the Ukrainian midfield. A bad giveaway by Zagorakis saw the home side break quickly, but substitute Andriy Voronin blasted over later in the half.

This was a good Ukrainian side, but one that looked there for the taking on the night. It was then so perplexing when Greece emerged from the locker room for the second half, they looked a completely different side. The confident first half performance gave way to a tentative second half showing. The pressing was gone and defensively the commitment shown in the first 45 minutes looked to have disappeared. Ukraine opened the scoring just six minutes after the break. Gennadiy Zubov curled in a precise cross to Andriy Vorobey. With the Greek defenders sitting off the attacker, Vorobey was free to head the ball down in the box, allow it to bounce and set himself up for a side volley that flew past Nikopolidis to the far side. It was a real sucker punch for the Greek players. And they looked shell-shocked the rest of the way. The effort was not in question, but the mental strength certainly was. Even at only 1-0 down, Greece never showed that they truly believed they could come back. A terrible second half performance began to materialize. The match seemed over as a contest by the time Voronin, having played a sharp give-and-go with Mayxm Kalinichenko that obliterated the Greek defense, dribbled into the area uncontested and shot past Nikopolidis to make it 2-0 in injury-time.

Two games played, two defeats against the main rivals for qualification left the Ethniki in a precarious position at the start of qualification. Spain had defeated Northern Ireland comfortably 3-0 in Albacete and had taken early control of the group with six points, while Ukraine were already on four.

The press had a field day with the team and Rehhagel in the aftermath of the Ukraine match. There was plenty of blame allocated to Rehhagel, both for his tactics and personnel choices. The players were not spared either. There was no longer allowance that this was a new group building toward something good. After losing to Ukraine and falling behind so early in the qualifiers, the prevailing belief was that these players were no different from their predecessors, that they did not have the mental strength nor the character to find success with the national team.

It was not only the media and the public from where criticism came. There were real issues within the EPO with regard to the way qualifying had begun. Disappointment reigned, though it was still a shock to hear the Federation president Gagatsis slam the team in the days following the Ukraine defeat. In a radio interview on the eve of the next qualifier against Armenia, Gagatsis unloaded on the national team players, while protecting his coach. "This story about the mistakes of the coaches has to stop. In the past we had other coaches, but we did not see anything different. Maybe we are unable to accept responsibility. Maybe this is the limit of our abilities," lamented Gagatsis.

For a politically savvy individual like Gagatsis, normally that might have been enough, but he decided to further attack the players. "I am furious, bitter, and saddened. I have all the emotions that someone who believed in this team could have. The question needing answering is whether we should continue to believe. In the Ukraine, the Ethniki showed it could take the game. And that is what frustrates me. However, after they scored, we became a neighborhood team from the fourth division, an uncommitted tournament side," riled the normally measured Gagatsis in front of the assembled Greek media.

The harsh words were all part of a coordinated effort by Gagatsis to test the players' pride. He knew they would not be happy with him, however he banked on the players to respond on the field. Many team members were angry with the EPO president, some proceeded in going months without speaking to him. Gagatsis knew this group and as he stated on numerous occasions believed greatly in their ability. Even he knew however that Greece's qualification hopes were hanging by a thread. His public outburst was his attempt at inspiring a reaction.

Despite the difficult atmosphere surrounding the team, Rehhagel did not seem worried. His unflappable demeanor had been taken by some in Greece as an indicator that he did not care. However, it was a characteristic built on 30 years of experience coaching at the top level. It was not that he did not care about the defeats, he simply had been there and done that. He had survived defeats in finals, crucial losses at the end of league campaigns, and catastrophic results like the 12-0 reverse to Monchengladbach that saw him lose the Dortmund job. Just the same he had won big matches throughout his career. In describing Rehhagel following the Spain and Ukraine results, Topalidis paints a picture of a man who simply kept moving forward. "Rehhagel did not believe that qualification was lost. We always were realists and the reality was that we lost to two teams who you could lose to. Spain and Ukraine were two very good sides that Greece could lose to. It was as simple as that. We still had matches to play."

It was undeniable that Rehhagel was under pressure, whether he felt it or not. Supporters hoping for a fresh, new national team were beginning to doubt Rehhagel's ability to make that happen. The media seemed out for blood as the defeats in qualifying began to pile. Gagatsis had no plans to get rid of his manager, but even he would be forced to consider Rehhagel's future if Greece failed to defeat Armenia.

Just two matches into qualification, the Ethniki had their backs to the wall. Four days after the loss in Kiev, it was time to face the Armenians at the Leoforos. Only a win would suffice if the dream of Euro 2004 qualification was to be kept alive.

Chapter 9

The Search For Oxygen

Rehhagel hated losing. "My first impression of Rehhagel was that he was a realist. It was all about substance. He took great care in showing us the way we could win. He never liked us playing well, but still losing. He always looked for the win," insists Karagounis.

In the press conference before the Armenia match, Rehhagel did not hide the fact that his team had no option, but to win. "We need to win so that our attempt for qualification has oxygen," said an under pressure Rehhagel. The manager evaded media questions about his future, indicating Greece was a democracy so he could answer what he wished and that since he did not know Greek he was not worried about what was being written about him.

Rehhagel also attempted to deflect questions regarding the team's defensive displays. He was quick to admit that Dabizas and Dellas had both committed errors in the first two qualifiers. However, he highlighted the good work they had done and believed dropping them would disrupt the team's chemistry.

Hoping to give the starting eleven a spark, Rehhagel made three changes to the line-up as compared to the Ukraine match. Zagorakis, Lakis, and the suspended Karagounis made way for Basinas, Pantelis Kafes, and Giorgos Georgiadis.

The defeats to Spain and Ukraine subsequently gave the public difficulty in seeing a path toward qualification for Euro 2004. The pessimism was back with regard to the Ethniki. This managed to keep the fans away as the night of the Armenia match came. Just 6,000 supporters were in the stands as the match kicked off. Armenia entered the qualifier in good spirits following their 2-2 home draw against Ukraine. Oskar Lopez had been appointed manager before that match after impressing in a stint with Armenian club Pyunik Yerevan, whom he led to a league and cup double in 2002. Lopez, a midfielder of decent standard during his playing days, having featured for the likes of Independiente, Boca Juniors, and Quilmes, had been a journeyman coach who had worked with a number of Argentine clubs since the 1970s. Lopez's stint with Armenia would be short-lived. A pay dispute in the ensuing months saw the Argentine leave the Armenia job after only two matches.

Greece were in dire need of a momentum shift and it came early against Armenia. A minute into the match, a sharp give-and-go between Basinas and Georgiadis saw the latter explode forward only to be fouled just outside the area. The ball was in perfect position for a shot on target from Tsiartas, a player who scored several free-kick goals throughout his career. The expected effort never came though as Tsiartas instead sent a deft cross into the box where Nikolaidis rose unmarked to head past Armenia goalkeeper Roman Berezovsky from eight yards. 1-0 to Greece inside two minutes. It was a start that Greece desperately needed.

Tsiartas provided the element of surprise and Nikolaidis the finish, but credit had to go to Georgiadis for winning the foul the goal came from. He was a player who was selected often by Rehhagel, but almost always as a substitute off the bench. In fact, the Armenia match was the only time Georgiadis ever started a game in nearly three years under Rehhagel.

* * * *

Georgiadis was born in Greece, though he grew up in Germany after his family emigrated there. He played football as a youngster in Germany before returning to Greece as a teenager and signing with Doxa Drama as a 17-year-old. While playing for some select sides in the city of Kavala, his place of birth, Georgiadis counted amongst his teammates then both Zagorakis and Vryzas. Georgiadis came from a football family, his father Charalambos having played as high as the second division in Greece.

A couple seasons for Doxa and Georgiadis quickly became one of the hottest talents in the Greek game. His pace and ability to score goals from his right wing position were apparent and traits that Panathinaikos found appealing, signing the player in 1992. Georgiadis spent six seasons with the 'Prasini', winning two league titles and three domestic cups. In 1995, he was chosen as the Greek Footballer of the Year. After going on a tear in the 1997/98 season where he scored 21 goals in all competitions, Newcastle became interested. Georgiadis was a personal selection of then Magpies boss Kenny Dalglish and was signed ahead of the 1998/99 campaign. Unfortunately, his move to the Premier League did not go as hoped. Dalglish was sacked just two matches into the season. His successor, Ruud Gullit, rarely picked the player as Georgiadis made just ten appearances for Newcastle that season. He did manage to score the game-winner against Everton in an FA Cup quarter-final. He returned to Greece for PAOK, continuing where he left off with some superb form during his four years there. In the lead-up to the Euro 2004 qualifiers he joined Olympiacos. He would go on to win a league and a cup in Piraeus before going to Iraklis for a season and finishing off his career back at PAOK between 2006 and 2008. Georgiadis never made the pitch in Portugal and he was even substituted at halftime against Armenia, but he was someone Rehhagel called upon often to provide a spark and he did just that to help Greece take the lead in their third qualifier.

* * * *

Greece certainly looked buoyed by the early goal, the team's pressing causing the opposition headaches and it was nearly 2-0 when Nikolaidis fed Charisteas only for him to see his well-hit drive turned away by Berezovsky. Everything pointed to an easy win in the early stages. This Greek team, however, was not yet the finished product. The belief and solidity that came to symbolize the team throughout the next year and a half was not yet cemented. The balance of attacking and keeping things tight at the back had not yet been found. Perhaps this is the case why it was Armenia who came close to scoring on many occasions in the first half. Nikopolidis had to be at his most alert off the line in order to clear two dangerous, defense-splitting passes. After Charisteas skied a fine cutback from Georgiadis, Armenia threatened again as Artur Petrosyan and Arman Karamyan sliced through the Greek defense only for the latter to miss high and wide from inside the box. The half ended with Nikolaidis missing a double chance, his initial effort saved and his follow-up seeing him miss the ball completely with the goal at his mercy. Nikolaidis was denied again as his header from a Basinas corner was cleared off the line.

After the break, the physical nature of a match that featured 42 fouls was on full display. Greece did look a bit more composed as the half wore on. In the 59th minute, Charisteas lost possession of the ball in the Armenian penalty area from a Seitaridis throw-in. Armenia tried to play out of the back, but center-back

Harutyun Vardanyan's stray pass was picked off by Basinas whose second touch found Nikolaidis. The striker coolly chipped the onrushing Berezovsky to make it 2-0. That goal was decisive and allowed Greece to play more freely for the first time in their qualifying campaign. Nikolaidis' efforts to become the first Greek player to record a hat-trick since Dimitris Saravakos scored five goals against Egypt in 1990 fell short despite a great opportunity late on. Greece held on for the victory, their first in qualification.

Even though he usually exuded confidence, even Rehhagel seemed relieved after the match. "We had to win any way possible. It was important for us to get the first three points in order to challenge for qualification," said the Greece coach. More good news followed as word reached of Northern Ireland and Ukraine drawing 0-0 in the group's other fixture. While that first win of qualification was welcomed, criticism of Rehhagel would not go away. Defeating Armenia did little to enhance his standing with the media. His inability to speak Greek, the choice not to live in the country, and his tetchy demeanor in press conferences all played a role in sustaining if not a combative relationship with reporters, then at least one built on suspicion and frustration.

Attacking midfielder Tsiartas made headlines after the match as he launched a stinging rebuttal against the EPO. While he did not name Federation president Gagatsis specifically in his comments, it was clear he was taking aim at Gagatsis' recent criticisms of the team following the Ukraine loss. Tsiartas responded to claims that the Ethniki had been given everything in their preparations for the qualifiers against Spain and Ukraine as "a fairytale." "There were many holes in our preparations for the matches with Spain, Ukraine, and the latest against Armenia," Tsiartas told journalists at the time. He went to target the team's new training center that had been much lauded by the EPO revealing what the players felt about the completion of that project. "In regard to the new facilities in Agios Kosmas they're still only half-finished. And every time we train we risk injury." Tsiartas went on to say that the grass was 15cm high in the team's training sessions before Ukraine. The playmaker also appeared unimpressed by the media's claim that he had fallen out with Rehhagel after being subbed off at halftime. "Under no circumstances do I have any problem with my coach," said a clearly irritated Tsiartas.

2002 ended with two friendly matches for the team. The first was against Ireland in November at the Apostolos Nikolaidis Stadium. Ireland's troubles at the time certainly lessened the worthiness of the match. Eleven of the 28 players called up by caretaker manager Don Givens had withdrawn from the side. Givens was a temporary replacement after Mick McCarthy had resigned following the team's poor start to Euro 2004 qualifying. It was a scramble for Ireland to even find a squad of 18 players. Once they did, the roster included three goalkeepers, five center-backs, and in striker Glen Crowe, the first Ireland-based player to represent the country in 16 years.

It was unsurprising then that the friendly proved to be a fairly uninspiring match that finished 0-0. The first half was terrible as both sides tried to come to terms with a bumpy pitch. There was improvement from Greece after the break, especially from substitutes Ioannis Amanatidis, Dionysus Chiotis, and Dimitris Papadopoulos. All three were making their national team debuts. There had been mounting pressure to include Chiotis in the squad, after the AEK goalkeeper had been in impressive form, especially in the Champions' League during that period. Amanatidis was born in Greece, but raised in Germany. He was a young, up-and-coming player who eventually missed out on Euro 2004, but did eventually win 35 caps for his country and play for Greece at Euro 2008.

* * * *

Papadopoulos was playing in England for Burnley and had been brought in to bolster Greece's attacking options. He was born in Uzbekistan, but grew up in Kazakhstan where he lived until the age of seven. In 1989, just before the USSR broke up, he and his family (two parents and three siblings) emigrated to Greece. The journey to Greece lasted seven days with his father at one point needing to run to catch the train after it had made a brief stop. After his family settled in Greece, Papadopoulos began impressing on the football pitch. He began in the lower divisions for Akratitos, where his performances saw him selected for Greece at youth level.

A goal versus England in a 3-1 victory at the U-21 level saw Burnley take interest in the player. He made the move to Turf Moor in 2001 and stayed there for two years. "Pap" used his time in England as a crash course in football education and what it took to be a professional. A move to Dynamo Kiev beckoned however he eventually signed with Panathinaikos. A journeyman player, Papadopoulos played for twelve different teams during an 18-year career, including stints for clubs in Italy, Spain, and Croatia. At Panathinaikos, he not only stayed the longest (2003-2008), but he also played the best football of his career. Although he was initially not on Rehhagel's radar and other strikers were better known, Papadopoulos' displays for Panathinaikos in the 2003/04 season, where the team won the double and the player finished as the league's top scorer came at the perfect time. He was an in-form striker whom Rehhagel could simply not bypass and thus he ended up in the squad for Euro 2004.

* * * *

In the days following Christmas, the Ethniki participated in an unofficial friendly against top-flight side Xanthi. The game was a charity match in support of footballer Makis Tzatzos' son, Anastasis, who had fallen ill. It was a wonderful gesture by the national team players, who donated their December wages to Tzatzos so his son could go abroad and receive treatment. Many players vowed to continue participating in matches like these, and that promise has been held. Even after retirement, the members of the Euro 2004 winning side have played yearly matches benefitting various causes under the team name Greek Legends 2004. For the record, the Ethniki won that match 1-0. Rehhagel and the players all expressed their happiness to support their colleague and in doing so provided another example of the growing unity within the team.

Greece's next qualifier would once again take on a must-win feel. They would travel to Belfast to play Northern Ireland in early April 2003. Before that, three friendlies were played in order to properly prepare for the fourth qualifier. In January, Greece defeated Cyprus 2-1 in Larnaca thanks to goals from Fyssas and Choutos. That match was not played on a FIFA-sanctioned date and thus only domestic players were chosen. There were debuts for the likes of Anestis Agritis and Spyros Vallas for Greece, while fringe players such as Choutos, Dimitris Nalitzis, Nikos Liberopoulos, and Pantelis Konstantinidis were also chosen. Konstantinidis was an early favorite of Rehhagel, appearing in the German's first twelve matches as Greek manager. His cap against Cyprus was the last of his 20 appearances for Greece. Rehhagel showed a certain ruthlessness as he moved forward toward Euro 2004. The coach certainly had a tendency to stick with a core group of players, but that could change if he believed better players existed. Konstantinidis fell behind in the pecking order of wingers as Rehhagel preferred the likes of Giannakopoulos, Georgiadis, and Lakis.

Norway were chosen for a February friendly in Heraklion, Crete. The opposition were selected for their similarity in style to Northern Ireland.

The match would prove to be perfect preparation for Greece's next qualifier. Rain had pounded Crete in the days preceding the game, local authorities using the fire department and a helicopter in an attempt to dry the pitch the day before the match. The Norwegian officials expressed concerns about playing the friendly, but the match was given the go ahead. Greece emerged victorious 1-0 on a Sotiris Kyrgiakos goal after 25 minutes. The quality of the performance may not have been extremely high due to the adverse conditions, but something stood about that match. The Ethniki impressed with their passion. It was another sign of something special beginning to take shape. Despite the fact that no real football analysis of that match was possible due to the poor state of the pitch, this was an indicator that a strong team had begun to form.

Fighting it out in the mud against a mid-level European side may not have foretold of the success that was to occur some 17 months later. However, whereas previous Greek teams might have seen a friendly with that type of severe weather as a bother, this group of players appeared to relish the challenge. Rehhagel had not yet fixed the defense, had not yet settled on his preferred lineup or even formation, but he had built a team willing to fight. One whose members were ready to break down stereotypes of players who did not play for the shirt, of individuals who placed club loyalties above country. The result and display were secondary that day to the application. As friendlies go this quickly became a forgotten one, but in hindsight it was exactly a match like this that showcased the new mentality Rehhagel had managed to instill in these players.

A month later, Greece blew a two-goal lead in Vienna against Austria (2-2), a week before facing off against Northern Ireland. It might have seemed like old habits had returned. Rehhagel made eight substitutions from halftime on and Greece also had some absences in defense. The failure to hold on to that advantage, given by goals from Tsiartas and Kafes, led to disapproval from some quarters. It also distorted what had been a good performance by Greece. There were several chances created as Tsiartas ran the game in the Greek midfield. The Austrian comeback left a bad taste in the mouth as far as the result. Those who looked specifically at the performance remained satisfied. The team's evolution and progression was on track.

Many commentators remained convinced that Greece's chances for qualification for the European Championship had been lost in the first two defeats to Spain and Ukraine. The initial wave of optimism shown as the qualifiers started had long disappeared. There was scant coverage by the press for the victory over Armenia and the friendlies that followed in preparation for the Northern Ireland game. The public also displayed little interest. Crowds were down. The Norway friendly in Crete drew a crowd of less than 3,000. That was a surprise, the terrible weather notwithstanding. Emphasis was back to club football and the close title race that had developed. The average Greek fan had seen this story before with the Ethniki. There would have been few who continued to harbour hope. Instead of bracing for disappointment, a general apathy had returned when dealing with the team.

Ukraine's 2-2 draw against Spain at home, featuring an injury-time equalizer, was a bad result for Greece ahead of their next qualifier. As the Ethniki continued to see the possibility for second place in the group, they needed their main rivals for that spot to drop points.

Rehhagel faced an injury crisis heading into his side's next qualifier. Dellas, Seitaridis, Patsatzoglou, Basinas, and Goumas were all ruled out of the squad. It was a nightmare as most were defenders and Basinas himself, a defensive midfielder. Even the players called in as replacements were going down such as central defender Spyros Vallas from Olympiacos, who suffered a season-ending knee injury against Austria.

If there were any good news at all it was that Greece were playing Northern Ireland. Sammy McIlroy's team were undergoing one of the worst periods in their history. The atmosphere surrounding the team was negative. Several players had called quits on their time with the national team in recent months including former captain, Neil Lennon. The Celtic midfielder ruled himself out of international duty after he received death threats the previous August for saying he would be glad to play for a united Ireland side. Northern Ireland enjoyed a rich football history. George Best, widely considered as one of the greatest footballers ever, appeared 37 times for the country in the 1960s and 1970s. The golden era of the national team occurred during a wonderful run in the 1980s, as the team qualified for both the 1982 and 1986 World Cups. In Spain at the 1982 World Cup, the Northern Irish team shockingly defeated the host side en route to a quarterfinal place where they lost to France, 4-1. Those heady days were long gone by April 2002. McIlroy, a former Manchester United midfielder who was capped by Northern Ireland 88 times, had overseen a side that had failed to score in their last 702 minutes, some 17 months of football.

Still, McIlroy seemed unfazed by his team's inability to score goals. In the press conference before the match he blamed a massive absence of luck for his strikers and believed things would turn around against Greece. The Ethniki had undergone a mini training camp in Frankfurt following the Austria friendly. As the team travelled to Belfast, Rehhagel challenged his team to play like 'patriots' and "with passion and strength to achieve our target."

An expectant crowd at Windsor Park was in singing voice as the match kicked off on 2 April. Northern Ireland had just lost to Armenia and were themselves needing a result to give them any chance of challenging for second place. And the hosts began brightly as mere seconds into the game, Keith Gillespie evaded Venetidis down the right and crossed for Grant McCann, who headed straight at Nikopolidis from close range. Greece responded quickly, Tsiartas' free-kick from a foul on Karagounis leading to a chance from Giannakopoulos that was saved by Northern Ireland goalkeeper Maik Taylor.

Greece did not have to wait long for the breakthrough. In the second minute, Tsiartas lost possession at midfield, but chased the ball down and won it back. He dribbled uncontested through the midfield and played a magnificent through ball into the path of Charisteas. The young striker took a touch past the onrushing Taylor, rounding the goalkeeper and finishing into an open net.

The early goal unsettled the home side and Tsiartas was running the show, putting in numerous balls over the top of the opposition backline. One such pass saw him pick out Giannakopoulos, operating as a right wing-back due to the numerous injuries to defenders, who crossed for Charisteas, but his effort was right at Taylor. The Ethniki were seeking the second goal that would go a long way in killing off the game. The remainder of the first half saw an escalation in the physicality of the match. Zagorakis could be seen jawing with the Northern Ireland players on many occasions, while the individual battles, such as Gillespie against Venetidis on the right flank and center-back Kyrgiakos against forward James Quinn, threatened to spill over at times. The match flow was disrupted by numerous fouls. Greece did play some decent football in spurts, showing their adeptness at maintaining possession in tight spaces.

Rehhagel's side were fortunate to have escaped punishment when Kyrgiakos stiff-armed Quinn in the box, but Northern Ireland too were playing on the edge, evidenced by a wild challenge from Mark Williams on Nikolaidis. It was of little surprise then when seven minutes before the interval a red card came out. Polish referee Grzegorz Gilewski gave Quinn his marching orders after a late tackle on Karagounis. Nikolaidis went off just before halftime, unable to shake off the after effects of Williams' challenge. And in a clear indicator of the ill-tempered nature of the game, the two sides clashed as they went off the pitch for the break.

Just ten minutes into the second half, Greece sealed the game. Defender George McCartney played a loose back pass after pressure from Karagounis. The errant ball was latched onto by Charisteas as he burst into the box with one touch and fired past Taylor with the second. The momentum and belief was all with Greece after that. Northern Ireland were reduced to nine men with 20 minutes remaining as Gillespie picked up a second yellow card for late hit on Kyrgiakos. The Ethniki did receive one scare late on as Williams found space at the back post off a set-piece, but could only steer his shot onto the crossbar. In all actuality, Greece should have added to their lead as the likes of Charisteas, Karagounis, and Vryzas all missed good opportunities in the latter stages.

Dabizas, one of Greece's standout performers on that night, believes that was one of the most crucial in qualifying for Euro 2004. "The match I remember most vividly was the one against Northern Ireland. We knew that failure to win there meant most likely we would wave goodbye to qualification. That night was very intense," Dabizas continued, "The conditions were very difficult and Northern Ireland were a tough team. They were also a very physical side, a real team of battlers. We knew a loss would end our qualification hopes, perhaps even mathematically. But, the characteristics we have as Greeks, that of fighters helped us through. There was anxiety, but we overcame that."

The 2-0 win was Greece's first competitive away victory in three-and-half years. It was a professional performance by the players. The early goal, like against Armenia, set the tone and Greece looked very comfortable playing with the lead. Northern Ireland's physical play was matched up to. The Ethniki refused to be pushed around and on display were certainly characteristics of a team that had developed a battle-hardened spirit.

Chapter 10

Four Days In June

Victory in Belfast suddenly saw Greece thrust back into contention for second place. Spain were firmly in control of Group 6 with ten points after four matches, their only blemish a draw in Kiev. Greece and Ukraine followed with six points, Armenia were on four points, while Northern Ireland had one.

Instead of enthusiasm at this qualification comeback, there was virtually no sense of trust from fans that this team could continue to turn things around. In general, apathy remained and that applied to the media as well. Journalist Giannis Koukoulas produced an editorial piece at the time for daily newspaper Kathemerini. In it he encapsulated much of the prevalent thinking at the time. Basically, that few believed the win over Northern Ireland had proven much at all. Koukoulas had taken aim at Rehhagel's post-match comments following the Ethniki's latest qualifying win. Rehhagel had expressed his satisfaction for a "very important win." He went to suggest that failure to have claimed the three points would have made qualification impossible, "If we didn't gain that win, it would have knocked us out of the running for second in the group." Koukoulas felt as though the manager had made too much of that result, sarcastically writing "What qualification for the 2004 European Championship? We have achieved that already. The next goal is winning the trophy. The only thing to think about is...who is going to be our opponent in the final." Rehhagel had the "expression of a trophy-winner", said the journalist.

In hindsight, the irony of Koukoulas' commentary might bring a smile to one's face. However, during that time, his view represented the majority, a sort of collective 'you beat Northern Ireland, so what?' The players of course felt differently. While two big tests awaited in the next qualifiers, confidence had grown as such that the group believed in qualification, that at least it was in their hands. DABIZAS QUOTE.

Greece's next two qualifiers were always going to be the team's toughest remaining stretch of qualification. Away to Spain and home to Ukraine in the space of four days in June represented a daunting challenge. The team prepared for those encounters with a final friendly away to Slovakia in Zilina at the end of April. A 2-2 draw was not a terrible result, but it was another Jekyll and Hyde performance from the team. Greece produced moments of good football, but were undone by many individual mistakes. A Vasilis Tsiartas penalty and Lambros Choutos goal twice gave the Ethniki the lead, only for Slovakia to equalize quickly both times through Szilard Nemeth. The poor pitch did not help either side. Despite being pegged back twice, Greece did create numerous chances, including a Dellas header that hit the post and a Basinas penalty that was saved late on.

Rehhagel outlined the individual errors in his post-match comments, but said he remained pleased with the players' overall effort. Soon after, the manager made his squad selection for the qualifiers against Spain and Ukraine. Five regular members of the team were out through injury, including Nikolaidis, Georgiadis, Patsatzoglou, Antzas, and Kafes. Central defender Michalis Kapsis was drafted in to replace Antzas. Meanwhile, two new faces were called up. Young AEK midfielder, Kostas Katsouranis, joined up with the national team for the first time and Olympiacos goalkeeper, Fanis Katergiannakis, was recalled to the team for the first time under Rehhagel. Both players were rewarded for their strong club displays in a very tight title race in Greece that season.

Before departing for Spain, Rehhagel spoke to the media and did not hesitate to call Spain the clear favorite. He did throw out a warning to the Spanish side. "I have belief in my players," said the Greek boss, "With the proper strategy, tactics, and mental preparation and the necessary patriotism, they can take a result."

The actual trip to Spain was fraught with problems for the team. A delay leaving Athens of more than two hours due to a strike by French air traffic control workers meant that the Greeks did not reach Barcelona until midnight. There, the Spanish authorities were kind enough to hold their connecting flight to Zaragoza, the site of the qualifier. Tsiartas later did not shy away from public criticism of the EPO and the decision to book a commercial flight instead of a chartered plane for the team.

In the days preceding the game, Rehhagel reiterated in training that everyone had to be extremely focused, especially in defense. The coach spent training sessions in Zaragoza reminding his players of Spain's pressing ability. Playing the ball out of the back or combinations in Greece's own half were not necessary according to Rehhagel if Spain was pressing high. The preferred option in those cases was to get rid of the ball quickly. The German saw first-hand what the Spanish pressing game did to Greece in the first qualifier and wanted to avoid giving up any easy goals. He told the players to make their mistakes in midfield and attack, but not in defense, as it could be deadly.

A minor knock to Charisteas meant he would be a game-time decision, while for Spain they would be devoid of Real Madrid's Guti. His place would be taken by Barcelona midfielder Gabri.

On 7 June 2003, 30,000 fans packed in to the Estadio La Romareda in Zaragoza to watch Spain take on Greece. Spain had defeated Greece in all four matches the two countries had previously played, including a 2-1 friendly win in the same stadium nearly 33 years earlier. A similar result would have been a big blow to Greece's qualification hopes for Portugal.

On a warm night in northeastern Spain, the home side began the match with a very attack-minded line-up. Greece meanwhile, had to make four changes from their previous qualifier against Northern Ireland due to their injury problems, though Charisteas was deemed fit enough to start the game.

Spain began the match with a confidence resembling a side that had not lost a home qualifier in years. The plan at the start was clear to see, Inaki Saez's team was trying to attack down the flanks through Joseba Etxeberria and Vicente in order to provide service to the superstar attacking duo of Raul and Fernando Morientes.

Spain attempted to overwhelm the visitors as they searched for an early goal to set the tone. Etxeberria looked lively and cut past Venetidis in the opening minutes serving up an inviting ball for Raul whose first-time shot flew just over the goal. Nikopolidis was forced into action soon after, tipping over Etxeberria's clever shot as the Ethniki struggled to cope with Spain's pace and ball movement.

The irresistible Etxeberria glided past Venetidis in open space on 15 minutes and was brought down from behind earning a yellow for the Greek left-back. By the time Greece created their first opportunity in the 20th minute, a Vryzas half volley from a knockdown by Charisteas that Carles Puyol scrambled to block, Spain had already had 65% possession, created numerous chances, and won five corner-kicks. Greece were barely hanging on. "Look the key in these matches is not to concede a goal as long as possible. The first 15-20 minutes are very important so you can gain that self-belief as a team. You then begin to gain ground on the pitch by finding your footing as a team so you can get something out of that game. That's what we did," said Stelios Giannakopoulos, the player that would provide the game's most decisive moment.

Giannakopoulos had made his way to the national side following a fine start to his club career at Olympiacos. It was a team he was never supposed to play for. His father, Alekos, had played for Panathinaikos. Stelios grew up supporting his father's club and as he rose through the ranks and showed his incredible potential at Paniliakos in his early 20s, it seemed imminent that Panathinaikos would be his next destination. "Sometimes life brings us things that we don't expect. You cannot order things in life sometimes the way you would like and that was what happened with my situation," recalls Giannakopoulos. "My father played for Panathinaikos. Everybody believed that I would also go there, and many knew I was a step away from going. I had already spoken with Panathinaikos, and the club had already spoken with Paniliakos."

Luckily for Olympiacos, they did not believe Giannakopoulos to Panathinaikos was a done deal. In July 1996, the *Erythrolefki* went hard after Giannakopoulos and his teammate at Paniliakos, Predrag Djordjevic. The two wingers were eventually signed and they helped change the course of Olympiacos' football history. The duo are considered amongst the major catalysts in ending a barren spell of ten years without a title for the club and beginning a run of seven consecutive championships.

Giannakopoulos endeared himself immediately to the Olympiacos supporters. His work rate on the right flank along with a healthy contribution of goals and assists made him a fan favorite. "The joys which I took from Olympiacos cannot be put into words and remains to today. The love which I received from Olympiacos supporters is so great," says Giannakopoulos. In September 1997, he scored Olympiacos' first-ever Champions' League goal, a memorable half volley from nearly 40 yards to seal a win over Porto and give the Piraeus side their first win in the competition. In the 1998/99 season he was one of the most important players in a side that came within minutes of a place in the Champions' League semi-finals (Juventus advanced 3-2 on aggregate with a late goal at the Olympic Stadium in Athens).

As the titles came, so did his stock continue to rise. In 2003, he was selected as Greek Footballer of the Year. That same year signaled the right time to make the move abroad. The Premier League emerged as the preferred destination. Bolton manager Sam Allardyce was adamant on signing the player and a deal was completed with Olympiacos. "In England, I grew and became a complete footballer. I arrived there at a very good and mature football age at 29 after leaving Olympiacos," says Giannakopoulos. The player spent five years at the Reebok Stadium racking up over 175 appearances and scoring 28 goals in all competitions. He was part of one of the best spells in Bolton's club history. Giannakopoulos adapted very well to the English game, so much so that the bigger clubs began to come in for him. Manchester City wanted him, and he came extremely close to a switch to Liverpool in 2005. "I was within touching distance of a move to Liverpool. During that time period, Rafa Benitez was calling me virtually every day telling me to be careful in training and not to get injured. It was basically a matter of time before I signed," remembers Giannakopoulos. Bolton held firm though and offered the player an improved contract. Giannakopoulos stayed until 2008. He moved to Hull for a short time before ending his career back in Greece with Larisa.

Giannakopoulos made his debut with the Ethniki in 1997 against Cyprus after having represented Greece at U-21 level. After beginning his international career strongly, he subsequently lost his place in the team for nearly two years. That all changed as soon as Rehhagel came in. The new manager instantly began picking the winger. "I believe Rehhagel saw a player who gives everything when he plays for the Ethniki. In me he saw willingness, drive, and passion along with good performances," says Giannakopoulos. Rehhagel's appointment helped Giannakopoulos rejoin the Ethniki and the player saw a marked difference from his previous time with the national team. "When the German came, I believe the organization improved to a very high level. Our collective discipline was also very high, whatever egos and issues we had between us had dissipated. The Federation and the manager worked well together, there were no conflicts that affected the team. All these things worked together to benefit the Ethniki and allow us players to concentrate on our goals."

* * * *

As the half wore on, Greece settled and began to possess the ball in a more effective manner. Morientes and Raul continued to have good opportunities, but on two occasions Nikopolidis made important interventions. The Greek goalkeeper held on to Raul's close range shot and came off his line quickly to intercept a Morientes ball for his strike partner.

Just after the half hour, Rehhagel decided to make a rare coaching move. Wanting to make his midfield more mobile in order to close down the Spaniards quicker, he made two substitutions. Lakis came on for Charisteas in the 34th minute and two minutes after that Tsiartas was taken off in favor of Karagounis. Tsiartas was visibly frustrated with the move as he continuously shook his head while walking off the pitch. He may not have liked the decision, but soon Rehhagel's switch would pay dividends.

Three minutes before halftime, Seitaridis won the ball near the center circle on the right and played it to Lakis. Good close control by Lakis saw him evade a tackle and pass to Giannakopoulos. He took a touch and played it out to Venetidis on the left. Giannakopoulos initially ran toward the penalty box only to come back and offer support to Venetidis. The ball was played square to Giannakopoulos as the Spanish defense sat off for a moment with Venetidis dragging his defender with him on a run down the left. Giannakopoulos with time and space at the top of the area took a touch to set himself up and then struck a bullet of a shot from 22 yards that beat Casillas in the Spanish goal, low to his left side. Greece were up 1-0 with a goal that no one would have expected, except perhaps Giannakopoulos himself.

"It was something we worked on all week in practice," revealed Giannakopoulos. "It was the first time I had changed flanks, I was playing on the left side. It was something that took me by surprise when I found out I would be starting on the left instead of the right. It was the first time in my career that I played there in an official match. There was a reason though. Michel Salgado, Spain's right-back, could not defend as well with his left. The plan was then, if given the chance, to cut inside to my right foot, meaning he would have to defend with his weaker one. That's why so many players in football play on the opposite flank, so they can cut in and take shots. That's what I did when I saw the opportunity."

The half ended with Greece ahead and Spain left wondering how they had not scored despite their eight shots on goal and overall superiority. In the locker room, Rehhagel called on his players to focus on holding on to the ball more. "The coach wanted us to keep our lines tighter and closer together. He also made reference to breaking up Spain's possession by having us keep the ball better. We knew we had to possess the ball and slow the tempo of the match because Spain was going to put us under lots of pressure," said Giannakopoulos. That is exactly what happened as soon as the second half kicked off. Morientes had a chance immediately, but blasted wide when in a good position inside the box. The Ethniki were effectively already in a backs-to-the-wall defending mode. There was a palpable feeling that this could be a pivotal moment in qualification.

Saez made a double change just before the hour. The Spanish boss going for a straight swap of his wingers with Javier De Pedro and Joaquin replacing Vicente and Etxeberria, respectively. Spain continued to look for openings. It was clear though that frustration had begun to creep into their game. Rehhagel's players were putting forth a clinic in defending a lead.

With eleven minutes remaining, Greece were reduced to ten men as Venetidis saw his second yellow card, this time for fouling Joaquin from behind. Minutes earlier, Saez had used his final substitution to bring on midfielder Sergio Gonzalez for center-back Carlos Marchena. Spain were now pushing players forward in a fierce attacking onslaught. The ball was constantly being played to the wings and countless, dangerous crosses had to be dealt with by the Greek backline. Nikopolidis had to be at his best on several plays, denying Raul, stopping a De Pedro free-kick, and saving from Sergio late on. In the dying stages it was Greece who actually had the biggest chances to score. On swift counter-attacks, both Karagounis and Lakis were unable to convert chances.

The final whistle saw the Greek players become one. It was a historic result for Greek football. No Greek side, club or national team, had ever won in Spain. The team bent quite often over the 90 minutes, but never broke, showing an incredible resilience in the face of incessant Spanish attacks. It was a performance that truly showed how much of a team this group had become under Rehhagel. The players had bought in and had become accustomed to doing whatever they had to do.

Giannakopoulos, who played as a left-back after the red card, said, "It was the first time in my career that I had played left-back. It was an experience, but we all had sacrificed. It was a strong and intense night that we came through together. We defended as a unit and fought for each other."

Ukraine defeated Armenia 4-3 in a topsy-turvy qualifier on the same night, winning the game with a 93rd minute goal from Serhiy Fedorov. Spain stayed atop the group with 10 points despite their loss, while Greece and Ukraine moved to just a point behind. This set up what essentially amounted to a final in the next qualifier, between the two teams in Athens.

The incredible win in Zaragoza saw a surge of excitement in Greece with regard to the Ethniki. Whereas the Spain game had warranted only scant coverage in the lead-up in the papers, suddenly with qualification now a distinct possibility, the interest in the match versus the Ukrainians was visible on the front pages. Tickets for the match sold out immediately after the victory against Spain. Not only did the team see this as the time to seize the momentum, long-suffering Greek fans were also aware of how close their country now was to a major tournament.

Venetidis' red card meant that he would be unavailable for the next match. He was set to be replaced by Takis Fyssas in the line-up. Ioannis Amanatidis, an attacking player from the U-21's, joined the squad. Ukraine came to Greece without their captain, Oleg Luzhny, who had to miss out due to suspension. The away side did welcome back stalwarts Andriy Husin and Anatoliy Tymoschuk from one-match bans and defender Yuriy Dmitrulin, a defender recently recovered from an appendix operation. Unlike the first qualifier between the two teams in Kiev, Greece would now have to face Andriy Shevchenko, one of the world's top strikers.

Rehhagel indicated in his pre-match comments that Greece would undoubtedly play differently than they did in Zaragoza. Still, he made it painstakingly clear that "while we owe it to be creative, we will not be so in an uncontrollable way." The manager also warned of the speed and quality of Shevchenko and teammate Andriy Voronin. Rehhagel appeared optimistic, but also sent out a warning. "The enthusiasm is big amongst everyone, but the match is not easy. We must have self-belief to overcome the past," said the German, clearly referring to past campaigns where Greece managed to falter in the crucial stages.

This team did not however appear to be feeling weighed down by previous failures. "I do remember the desire of all of us and the fans for the match against Ukraine. People in Greece were so excited, as were we, wanting to take that next step toward qualification," said Giannakopoulos, adding, "There was some anxiousness, but it was a more positive anxiety in the group. The pressure was there finally to qualify, instead of not qualifying. So, for us the anxiety was more of a positive thing rather than a negative feeling of not being in that position, which we all had experienced many times before." These were players that had become used to losing, to coming so close, only to find disappointment time and time again. The view was that this match was a shot at changing the narrative that had been created to describe them.

The atmosphere at the Apostolos Nikolaidis Stadium on 11 June certainly felt like that of a final. And unlike against Spain, it was Greece who began on the front foot. In a confident opening period, it was the home side asking all the questions. 15 minutes in and the Ethniki were rewarded for that endeavor. Zagorakis found Fyssas streaking down the left. He brought the ball down with a sublime first touch, cut inside nicely into the box and was brought down by Rebrov inside the area. Penalty for Greece. Giannakopoulos, the hero in Zaragoza, stepped up to take the spot kick. He chose power, but Ukrainian goalkeeper Shovkovskiy, dove to his right, raised his left hand and beat the ball away.

The missed penalty was a letdown for Greece and its after effects could be seen in the following minutes. Kapsis misjudged a long ball to Shevchenko, but luckily for the Ethniki, the opposition striker could only tamely head the ball wide. Still, the home side's first half performance remained good until the interval. Rehhagel's side created some fantastic opportunities and Shovkoskiy had to be at his best to make a double save from Fyssas on the half hour after terrific build-up play by Greece. The Ukrainian goalkeeper then got two solid fists up to punch away a powerful Dellas free-kick.

Ukraine began the second half in much improved fashion. An errant pass from substitute Charisteas was picked off by Rebrov. He found Shevchenko's diagonal run. The AC Milan attacker burst into the box and unleashed a venomous drive that Nikopolidis did superbly to push over the bar.

As the half continued, both sides upped their game, knowing full well the magnitude of a victory. Karagounis' sliding tackle on Rebrov in midfield was symbolic of the passion shown on the night. Rehhagel was admonished by the fourth official for chasing down a ball outside his technical area and trying to give it to his players quickly.

The tension grew as the minutes passed. Rehhagel brought on Choutos for Lakis as well as Tsiartas for Zagorakis with about twenty minutes remaining. Zagorakis had run the midfield superbly the entire match, but Rehhagel installed Tsiartas, seeing his side could use some of midfielder's playmaking ability.

Dellas made the tackle of Greece's qualifying campaign as he slid through to deny Shevchenko who would have been clean through on goal. Seitaridis picked up the loose ball and embarked on a 30-yard run. That ended with the team's best chance of the match as Seitaridis' shot was blocked into the path of Choutos who touched the ball past Shovkovskiy, but the ball was eventually cleared away and Seitaridis' follow-up flew well over. It was a chaotic sequence that showed just how finely poised the match was. A break either way looked like it would decide the game.

* * * *

The Ukraine match showed the increasing influence of Traianos Dellas in the Greek defense. Injuries had halted the player's progression in the early stages of his career. A move to Sheffield United after a few seasons for Aris and Panserraikos (on loan) looked like the defender's big break. With fellow Greeks, Vasilis Borbokis and Dimitris Markos, also on the books at the club and the physical nature of the English game seemingly perfect for the 6'5 Thessaloniki-born Dellas, the switch abroad shaped up to be a big success. It turned out to be difficult period for Dellas. Injuries kept him from getting a decent run in the side and his time at Bramall Lane was full of frustration. He did manage to memorably come on as a substitute striker to score twice in a comeback win over Tranmere. To those who knew him best, Dellas' attacking abilities were of no surprise. His youth career saw him begin as a right winger before going away one summer only to return some 20 centimeters taller the following season. The massive growth spurt effectively forced him to become a center-back.

Following his two seasons in England, he came back to Greece to play for AEK. In two years for the Kitrinomavri he managed 56 appearances and helped the team win the 1999/00 Greek Cup. Changes at AEK and an overabundance of defenders saw him become one of the odd men out ahead of the 2001/02 season. Told to find a new club just days before the transfer window closed, Dellas caught a lucky break as Zisis Vryzas, playing then for Italian side Perugia, had told his employers about Dellas' ability. He was invited to train with the team and play a friendly. Though Perugia balked at the move initially, a 5-0 defeat at the hands of Inter Milan a short while later suggested they needed more defensive reinforcements than they thought. Dellas signed and played exceptionally well for the first half of the season. Then, a contract dispute saw him banished to the reserve team for the remainder of the campaign. Dellas had refused to immediately accept a new contract, preferring to wait, just as Perugia had waited before finally signing him. He was frozen out of the team and suffered a great deal of abuse from Perugia supporters as he left training sessions.

The player showed incredible character to continue training with the youth side and maintain his silence despite the vitriol thrown his way.

His Perugia days were done at the end of that season and a return to Greece would have seemed the likeliest path. Dellas had done so well however in the first half of the season that he had attracted the interest of the biggest Italian clubs such as Milan, Inter, Juventus, and Roma. Dellas eventually signed for the capital side and remained at the *Giallorossi* for three seasons until a return to AEK in 2005. His club career would end in 2012 with a third spell at AEK, after two seasons in Cyprus for Anorthosis.

While Dellas was first called up before Rehhagel's time, making his debut in a 2001 friendly versus Croatia, it was under the German boss that he made the vast majority of his 53 caps for Greece. By the time the Euro 2004 qualifiers hit the halfway mark, Rehhagel saw in Dellas the man who could become the team's undisputed leader at the back. The manager called the player 'the Colossus of Rhodes' and filled him with supreme confidence. Rehhagel valued Dellas' ability to not only engage in the physical part of the game, but also to distribute effectively from the back. At Euro 2004 his performances as a sweeper were unforgettable. Dellas' masterclass displays in defense were a vital part of Greece's success and on an individual level earned him honors as one of the tournament's best eleven players as voted for by UEFA.

* * * *

Half-chances continued to come for both teams in the closing stages. Charisteas fired over a half-volley after a Giannakopoulos free-kick hit the wall. With four minutes remaining, the goal the Ethniki had so desperately been searching for finally came. Dabizas passed to Tsiartas, he played the ball to Karagounis. Tsiartas took off down the left and Karagounis promptly played an inch-perfect 25-yard diagonal pass into his path. Tsiartas had a lot of work to do still, but nothing that his magical left foot could not figure out. He crossed into the heart of the box on the half volley where Charisteas slid through to knock the ball past Shovkovskiy. The goal cued scenes of bedlam inside the ground.

It was now just a matter of seeing out the final minutes, something that the Ethniki nearly failed to do when late on in injury-time Husin touched in for Shevchenko for a one-on-one, but Nikopolidis came to the rescue to deny the chance.

The final whistle saw the crowd inside the Stadio Leoforos engaged in pure jubilation. The players were no different. They had come through a crucial stretch of games. The Ukraine game brought to an end a historic four days for Greece. It was the first time the country had ever won two straight qualifiers in such a short span. The victory against Ukraine marked Greece's fourth consecutive win in qualification, another first for the national team.

The good news was not over though. Soon after the match, word reached the team that Spain had been held to a 0-0 draw in Belfast against Northern Ireland. That meant that Greece now stood alone atop of Group 6 with 12 points. Spain fell to second, a point behind, while Ukraine stayed in third, three points adrift of the leaders. The next day, Spanish newspaper El Mundo Deportivo led with the headline, "Complete Misery." Greece would now automatically qualify for Euro 2004 if they could manage to defeat Armenia and Northern Ireland in their final two qualifiers.

The stereotype of Greeks having emotions that go from one extreme to the other could be found in the aftermath of the team's win over Ukraine. Suddenly, support of this team was found everywhere from greater coverage in papers and websites to conversations in cafes and on the street. It was an amazing contrast from the beginning of the qualifiers and the two opening defeats. In the eyes of a nation, Rehhagel and his players had initially been branded as hopeless losers. With qualification now so close, they had evolved into heroes in waiting.

Rehhagel called the conquest of Spain one of the biggest achievements of his career. He insisted however that a victory over Ukraine was a must if his team wanted to qualify. The Ethniki had defied the past and succeeded where many thought they would fail. Rehhagel began to convince the skeptics of the quality of his work. And the players proved that they truly cared about the national team and could function together as a group. Two matches remained. Rehhagel and his players held the keys to Portugal in their own hands.

Chapter 11

Qualification Achieved

The importance of the victories versus Spain and Ukraine were vital in Greece qualifying for Euro 2004. Those successes were also the ones that kept Rehhagel in his job. After Greece's poor start to qualification, there were growing calls for the German to get the sack. EPO supremo Gagatsis stood by his man and was not swayed by the pressure exerted to dispose of Rehhagel.

In early 2003, an extremely lucrative offer had been made by Bayer Leverkusen toward Rehhagel to become the club's new technical director. Before Greece had played Northern Ireland, Rehhagel and Topalidis met with Gagatsis to discuss that offer and their futures together. Rehhagel himself knew that public opinion, many sections of the media, and a good deal of high-ranking officials in the EPO were increasingly against him. He asked Gagatsis whether it would be better for him to leave his post after all that had been said and done. Gagatsis dismissed the notion. He insisted that the team could still go to Portugal and that the two sides would discuss after that what would happen. "Yes, it's true that he came to me and said that he had a mythic offer from Leverkusen and if he should go. I heard him and simply said no, you will remain and we will go to Euro 2004 together," reveals Gagatsis. The support the EPO supremo had offered was enough to convince Rehhagel that he should stay.

He was ultimately vindicated for that decision, however it was the two victories in those June qualifiers that made the difference. According to Topalidis, it was in Zaragoza where the turning point occurred. "The losses to start qualifying meant that Rehhagel was increasingly closer to being let go or leaving the job himself. When we went to Spain we were still under pressure. If we lost, it was certain that Rehhagel would have been gone. There were people in the stands watching the team, ready to take over. Specifically, Ioannis Kyrastas was in line to be Rehhagel's successor," said the assistant manager.

Kyrastas was a former Greek international who played his club ball for Olympiacos and then Panathinaikos. He was a defender of some repute, winning seven league titles and six domestic cups. He was perhaps best known for his managerial career, specifically two stints at Panathinaikos. Though he failed to win a title, his methods, particularly helping nurture many of the Euro 2004 players who passed through Panathinaikos, are fondly remembered by supporters of the club and many others who admired his contributions to the Greek game. Kyrastas passed away in April 2004, after complications from Sepsis, just two months before many of the players he helped develop played in the European Championship.

Gagatsis disputes any suggestion he was ever ready to sack Rehhagel. "There was never a chance I would have let Rehhagel go, even if we did not manage to qualify for the finals in Portugal," Gagatsis assures. "That was simply reinforced in Spain when I was assured once again that we had a top manager. Not only because we win, we could have lost. However, when you see your coach take off two of the biggest names in the team in the first half in Tsiartas and Charisteas, I knew right then we were going on to do big things. Maybe I did not expect how much we would achieve, but at that moment, with that move I was convinced that was the exact manager I wanted for this team."

In hindsight, Greece's two victories over Spain and Ukraine were a product of nearly two years of work. Rehhagel trusted a core group of players whom he rarely changed. New faces were considered and assessed, they were not however called into the squad too often. Greek journalist Sotirios Triantafyllou explains Rehhagel's policy, "Rehhagel's philosophy involved a lot of discipline. He also made the Ethniki a club in the sense that he did not change players often and it was not easy for a new player to be called in." It was the trust in those players that he did play that ultimately changed the course of qualification and Greek football history. "He supported his players, even when many of those were not starting for their clubs, not playing often for their clubs, or in some cases did not have a club," states Triantafyllou. "The result were players who drank water in his name, giving their all, not only for the team and the Greek flag, but also for their manager."

Trust was a big part of the relationship between Rehhagel and his team. Just as important was Rehhagel's protection of his players. It was not only that

Rehhagel would deflect any blame thrown his players way. He kept them away from outside influences he deemed unnecessary. "Rehhagel fortified the environment surrounding the players. Imagine that the national team always stayed in a different hotel than officials and journalists who travelled to away matches. Very few people had access," says Triantafyllou. "All this produced a like-minded group of players who knew each other well, both on and off the pitch. Add to this the fact that Rehhagel encountered a talented generation, then all these steps along with a little luck helped bring about successes that Greek football had never had."

The togetherness that Rehhagel helped foster was in direct contrast to the animosity permeating Greek football at the time. With Olympiacos dominating the top-flight, but being heavily challenged by strong Panathinaikos and AEK teams, there was no love lost between the country's big three clubs. The 2002/03 finished amidst an acrimonious air. Olympiacos won the title, their seventh straight, after finishing on 70 points, even with Panathinaikos, but with a better head-to-head record. On the penultimate weekend of the season, it was Panathinaikos who held a three-point lead as the teams met at the Rizoupouli Stadium. Olympiacos were using the ground on a temporary basis as their new Karaiskakis Stadium was being constructed. Panathinaikos had won 3-2 the first time the two teams met. They merely had to win or draw in order to win the title. Even a one-goal loss would have kept their title hopes alive with a playoff decider a real possibility.

The match suffered from chaos before it even began. The Panathinaikos team bus was attacked by Olympiacos supporters on the way to the stadium with various missiles and flares. The two sets of supporters in the ground combined to create a hostile atmosphere, which was only exacerbated by the events occurring outside the stadium. Panathinaikos' players struggled to get out on to the pitch in order to warm-up. Some of the team's foreign players would later say they feared for their lives inside the locker room. On the pitch, Olympiacos dominated the match, winning 3-0 and going on to claim the title on the last matchday. Many observers agreed the match should not have been played considering the conditions prevalent ahead of kick-off. Others pointed to the fact that nothing happened during the match and that Olympiacos won fair and square. The match, which became infamously known as "The Derby of Rizoupouli", was a snapshot of Greek football at the time. Club rivalries were intense if not downright hostile, especially between Olympiacos and

Panathinaikos. Considering the prevailing state of affairs, it was a notable accomplishment how Rehhagel managed to keep the enmity at club level far away from the Ethniki. The more hatred the clubs harbored for each other it seemed, the closer the Ethniki became.

Greece picked up a 2-1 friendly victory away to Sweden in August 2003 in the lead-up to their next qualifier, away to Armenia. Giannakopoulos and Pantelis Kafes scored the goals in the comeback win. Kafes was a utility midfielder who had just moved to Olympiacos from PAOK. Rehhagel appreciated Kafes' versatility, the Veria-born player as comfortable in a defensive midfield position as he was further forward in the middle of the park. He appeared in two Euro 2004 qualifiers and eventually made 41 appearances for Greece. He was unique in that he wore the number one throughout his club career even though he was an outfield player. Kafes was something of an iron man in Greek football as he enjoyed a 17-year career that saw him play just shy of 600 matches.

Bigger clubs began taking notice of Kafes while he was on the books of local club Pontioi Veria. In 1997, PAOK beat out other interested team to the player's signature. He immediately began to feature in the starting line-up for the Thessaloniki side. After six seasons and two Greek Cup successes at the Toumba Stadium he made his way to Olympiacos. The reigning Greek champions had been swayed to move for Kafes, not only due to his tenacious work in the midfield trenches, but also his knack for scoring. Kafes scored more than 80 goals over the course of his career, including some fantastic strikes against major European clubs such as Real Madrid and Lyon. He later moved to AEK where he played four seasons before going back to hometown to quietly end his career with Veria in 2013. It was no surprise he never announced his retirement. Kafes was a low-profile individual and that along with his obvious quality is what saw him have such a long and respectable career.

* * * *

The performance against Sweden was a very good one by the Ethniki. It was a complete display in so far as the team looked very stable defensively and impressive going forward. It was a controlled outing that once again showcased the new-found resilience and desire of this group to try to get results, even in friendly matches. Attempting to win every match they played was now part of the culture. The environment surrounding the team was one of growing belief and unity. The celebrations of Nikolaidis on the bench after the goals, an example of a team that was invested in the game and in each other.

In early September, the team travelled to Yerevan for the next match against Armenia. Giannakopoulos and Antzas were injury concerns, but both made the trip. Katergiannankis kept his place as back-up goalkeeper. The most worrying bit of news for Rehhagel was the absence of Tsiartas. He was the sort of player that possessed that extra little genius that occasionally could unlock packed defenses.

Two players that did not get called up were Choutos and Patsatzoglou. For Choutos, the match against Ukraine would be the last he would play in a Greek jersey with Rehhagel preferring his other attacking options. Patsatzoglou's case was different. He was a Rehhagel favorite from the start. The German was a big fan of the player's attitude, versatility, and overall ability. He missed the Armenia match and later on all of Euro 2004 due to injury. Years later, Patsatzoglou would place the blame on a misdiagnosis of that injury. The player was treated for bone spurs, instead of a heel problem incurred from eight consecutive seasons of playing without stop. An ensuing procedure left him with an infection and the bad luck began to pile up for a player Rehhagel said he would have taken to Portugal if he could even walk. For nearly three years Patsatzoglou struggled to find fitness, not only missing out on Portugal, but also a transfer to a major European club (Manchester United representatives had gone to Athens in 2003 to make an offer for the player only to be rebuffed by Olympiacos president, Sokratis Kokkalis). He eventually recovered in the latter stages of his career making the Ethniki squads for Euro 2008 and the 2010 World Cup.

Armenia had given a positive showing of themselves in the group up to that point. Any Greek player who spoke about their upcoming opponents before the match were adamant that this would not be an easy contest. Rehhagel led this charge. On the eve of the game, he barricaded the players in the team hotel. Only team members were allowed in the facility and no one else, demanded the German. There he held discussions with the players, reiterating how difficult the match would be. In the last training session before the game, Rehhagel ordered his players to conserve energy and not to do any needless running in the hot conditions and elevation of Yerevan.

As the qualifier kicked off, Nikopolidis was forced into an early reaction save at his near post. It was a reminder that this would be no stroll in the park.

Giannakopoulos had a header go wide at the start of the match, yet Greece were having trouble creating chances against an organized Armenian side. There remained a patience in the Greek team, a certainty that the opening would eventually come. That occurred on 35 minutes.

A Basinas free-kick was soon cleared away with a bicycle-kick by Arman Karamyan. The ball landed at Seitaridis' feet and he released a ball out wide that Charisteas dummied for Dellas. The center-back looked up and measured his cross and picked out Vryzas, who gave Armenian goalkeeper Berezovsky no chance with his header.

* * * *

'Zisis the end'. That was the headline The Times of London ran with after Vryzas' late goal had helped PAOK knock Arsenal out of the UEFA Cup at Highbury in September 1997. Vryzas' goal, a sublime finish past David Seaman that began with him bamboozling Arsenal center-backs Tony Adams and Steve Bould, would become one of the most celebrated in PAOK's history. Ironically, a few years later he would leave the Thessaloniki club with a section of supporters unhappy with his lack of goals.

The truth is that Vryzas was never a prolific, goalscoring striker. He was a player who instead relished the battles in the trenches. After making his debut for Xanthi in 1992, he slowly became the best target forward in Greek football. The main hallmarks of Vryzas' game were his hold-up play and his ability to make runs to open up space for others. Some did not appreciate all of his dirty work, preferring to focus on his average goal stats. In 2000, he went abroad in search of a place where his style of play would be a better fit. He ended up at Perugia in Italy. Vryzas thrived in Umbria, nailing down a place as a regular starter for Perugia and helping lead the club to their first UEFA Cup appearance in nearly a quarter century. He further endeared himself to PAOK supporters by revealing a PAOK shirt under his Perugia jersey while celebrating a goal in a UEFA Cup victory over PAOK's big city rivals, Aris. That period of time was one of the best in Perugia's history, Vryzas playing a big part in victories over clubs such as AC Milan. While his strike rate at Perugia was no better than his career average of one goal every five matches, he became a highly-rated striker for what he brought to the table besides goals. His performances eventually saw him move to Fiorentina in 2003. The move to the Stadio Artemio Franchi did not pan out as well and featured two loan moves to Celta Vigo and Torino. Vryzas returned to Greece in 2006 and finished his career with a season each at first clubs Xanthi and PAOK.

Vryzas was a Rehhagel favorite and an ever-present in the German's line-ups. Vryzas' reliability and unselfishness was a key factor in Greece's qualification for Euro 2004 and he played a big role in the tournament itself in an understated manner that symbolized his career.

* * * *

After the break, Nikolaidis came on for Charisteas and proved to be a handful throughout. The Atletico Madrid striker conjuring up three big chances, the best being a header that Berezovsky pushed onto the post. Armenia put together some dangerous attacks, but the Greek defense denied their opponents any clear, goalscoring chances. That was until the final moments of the match. It was then when Ara Hakobyan found Galust Petrosyan completely unmarked at the far post. Much to the relief of the Greek players, Petrosyan's powerful header bounced off the ground and over the crossbar.

Greece held on and had accomplished their task in Armenia. A few days later the team were assured a spot in the qualifying playoffs as Spain had eliminated Ukraine from contention with a 2-1 win. Greece were on 15 points and Spain on 14 going into the final qualifier in October.

There was as much relief as joy on the faces of the Greek squad as they made the trip back to Greece. The win that effectively set-up a final against Northern Ireland in the last qualifier could not be fully appreciated. That is because a strange story emerged following the game.

Ruben Hayrapetyan, the president of the Football Federation of Armenia (FFA) made claims to the UEFA match delegate that approaches were made to Armenian players to fix the match against Greece. The FFA claimed that some of its players had received calls from unidentified people offering them money to allow the Greeks to win. Yervand Sukiasyn, a former Armenia international, living in Greece after playing for Iraklis, was at the center of the accusations. The story followed that Armenian U-21 manager, Karen Artunian, received a call from Sukiasyn, who claimed he had been ordered by EPO president Gagatsis to offer money for Armenia to throw the game. Artunian told this to Hayrapetyan, they both went to the FFA offices, and recorded a call to Sukiasyn. It was then claimed that Sukiasyn, working as a football agent for Armenian players in Greece, offered USD 1 million for a Greek win.

The FFA went straight to the Associated Press (AP) with the accusation. The AP promptly ran the story. Sukiasyan immediately denied taking part in any bribe, calling the accusations "shameless lies and a product of fantasy." He also said he did not even know Gagatsis. The day after the story broke, UEFA issued an official statement regarding the matter. It said that the European football governing body would launch an investigation. As soon as the EPO found out about the situation, Gagatsis contacted UEFA directly and asked that the investigation begin immediately so as to clear Greece's name and not to put the Ethniki's potential qualification in jeopardy. The Royal Spanish Football Federation (RFEF), themselves plenty to gain from a possible suspension of Greece, reached out to the EPO directly and offered their full support. The top officials at the RFEF stated they believed the Greeks and this was all a fabrication.

UEFA appointed Austrian Gerhard Kapl, a disciplinary investigator for the organization, to head up the case. The investigation did yield a tape. However, it was soon discovered that the recording of the phone call had been doctored many times over and was a fake. Before the last round of qualifying fixtures, UEFA released another statement. It read, "UEFA has found no indication that the EPO had been involved in any irregularities. As the situation stands at present, it is clear that there was nothing irregular about the Euro 2004 qualifier in question." This meant that the state of group play would be unaffected.

Despite the fact that most involved with the Ethniki did not take the Armenian claims of match-fixing seriously, it was still a relief to be able to put that issue to bed. Now, everyone could focus on the best possible preparation for Greece's final qualifier against Northern Ireland. With qualification to Euro 2004 so close, the media coverage of the build-up was comprehensive. This was in stark contrast to the rest of the qualifying campaign. Everyone had jumped on the bandwagon by this stage.

Many similarities were made in news reports before that game comparing the upcoming qualifier to Greece's final qualifier for the 1980 European Championship. 24 years before, Greece had needed a win in their final match to advance and they did so in the same stadium that the national team would host Northern Ireland.

The remarks of the players before the match showed clearly that their heads were not in the clouds. Dellas described the encounter as containing "hidden pitfalls." Giannakopoulos called for "seriousness, discipline and respect for the opposition", while Charisteas said "it would be a shame for something to go wrong now, after a huge effort." Rehhagel expressed his confidence that Greece would score, but did tell reporters that his team needed to be steady at the back and "at their highest level, both in spirit and body." He went on to call the occasion "a historic moment where the players understand they can write history."

Northern Ireland were coming to Greece at the end of a terrible campaign. McIlroy's men had still not scored through seven qualifiers and had gone twelve matches in total without a goal. With nothing to play for, McIlroy stated that the pressure was all with Greece and that his team would try to disrupt the party. The Greek press latched on to comments made by Northern Ireland captain Keith Gillespie who said, "These countries know how to play-act on the pitch. Some ridiculous happenings took place in the first match." It was no surprise then that Gillespie was booed every time he touched the ball in his 64 minutes on the field in that final qualifier.

The only injury concern for Rehhagel was a knock to Kapsis in the days leading up to the game. Perhaps, the biggest worry was the lack of match fitness for some key personnel, specifically the foreign-based players. While the likely striking duo of Charisteas and Vryzas had been playing regularly at Werder Bremen and Perugia, respectively, others abroad had not. Giannakopoulos had played only four matches all season for Bolton, while the likes of Dabizas, Dellas, and Nikolaidis had virtually no game time at all for their clubs. Rehhagel's trust in these players was absolute. When pressed about their ability to perform, he simply stated he was not concerned and he believed in them. Form and fitness were other issues. While it was October and relatively early in the league season, players such as Nikopolidis, Basinas, Karagounis, and Kapsis were either fighting through some tough patches of form or a long time on the sidelines. Karagounis, in particular, still did not appear to be fully fit following his long injury layoff.

In another hiccup before the game, there were ongoing problems with the training facilities at Agios Kosmas. Rehhagel decided not to risk anything. The decision was made to hold the last few training sessions at the Rizoupouli Stadium, though incredibly the team was denied time on the pitch. The reason given was that the facility was booked with practice for academy teams. The Ethniki ended up at club side Ionikos' stadium, Neapoli, in Nikaia, a suburb of Athens.

There was undoubtedly a readiness amongst the packed crowd inside the

Leoforos on 11 October 2003 to celebrate. The pre-game festivities included a marching band and even a song made for the team by legendary Greek composer and football lover Makis Theodorakis. Several former national team members were in attendance as were other high-profile guests such as the President of the Athens Organizing Committee for the 2004 Olympic Games, Gianna Angelopoulos-Daskalaki.

Kapsis was ruled out so Dabizas took his place in the starting eleven. In a small surprise, Tsiartas was opted for instead of Karagounis in midfield. Nikopolidis had lost the starting job at Panathinaikos, but for Rehhagel, he was well-established as the national team's number one. The opening whistle saw Gillespie nearly played through in a nervy first minute for the home side. The Ethniki quickly settled and were holding the ball well in the early stages. Northern Ireland's plan was crystal clear, defend en masse and hit on the counter-attack. Greece focused their attacks mostly on the right side as the likes of Seitaridis and Giannakopoulos probed in hopes of getting into the box or providing crosses for Charisteas and Vryzas. Rehhagel's men had the bulk of the possession in the opening 20 minutes. Despite enjoying a lot of the ball there were only half chances to speak of. At one point, Charisteas lost possession in the Northern Irish half and picked up a silly yellow card for a clumsy challenge. It was an example of a team trying to do too much as frustration had crept in to Greece's play.

Just after the caution, Charisteas atoned for that act with the game's first real chance. The striker producing a hard, low shot that Northern Ireland goalkeeper Maik Taylor pushed out for a corner. Seitaridis then went on a mazy run down the right, cut inside and forced Taylor into another save. Greece appeared to be coming closer to the goal they so desperately were looking for. Dellas came up with an important intervention just after the half hour to concede a corner. It was the first real counter-attack from the visitors, but a reminder that Northern Ireland were not going to go down easy.

Rehhagel, as per usual during the qualifiers, did not hesitate on making big decisions early. At halftime the Ethniki boss went forward with a double change. Charisteas was substituted for Nikolaidis and Dabizas pulled off in favor Venetidis.

* * * *

The German settled on his preferred left-backs early on in his tenure. Fyssas would be the first-choice on many occasions, but Rehhagel appreciated what

Venetidis brought to the table. Venetidis' fully committed displays had a place in Rehhagel's Ethniki. It was not just his effort that convinced the manager. Venetidis was a solid full-back, but he could contribute in attack as well. The player added another dimension to Greece's games with his overlapping runs and excellent deliveries from the flanks. Born in Orestiada, Greece's northeastern most city, located just a few kilometers from the Turkish border, Venetidis began his career as a youngster with local club, Orestis Orestiada. Two seasons of fine performances in lower-league football was all that Xanthi needed to snap up the promising left-back. Venetidis had no trouble making the jump to the top-flight and he became a starter for Xanthi immediately, registering over 100 appearances over three seasons. Venetidis continued his rise to the top Greek clubs by moving to Thessaloniki in 1999 to join PAOK. He won his first silverware there as a player by helping his team to the 2001 Greek Cup. Olympiacos, the team PAOK had defeated 4-2 in that cup final, desperately wanted the player in the wake of Grigoris Georgatos' move to Italy. Ironically, Venetidis ended up replacing Georgatos at club level and with the Ethniki as well with Rehhagel choosing him as the defender who would take Georgatos' place after that duo had fallen out. Five seasons at Olympiacos yielded four league titles and two cup successes. He finished off his career with six seasons at Larisa, a stint that brought about another Greek Cup victory in 2007.

* * * *

After the break, the match took a similar look to that of the first half. The Greek effort was visible, however despite the passion and effort on display, there was still no incisiveness. Tsiartas was setting the tempo in the midfield and he continuously was trying to play balls behind the Northern Irish defense. It was to no avail against a side that was defending so deep.

As the time passed, the tension grew. The crowd, in full voice to start the match, had become quieter. The nervousness could be heard in the growing moments of a collectively held breath. Seitaridis continued to make inroads down his flank and produced a fantastic cross which Giannakopoulos knocked down. With the goal gaping, Vryzas just failed to prod the ball into the net. In the one instance the opposition risked a few more players forward, Greece were able to counter-attack just after the hour mark. A lighting quick burst saw Giannakopoulos fouled. Tsiartas then botched the ensuing free-kick leading to a counter from Northern Ireland. They had numbers on the break and it took a fantastic block from Dellas off of an Aaron Hughes shot to keep them off the board.

The match was not turning out how Greece would have wanted. And though Northern Ireland had little to show in an attacking sense, they had managed to create some dangerous moments in transition. The decisive moment in the match came in surprise fashion in the 65th minute. Just when Greece looked to be lacking the patience and ingenuity to break down Northern Ireland, the hosts won a penalty. Giannakopoulos played Vryzas through and as the striker burst into the box he was brought down by defender George McCartney. Portuguese referee Lucilio Batista showed no hesitation in not only pointing to the spot, but in also producing a red card for McCartney.

Vasilis Tsiartas had played the initial long-ball to Giannakopoulos to create the play that would define the match. Those who followed Greek football during that time period knew full well the high level of attacking quality Tsiartas brought to the field. The playmaker had a vision and passing range unique to the rest of the Greek squad. He could see the spaces others could not, find the holes that most did not think were there. His left foot was deadly whether shooting from long-range or scoring from free-kicks. He was a once-in-a-generation talent in Greek football. This is perhaps why he was known as 'El Mago' during his time in Spain with Sevilla.

Tsiartas began his professional career at Naoussa, close to his hometown of Alexandreia. As a 17-year-old he began to display the skills that would make him one of the country's most-sought after footballers in the early 1990s. In December 1992, he joined AEK after playing a big role in putting Naoussa into a position to be promoted to the Alpha Ethniki (they eventually would go up to the top-flight, spending one season there in 1993/94). His ability was evident and he was first called up to the national side just before the 1994 World Cup. His first cap came against Saudi Arabia in April 1994 where he was an impressive second-half substitute in a 5-1 win for Greece. Calls for his inclusion to the squad for that tournament went unanswered, which may have been a blessing in disguise for the player.

The playmaker's influence at club level grew and in 1995/96 he finished the season as leading scorer in the league, scored a hat-trick in the Greek Cup final, and ended the year as the Greek Footballer of the Year. In a time where there were very few Greeks playing abroad, Tsiartas was being scouted heavily by foreign clubs. He moved to Sevilla ahead of the 1996/97 season. The start of his spell in Andalusia was a mixed bag. He joined Sevilla in a difficult period of the club's history. His style of play divided opinion. Some saw a footballing genius while others saw a lazy player who could not be bothered to run. At his unveiling he flicked the ball up in the air twelve different ways prompting a local journalist to suggest that he was talking to the ball. As Sevilla toiled in the lower reaches of the Primer Division, Tsiartas' coach, Jose Antonio Camacho slammed the player for not running at all while speaking to the press. When a reporter asked Tsiartas about that, he replied "I don't need to run, the ball runs for me." The first season in Sevilla ended in disaster as the club were relegated to the Segunda Division. Tsiartas was made one of the scapegoats by supporters as many of the Sevilla high brass blamed him for being more concerned about his pay rather than his effort on the training pitch. Tsiartas' overall play had seen his stock rise though. The legendary Alfredo di Stefano once commenting to a newspaper that "the number ten of Sevilla is one player Real should be interested in." No move like that materialized, but Racing Santander were extremely close to signing the player, hoping the lure of remaining in the top division would be enough. Tsiartas wanted to make the switch and it nearly happened. It all fell apart in the end as Sevilla could find a worthy replacement.

The next two seasons would cement Tsiartas' place as a club legend, capping off a remarkable turnaround within the club and with the supporters. When Marcos Alonso took over as manager in January 1999, Sevilla were in twelfth place in the Segunda Division. The new boss improved matters quickly and Tsiartas' performances drove Sevilla toward promotion. In the promotion play-offs against Villarreal, Tsiartas scored a first leg brace away to give his side a precious 2-0 victory. He then provided an assist in the return fixture as Sevilla went back up to the Primera Division following a 3-0 aggregate win. His fourth and final season in Spain ended in disappointment once again as Sevilla went straight back down. He returned to Greece and AEK leaving a positive view of his contributions back in Spain where he managed 46 goals and 54 assists over four years.

Rehhagel consistently chose Tsiartas all the way up until Euro 2004. There, the German preferred packing the midfield with players who were more mobile and better at closing down the opposition. Still, Tsiartas was the man Rehhagel would bring on when Greece needed that extra bit of creativity and inspiration.

And the player accepted that role and featured in some of Greece's most pivotal moments during the tournament.

* * * *

Tsiartas stood over the ball and in front of Taylor, knowing full well that a goal could take Greece to Portugal. Taylor had been in superb form for Northern Ireland in the qualifying campaign. His performance against Spain became the stuff of legend after he produced a series of fantastic stops to deny the Spaniards and help his team to a 0-0 draw.

And as Tsiartas ran up and struck the penalty it appeared as though Taylor got the jump he needed to make the save. The penalty was struck so cleanly and with such precision that even though Taylor had guessed right and came close, the ball caressed the side netting after evading his reach.

Tsiartas had done it and Greece were finally ahead. This time there would be no stranglehold on the noise inside the stadium. The tension was lifted and the Greek fans were in full voice once again. The confidence had returned and qualification for Portugal was 20 minutes away. With ten minutes left, an uncharacteristic error by the otherwise terrific Dellas opened the door for Northern Ireland. The Greek center-back's mis-clearance falling at the feet of substitute Andy Smith, who somehow managed to smack his shot from six yards well over the goal.

Greece regained control of the ball and threatened themselves as Giannakopoulos' chip was pushed onto the bar by Taylor. In a chaotic finale, Dellas played through severe cramping while Basinas also was in pain after picking up a knock and eventually was subbed off by Zagorakis.

After three minutes of injury-time, Batista blew the final whistle. Greece had qualified for the European Championship for the first time in 24 years. It was the country's first qualification for a major finals in a decade. And the celebrations told of a country and group of players who were overjoyed to have succeeded in this achievement.

The Greek team celebrated in the middle of the pitch as one. Rehhagel and Topalidis right in the midst of all the players. Kostas Vernikos, the Greek commentator in charge of that match seemed to accurately describe the scenes. "Rehhagel taught these players how to play like Germans and they taught him how to celebrate like a Greek," said the clearly emotional broadcaster.

Those words encapsulated a lot of what had transpired in the previous 26 months. A underachieving, but talented group of players, had been given the discipline, strategy, and structure necessary to finally find success. In the process, they gave their manager the trust and loyalty he so needed in order to be able to celebrate another great managerial achievement.

Basinas spoke to the EPO's official site and made no mistake about what he believed led Greece to this qualification, saying, "We were able to surpass club differences, which we had in the past. And now we were only focused on the good of the national team." Rehhagel spoke about experience and his players. The proud manager stating, "I have great experience and knew how to handle similar circumstances. For me, the most important thing in the whole journey, and ultimately in the success, was the players." When asked by a reporter what he thought about Greece's chances at Euro 2004, Rehhagel showed he was not content with merely qualifying. "We want to go to Portugal and show that we were not lucky to come first in the group, that we are a strong team," said the German. Just having achieved such a momentous qualification, Rehhagel had already set the tone with regard to Greece's participation in that tournament. The preparation to do something special in Portugal had already begun.

Some of the travelling Greek fans in Lisbon.

The Greece team starting eleven pose for a group photo prior to the Final.

Back row, left to right:
Traianos Dellas, Angelos Charisteas, Takis Fyssas, Kostas Katsouranis, Michalis Kapsis, Antonis Nikopolidis

Front row, left to right:
Stelios Giannakopoulos, Zisis Vryzas, Giourkas Seitaridis, Angelos Basinas, Theodoros Zagorakis (captain)

Portugal's Cristiano Ronaldo takes off his shirt after taking the 1-0 lead during the semi-final against the Netherlands. Portugal went on to win 2-1 to set-up the final against Greece.

Forward Angelos Charisteas (R) struggles for the ball against Czech defender Marek Jankulovski during the semi-final between Greece and the Czech Republic in Porto. Greece won the game with a 1-0 'silver goal' during extra time to set-up the final against Portugal.

Greek defender Takis Fyssas (L) fights for the ball with Portuguese midfielder and team captain Luis Figo.

Greece team captain and midfielder Theodoros Zagorakis throws up his arms in triumph after the final.

Euro 2004 started as it finished, with a match between hosts Portugal and Greece. Greece's German coach, Otto Rehhagel, led the team to an impossible victory.

Greek fans gather in Athens the day after the final.

Chapter 12

Preparing For A New Challenge

In light of clinching qualification, there was a tremendous feel-good factor surrounding the team. The press coverage was extremely comprehensive and positive, perhaps even borderline sensationalized. There was widespread euphoria amongst Greeks with regard to making it to Euro 2004. While the national team had suffered through years of failure, the country maintained its passion for football. And now, finally people could watch a major tournament and cheer on their own team.

The players were widely praised for the way they handled the qualifying campaign. The character they showed in coming back from two consecutive losses to win six matches in a row, whilst not conceding a goal during that winning streak, was admirable. The view those in the football community had of this group had changed. The underachievers had become heroes in a matter of months. The team was handsomely rewarded for making it to Portugal. The players received a €2 million bonus (€1.4 million from the EPO and €600,000 from the government) and the Greek Minister of Culture and Sports prepared to offer the players a PRO-PO license. This would allow each player to set up a sports betting business when they retired. That was something that eventually could not be carried out so an additional €1 million was added to the collective bonus.

Rehhagel was the one individual who emerged with the most credit. Many saw in him the reason why this group of players were finally able to celebrate a successful qualification. Months before, his position appeared to be in question, but following the victory over Northern Ireland a discussion for a new contract began immediately. It took just a few weeks to nail down the details and in mid-November 2003, Rehhagel and the EPO agreed terms on contract renewal that would keep the manager in his job until the end of 2005. Rehhagel's yearly salary would be €600,000 with a bonus of over €400,000 should he steer the team toward qualifying for the 2006 FIFA World Cup.

Sorting out Rehhagel's future with the national team was key in the Ethniki being able to focus on preparing for the European Championship. As fate would have it, the team would get a taste of Portugal in advance of the competition. Greece had scheduled a friendly with Portugal months before for November. The match was to take place in Aveiro and be the first event to take place in the city's new Estadio Municipal de Aveiro. The ground was one of the new stadiums built specifically with Euro 2004 in mind.

The friendly on 15 November 2003 against the Portuguese was considered an important match by Rehhagel and the team. Not only because Greece would be playing the Euro hosts. The attention of many in Europe would now also be on Greece. The team was still a bit of an unknown quantity to many football fans throughout the continent. Some players who played abroad were known, however the lack of star power in general meant there were few recognizable names in the squad.

Lakis and Dimitris Papadopoulos were the new faces in the squad for the Portugal friendly. Vryzas was ruled out with a knee injury, while Antzas made the trip, but was unable to play due to a hip problem.

Portugal went into the match without regulars such as Nuno Gomes and Armand Petit. Young teenage sensation Cristiano Ronaldo was also unavailable. Fyssas was the central figure in this friendly on the side of the Portuguese media. The left-back had just agreed terms to join Benfica at the start of the January transfer window. The friendly finished 1-1 with Lakis giving the Ethniki the lead just after halftime and Pauleta drawing the home side level on the hour.

* * * *

Lakis was something of a rarity in Greek football at the time, a winger with speed and an ability to score goals. Perhaps only Giannakopoulos was similar to him in that Ethniki team. Lakis started his career in 1992 as a teammate with Vasilis Tsiartas at Naoussa, a modest regional side who shocked everybody when they managed to play one season in the Alpha Ethniki in 1993/94. His performances as a 17-year-old were a delight and one of the bright spots as Naoussa fell back down to the second division. By this point, his talent had seen him picked in the Greek youth national teams. Paniliakos was his next stop and he grew into one of the club's main attacking options before AEK agreed terms with the player in July 1998.

Known as "Turbo" due to his pace, Lakis continued to improve after landing at AEK and celebrated two Greek Cups in his first stint there (he would later rejoin the club between 2005-2007). He is perhaps best known in Greece for his goal in the 2000/01 Greek Cup quarter-finals against Olympiacos. In the first leg, Lakis took the ball from behind the half-field line and slalomed through the entire opposition defense before scoring an absolutely sensational goal. After Euro 2004, he played a season in the English Premier League with Crystal Palace before returning to Greece and finishing his career with spells at AEK, PAOK, and Kavala.

Greece once again had plenty to positives to take away from the Portugal friendly. The team succeeded in increasing their unbeaten run to thirteen matches. It was a result made more impressive by the fact that the Ethniki played a man down for nearly an hour. Karagounis had received his marching orders in the 31st minute after saving a goal-bound effort with his hands. Luis Figo's ensuing spot-kick was saved by Nikopolidis as was the superstar's follow-up attempt.

Two weeks after the Portugal friendly, Rehhagel and a Greek contingent travelled back to the country for the official Euro 2004 draw. Those proceedings were set to take place in Lisbon at the Pavilhao Atlantico on the banks of the Tagus River. The area used to be a rundown district that formerly contained old warehouses, a slaughterhouse, and an oil refinery. Holding the draw there was symbolic of Portugal's development and progress in recent time and ultimately their readiness to host such a big competition.

On 30 November 2003, the eyes of European football were all on Lisbon. A slew of officials and dignitaries were present, many of whom would help conduct the draw. The event itself was hosted by CNN Portuguese sports presenter Pedro Pinto and radio anchor Fatima Campos. They were assisted by outgoing UEFA Chief Executive, Gerhard Aigner, and his successor, Lars-Christen Olsson. Euro 2000 winner Laurent Blanc brought the trophy into the venue and was joined by Portugal's Hugo Viana and the country's greatest football ambassador, Eusebio. Early in the night, Adidas launched the official ball for Euro 2004, the Roteiro.

The draw seeding system was based on the performance of teams in qualifying for the 2002 World Cup and Euro 2004. Greece were in the lowest rank of seeded teams, in Pot D alongside Bulgaria, Switzerland, and Latvia. The draw commenced exactly 200 days from the start of the tournament's opening match.

That would be of great importance for Greece to know because they found themselves come out first and land in Group A. Portugal were team A1 and after Greece was selected, their place in the section was confirmed as A2. The opener was set as Portugal would play against Greece at the Estadio do Dragao in Porto. From Pot C, Russia ended up in Greece's group. All involved were hoping to avoid the Netherlands, a superb team who was in Pot C based on a below par performance in failing to qualify for the 2002 World Cup. Finally, the Pot B teams were next. Spain were drawn in to Group A. Portugal and Spain began as the overwhelming favorites against a Russia side with a history of underperforming and a Greek team who had not qualified for this tournament in roughly a quarter century. Greece would begin against Portugal on 12 June, then play Spain four days later at the Estadio do Bessa in Porto, before going to Faro-Loule on 20 June to face off against Russia in the group finale.

Reaction to the draw was swift from all sides. Portuguese manager, Luis Felipe Scolari suggested, "It is a balanced group, a very strong group." He reminded many that while the marquee match between his team and Spain would be last, that his team had to "concentrate on Greece and Russia beforehand." Spanish boss Inaki Saez also toed the line, stating his belief that the group was the one with the most similar teams, all with even chances to qualify. Russian coach Georgy Yartsev openly talked about the group favorites saying, "Portugal and Spain are obviously the favorites in the group and Greece and us are the outsiders." His concerns laid more with the fact that many of his players would head into the tournament with only eight to ten matches under their belts as the new Russian league season would not begin until early March.

Rehhagel seemed to take the results of the draw in stride. He cut the figure of a man who seemed almost giddy when analyzing Group A. "It is an advantage for us, as one of the outsiders of the group, to be playing the opening match against the host country," indicated the German coach. "The hosts are always under a huge amount of pressure in the first game, more than in the other games, and we will be under no pressure at all."

Rehhagel went on to call the prospect of playing in the opening match "a great honor." He also saw it as an opportunity for Greece to make a good start in the tournament, despite the fact that he deemed Portugal the big favorites. The players were already awaiting a difficult hand from the draw. Dellas confirmed this with his comments to the press after Greece learned of their fate. "Our job will not be easy. We knew that wherever we landed would be tough as we were in the lowest seeded group, but even that doesn't say much as its all the same difficulty for us. We begin as the outsiders, just as we did for the qualifiers, and we finished first," said Dellas.

The draw threw up some interesting groups. The dreaded 'Group of Death' tag seemed to go to Group D, which featured Germany, Netherlands, Czech Republic, and debutants Latvia. Italy found themselves in a section alongside Sweden, Bulgaria, and Denmark. English bookmaker William Hill slashed the Italian odds to win the tournament from 11 ½/1 to 4/1 due to the perceived easier nature of Group C. France began as the favorites to win the competition at 100/30 followed by hosts Portugal (13/2) and Spain (7/1). Greece's odd to lift the trophy were listed as 80/1, however some companies were offering as much as 150/1 or even 250/1. Only Latvia were consistently listed at longer odds to win the championship.

The Euro 2004 draw was met with mixed reaction back in Greece. Most gave Portugal and Spain the clear edge. The quality of those teams along with the fact that Portugal were hosts and Spain were nearby neighbors were also cited as important factors. The main concerns centered not on the fellow Group A participants, but rather the Greek team itself. The general hope was for a period of proper preparation and readiness so as avoid a repeat of the 1994 World Cup. The objective was a solid showing more than anything else.

In the wake of the draw, the EPO announced a trio of friendlies to be played in the lead-up to the tournament. There would be home matches against Bulgaria and Switzerland in February and March, respectively, and a very difficult test at the end of April, away to the Netherlands. Later, two final friendlies against Poland and Liechtenstein were announced. Those matches would be played near the team's training camp in Switzerland in the final week before arriving in Portugal for the tournament.

There was a host of work done behind the scenes for the remainder of 2003 and start of 2004. Rehhagel and Topalidis had travelled to both Portugal and Switzerland in order to find suitable base camps for the team. Bad Ragaz, a spa and health resort destination in the Swiss canton of St. Gallen, was selected as the team's pre-tournament training location. In Portugal, the coaching staff decided on a facility in Vila do Conde, a town on the River Ave near Porto, the site of Greece's first two matches.

The failure of the team members to show up for the annual Panhellenic Association of Sports Press (PSAT) Awards nearly caused a diplomatic episode of sorts and threatened to disrupt the feel-good factor surrounding the team. There was widespread criticism for the fact that not a single individual had not shown up to represent the national team, which was selected as the organization's Team of the Year for 2003. So as to atone for that error in judgement, in late January 2004, sixteen members of the team (the only missing players were those who were based abroad), along with Rehhagel, Topalidis, Gagatsis, and many other EPO officials visited the Greek President Konstantinos Stefanopoulos as a sign of respect and to apologize for having missed the PSAT awards.

Greece's first Euro 2004 warm-up occurred on 18 February against Bulgaria at the Apostolos Nikolaidis. Giannakopoulos was ruled out due to an injury. Nikolaidis was allowed leave from the game due to the birth of his daughter. Rehhagel recalled Chalkias, Papadopoulos, and Goumas to the team.

$$* * * *$$

Giannis Goumas' capable displays for Panathinaikos ensured he found his way into the Greek squad ahead of Euro 2004. Although he never was a first-choice regular for Greece, he did manage to be capped 45 times for his country between 1999 and 2008. Goumas was a reliable center-back who spent the entirety of his career at Panathinaikos. In 15 years with the *Prasini* he made over 400 appearances for the club. When he joined as a youngster in 1992 he was a highly-touted attacker. His early days in Athens were difficult and a bout of homesickness almost saw him return to his hometown of Ambelonas in Thessaly, near Larisa. He persevered and was able to make the grade. Goumas' time as a striker and right-sided midfielder as a teenager could explain his eventual goal output as his career unfolded. Despite being converted to a center-back early on in his professional career, Goumas scored 38 times for Panathinaikos. These included some spectacular efforts and goals against major continental sides such as Real Madrid, Juventus, and Rangers. Domestically, he also managed to score crucial goals, including one against Olympiacos in 2004 that helped Panathinaikos eventually win the league.

Never the biggest name on the roster or a star player, Goumas was a loyal servant for Panathinaikos and Greece whose performances for club and country were consistently of a good standard. He retired in 2009, having celebrated three league titles and two domestic cups with Panathinaikos.

* * * *

The Ethniki rolled over the Bulgarians in an extremely positive display, arguably the most complete under Rehhagel. The 2-0 win came thanks to goals from Papadopoulos and Vryzas. The performance coupled with the fact that it came against a team that had also qualified for Portugal brought about optimism. Everything seemed to be heading in the right direction.

One player who did not make the cut for the Bulgaria match was Paraskevas Antzas. The preceding months had seen Antzas step away from professional football. It appeared a surprising decision for the 27-year-old defender. Having played his way into Rehhagel's plans, Antzas had become a starter for the national team, a player included in the starting eleven in the final qualifier against Northern Ireland. A month after having helped qualify Greece for Portugal, Antzas left club side Olympiacos in favor of his hometown team, Doxa Drama. No public explanation was given at the time. Football fans were in awe that a player would step away from what was the peak of their career.

Antzas was always a reserved individual. When Xanthi showed interest in the player as a teenager, Antzas resisted initially, not wanting to leave his hometown and continue playing for his local team, Pandramaikos. It took his father's urging that he should try to play at Xanthi for Antzas to make the switch. The player looked at the move as a way to help his father work less. What followed was a rapid rise through the Greek game for Antzas. Three fantastic years at Xanthi saw him snapped up by Olympiacos. Antzas was a manager's dream, a ball-playing center-back just as comfortable building attacks from the back as he was in the game's physical battles. He was also versatile, able to play as a defensive midfielder. Antzas considered the top-flight easier than the third division, stating on many occasions that he found the lower levels much tougher and combative than the first division.

When he was 22, he lost his father and grandfather within months of each other. He continued to play and win titles at Olympiacos. However, as he revealed years later in an interview with sports site Gazzetta.gr, he was lost. He could not get over the passing of the two men he looked up to most and saw leaving the high-profile world of Olympiacos as the only way to help himself.

He joined Doxa Drama, a team playing in the Gamma Ethniki, the third division of Greek football. There was speculation that Rehhagel still might select the player for Euro 2004. Antzas' omission from the squad for the Bulgaria friendly showed that Rehhagel could find no place for him, the German saying, "We only call-up players playing in the top-flight." As a result, Antzas missed the Euro. He did come back to the professional ranks. The birth of his children gave him the motivation to play at the top level again. Three more seasons at Xanthi were followed by a return to Olympiacos for two seasons in 2007. He won back his place in the national team as well and Rehhagel selected him to Greece's Euro 2008 squad.

The victory over Bulgaria brought Greece's unbeaten run to fourteen. European football began to take notice of this streak. The Bulgaria win came in as the second headline on UEFA's official website. Rehhagel continued to select the players he trusted, the ones that helped achieve qualification. This meant giving playing time to those individuals who were getting little at their respective clubs. It seemed like a risky move. However, what it ultimately did was strengthen the bond between the manager and players. The atmosphere surrounding the team was so positive and in such good health that there was no sign of problems with Rehhagel's decision on who played and who did not. He had become a patriarchal figure whom the players had put their complete confidence into.

Chapter 13

The Final Stretch

Football infrastructure in Greece received a boost from the 2004 Olympic Games in Athens. The football tournament at those Olympics was to be held in various cities throughout the country. This meant several stadiums were renovated or reconstructed. In Crete, a brand new stadium was built in Heraklion named the Pankritio Stadium. At the end of March 2004, the Ethniki inaugurated that ground with a friendly against Switzerland.

27,000 fans filled the Pankritio Stadium for that encounter as Greece continued their strong performances in the Euro 2004 warm-up matches. Tsiartas, superb once again, scored the game's only goal in the 57th minute with a beautiful finish from a Vryzas cross. It was a solid display by the Ethniki who produced a high quality first hour of football. Tsiartas' goal saw him atone for a first-half penalty miss in a game where Greece created plenty and gave away very little in defense.

Swiss manager Kobi Kuhn was full of praise for the team in his post-match comments. "Greece showed experience, self-belief, and perhaps will be the surprise team of the upcoming Euro," Kuhn said. After seeing Greece he believed the team belonged amongst the darkhorses for the tournament. It was stunning to read that from a Greek perspective. However, the performances in the qualifiers and the unbeaten run, now at fifteen, had caused many to take notice of the team. Oleg Protasov, a former standout USSR international in the 1980s, who had led Olympiacos to the league title as manager in 2003, spoke to the Russian press during the same time period. Having seen the rise of the Greek side as a coach in Greece, he warned Russia by saying, "Greece needs to be dealt with. If they think it will be an easy barrier to cross against the Greeks, Russia will be making a big mistake."

* * * *

The Switzerland friendly saw Nikopolidis picked once again as Greece's starting goalkeeper. This would not have normally been news as Rehhagel had tabbed the 32-year-old as his number one early on in his reign. The problem was that Nikopolidis had not been playing at club level. A stalemate in the contract discussions between the player and Panathinaikos saw him marginalized by the club. Media reports at the time suggested Panathinaikos had offered the player €400,000 per year while Nikopolidis was asking for €600,000. After 15 years at Panathinaikos, Nikopolidis felt slighted by the club. The negotiations came to a halt as Nikopolidis refused to sign and Panathinaikos were unwilling to raise their offer. Nikopolidis was subsequently dropped in favor of Chalkias. This led to the unique situation of the back-up keeper at Panathinaikos being the starter for the national team and the number one for the *Prasini* as the back-up for Greece. It also caused a rift between the two men that was present at the beginning of the Euro 2004 preparations.

Nikopolidis began his career in the lower divisions playing for Anagennisi Artas as a teenager. He began as a field player and only played in goal due to his cousin needing to go to a wedding. Nikopolidis used his cousin's player card to be able to replace him in goal and liked it so much that he remained in that position. After two seasons for Arta, Panathinaikos signed the promising player and he moved to Athens at the age of 18. Nikopolidis' first eight years for the *Prasini* were a test in patience. Polish goalkeeper Jozef Wandzik was a club legend and had the starting role on lockdown. Wandzik's ten-year stay at Panathinaikos began just as Nikopolidis arrived. Wandzik went to Greece at the peak of his career and Nikopolidis was forced to wait in the wings. In eight seasons, Nikopolidis managed to make only twenty league appearances in total. He was already 26 before he began to play regularly in the 1996/97 campaign as Wandzik began to enter the latter stages of his own career. The common joke was that Nikopolidis had been signed by Panathinaikos with a full head of black hair and by the time he became the starter it had turned to gray. That look would lead to him being referred to as the "Greek George Clooney", due to his resemblance to the Hollywood actor.

Nikopolidis was always considered a reliable and unflappable goalkeeper. He debuted for Greece in an August 1999 friendly versus El Salvador. As with Panathinaikos, he had to bide his time to make his mark with the national team.

He split time with Elias Atmatsidis and then Dimitris Eleftheropoulos from 1999 to August 2001 when Rehhagel became manager. The German appeared to prefer Eleftheropoulos to begin with. The heavy loss at Finland along with Eleftheropoulos citing personal problems ahead of the qualifier against England in October 2001 saw Rehhagel put his full faith in Nikopolidis.

Just ahead of Euro 2004, Nikopolidis agreed to sign with Olympiacos. It was a shock move which Nikopolidis would later say was motivated in part by a desire for revenge. The player felt that Panathinaikos believed he was past his prime. He ended up finishing his career in Piraeus winning league titles in six of his seven seasons with the Erythrolefki. He announced his international retirement after Euro 2008 having represented his country 90 times.

The two other goalkeepers to be included in the Euro 2004 squad had been selected by Rehhagel consistently in the year leading up to the tournament. They were Kostas Chalkias and Fanis Katergiannakis. The 6'6 Chalkias was also a Panathinaikos academy product who cut his teeth with a stint at Apollon Athinon. He returned to Panathinaikos in 1998 and stayed three seasons. As Nikopolidis had to wait for Wandzik, so did Chalkias play second fiddle to Nikopolidis. Chalkias' desire for game time saw him move north to Thessaloniki where he played two full seasons for Iraklis. The opportunity for a third spell at Panathinaikos was too good to pass up and in 2003 Chalkias returned to the club.

Again, Chalkias reprised his role as back-up until Nikopolidis' problems with the club thrust Chalkias into the starting goalkeeper role. He helped lead the team to a double in the 2003/04 season and headed into the Euro with hopes of fighting for the number one spot. He later spent time abroad in rather unsuccessful spells at Portsmouth and Real Murcia before moving back to Greece to play for Aris and PAOK, completing the job of playing for all three major Thessaloniki clubs. After seemingly retiring in 2012, he came back to football in 2016 for two seasons at Panachaiki, finishing his playing days at the age of 44.

Katergiannakis spent the beginning of his professional career with Aris. He was a PAOK fan who never managed to play for his favored club. Aris supporters respected his loyalties and he was a fine player in his eight years there. "I believe if you are a one hundred percent professional and give no reasons otherwise, all fans will see that and respect you," says Katergiannakis. Injury robbed Katergiannakis of the opportunity to make his first cap when selected by Daniil in 1998. He eventually made his debut in 1999 against Bulgaria. "When I first wore the national team shirt I was flying in the heavens. It was a goal and life's dream, especially considering I was never selected in the youth national teams."

In a crowded field of goalkeepers he was never able to consistently play for the Ethniki. After moving to Olympiacos in 2002, he took ahold of the starting job there over Eleftheropoulos. He caught the eye of Rehhagel as a pair of safe hands with his assured performances in the 2002/03 season as Olympiacos won the league. Katergiannakis had also garnered a reputation as a penalty-kick specialist, registering a remarkable 47% save rate for his career when facing players from twelve yards. "There was no real secret behind my success at penalties. During that time period there was not much analysis. I kept my own statistics and folders on players who took kicks and tried to increase my chances in that way. That's basically what contributed to my success against penalty takers. I had help in amassing information from top statistician Stavros Petrakopoulos."

Nikopolidis' arrival at Olympiacos meant less playing time for Katergiannakis and decided to go abroad after Euro 2004. He ended up in Italy for Cagliari for a season in Serie A. He returned to Greece for the tail end of his career with time at Iraklis and Kavala. Katergiannakis was as well-liked as any in the squad. He became the team's unofficial photographer as Greece headed deeper into the tournament in Portugal. "We had some time off so I went shopping with Antonis (Nikopolidis). I saw this camera and said to myself since I'm not playing why don't I try my hand as a photo-journalist! I always would pick up a souvenir on my travels and it was a spur-of-the-moment decision," explains Katergiannakis.

After the Switzerland friendly, Nikopolidis blasted his employers in the press clearly saying that the decision for him being benching was not based on "sporting reasons." For Rehhagel, it simply did not matter. He refused to budge. Nikopolidis kept his spot and would continue to do so despite the situation between player and club dragging on for months.

Rehhagel was unshakable in his faith of Nikopolidis and chose him in every match leading up to Portugal. In fact, from October 2001 until February 2006, Nikopolidis made 56 consecutive starts for Greece. There was no clear choice with regard to the back-up. Many saw Chalkias as the number two, however Rehhagel would have likely made his decision based on the opposition. The taller, Chalkias would have likely featured against more direct sides as he was more adept at dealing with high balls while the quicker, Katergiannakis was stronger with the ball at his feet.

The tension between Nikopolidis and Chalkias due to the goalkeeping situation at Panathinaikos was palpable as the team gathered for the pre-tournament camp in Switzerland. Katergiannakis is not shy when describing his uneasiness in those circumstances. "It was a very difficult situation I discovered in Bad Ragaz. And the fact that we had no goalkeeping coach put me into an uncomfortable position as both were great guys and professionals." The ability of both players to eventually bury the hatchet helped foster an even greater team spirit according to Katergiannakis. "In training it was just us three, perhaps that was when I caught the coaching bug. I suppose it was not a bad start to have on your goalkeeping coach bio, winning a European championship. Seriously though, I had to help the atmosphere. Things were forgotten in time and it was perhaps the first example of the 'us above I' mentality we had."

Between the Switzerland match and the high-profile friendly with the Netherlands at the end of April, Rehhagel and Topalidis had a full schedule keeping tabs on their players. The duo were constantly travelling throughout Europe and Greece and checking on the status of the team members. Rehhagel decided to take another look at Zikos at Monaco as the team were embarking on an impressive run in Europe. Stoltidis was also being monitored though he had already shifted his attention. Stratos Apostolakis, the former Greek international, had become the coach of the Greek Olympic football team and asked Stoltidis to become one of the three overage players the team could select for the 2004 Olympic Games in Athens. Unable to see how he could be selected to the Euro 2004 side, Stoltidis accepted the offer.

As the match against the Dutch side approached, the media branded it a 'crash test'. This would be the best gauge yet as to how Greece would do in Portugal, playing away to a quality side, one of the contenders to lift the trophy come July. Indeed, the Netherlands had world-class talent spread throughout their roster. However, Dick Advocaat's side had injury problems ahead of the clash with Greece. Five players were out and they were all big names in European football at the time including Ruud van Nistelrooy, Edgar Davids, Phillip Cocu, Arjen Robben, and Andy van der Meyde. Greece would be missing out on Kapsis through injury, but Rehhagel could select from a full squad otherwise with Karagounis and Venetidis back from the sidelines and Fyssas and Goumas overcoming late fitness tests.

It was a typical Greek effort in the first 45 minutes at the Philips Stadion in Eindhoven. The home side carved out a couple of chances through striker Roy Makaay, but staunch defending by the Ethniki saw them head into the break at 0-0. Rehhagel must have been pleased as his team also had created a couple of chances with Nikolaidis and Vryzas. Rehhagel proceeded to substitute half his team after the interval, while Advocaat made only two changes. The Dutch seemed dead-set on using this match as a real marker for their Euro 2004 preparedness. And in the second half they showed, despite their injuries, that they would be one of the teams to beat in Portugal. The rash of substitutions had a serious effect on the rhythm of Greece. Though most of the changes were in midfield and attack, the destabilizing effects spread to the back. The collective concentration in defense had gone as clearly seen by Makaay's opener four minutes after halftime. Boudewijn Zenden was given all day to pick out a cross and Makaay was scandalously left alone in the penalty box to score. Four minutes later, Zenden was given too much space and his shot from the outside the area deflected off of Dabizas and flew past Nikopolidis. It was 2-0 just like that and on the hour a third came as John Heitinga scored on his international debut. Once again, the Greek defending was atrocious with Heitinga unmarked at the back post to prod home.

In twelve minutes, Greece had suffered a major blackout and conceded three times. While they managed to regain their footing, Pierre van Hooijdonk's 90th minute goal saw Greece go down to a heavy 4-0 defeat. It was the end of a 15-game unbeaten run that had lasted 18 months (the last loss for the Ethniki being the away qualifier against Ukraine back in October 2002).

There was widespread concern after the Dutch thumping. The ghosts of the 1994 World Cup had been awaken. The Greek press was united in saying that the Ethniki were simply not ready for the challenge of Euro 2004. Some more extreme observers called for Rehhagel to freshen up the team with new blood. Names such as Zikos and Stoltidis once again coming to the fore along with others such as attackers Yiannis Anastasiou and Ioannis Amanatidis. While columnists and reporters argued as to what actions needed to be taken, Rehhagel and the players tried to maintain their calmness and composure.

"Mistakes were made, that is why we play these friendly matches," explained captain Zagorakis. "We have seen these mistakes and will attempt to fix them." Charisteas spoke after the game saying that he believed it was better to have this result now rather than in Portugal. As usual, Rehhagel did not seem overly concerned. In success or failure, the German kept cool. Big wins were treated with a dose of reality and perspective, while losses were handled in the same way. "Greece played a good first half, and a not so good second half," said Rehhagel. "When you play against top teams, you are forbidden to make those mistakes. We made many in the second half. We must now concentrate, do our analysis, and not repeat the mistakes against the Netherlands in Portugal."

Rehhagel's measured responses helped bring reassurance. He had reacted similarly earlier in his tenure and continued to in response to whatever result occurred. The manager believed this was a process. The work of the last two years had convinced him of this team's potential. One friendly defeat was not enough to derail that view.

The Ethniki boss' ability to handle difficult situations would be put to the test just weeks before Euro 2004 was set to commence. And this time it was an event that could affect team unity, the foundation that Greece's success under Rehhagel had been built on. In late May 2004, just days before Rehhagel was to name his squad for Portugal, events at financially troubled AEK threatened to split the Greek team.

150 masked AEK supporters attacked their own club's training ground at Thrakomakedones, a town 16 kilometers north of Athens, destroying the club house, damaging cars, and looting personal items. AEK players remained bunkered in the changing rooms. Two players who were spotted by the angry mob, former Greek international Michalis Kasapis and Cypriot international Yiannakis Okkas, were both physically assaulted.

The attackers were targeting the players because of their refusal to get behind a plan to save the club. That plan was hatched by former AEK player and current national team member Demis Nikolaidis. AEK's debts had reached somewhere approaching €100 million. Nikolaidis' proposal was for a consortium of businessmen to be granted liquidation on special terms. Under Greek law, if 60% of creditors agree to drop their claims then the remaining 40% are required to follow suit. In order for Nikolaidis' rescue plan to work certain conditions had to be met. The players at the club would have to accept huge wage cuts and receive only 30% of the money owed to them. Some of the players had not been paid for 18 months.

The players were unified in objecting to the proposal. The attack appeared to be sparked after Nikolaidis issued a statement indicating that his plan to save the club could not move forward. The reasons given focused on the players' wages being too high and the consortium's inability to pay existing wages or the €8 million in outstanding wages owed to the players. Tsiartas, Nikolaidis' former teammate at AEK and current one on the Ethniki, led the players' objections to the proposal, initially calling it 'unethical' and a case of blackmail. After the incident at the training ground, Tsiartas gave public comments where he called Nikolaidis 'the ethical culprit' behind the attack. Nikolaidis fired back by saying he condemned any violent acts and that he was trying to do what was best for the club.

The incident at Thrakomakedones was a story picked up by major news outlets around the world such as CNN and Reuters amongst others. The overriding question was how this would all affect Greece's preparations for Euro 2004. It was feared the situation could put a rift in the Greek squad. Tsiartas was the most outspoken on the matter, but other AEK players were certain to go to Portugal including Zagorakis, Kapsis, Lakis, and Katsouranis and were all part of the equation. The tension remained in the following days with Tsiartas stating he did not know how he would be able to face Nikolaidis when Greece began its training camp. Tsiartas wanted to charge the perpetrators of the attack and expected Nikolaidis to keep a promise he gave of trying to bring the hooligans responsible to justice.

Rehhagel, the EPO, and Greek sports minister, Giorgos Orfanos believed the entire ordeal might cause internal divisions within the squad. All parties involved immediately tried to minimize the potential impact by demanding that Tsiartas and Nikolaidis spoke directly to one another. Rehhagel was especially alarmed at the direction this was taking. He decided to personally intervene. Ahead of the team leaving Greece for Poland, Rehhagel and Topalidis spoke to Tsiartas directly. Tsiartas reassured the coaches that despite not seeing eye to eye with Nikolaidis on how to secure AEK's future, he would not bring their dispute into the national team. Tsiartas was clear that he would not be causing any trouble ahead of or during Euro 2004. "The Greek fans are not charged with paying for our clash," Tsiartas stated to the media. "We do not go to a Euro every day. We will see what will happen after the tournament with Demis. From my end, not even the smallest issue will arise."

Rehhagel was satisfied with the player's response. And despite some pressure to leave one of the two players home, the manager picked both as part of his official squad selection in late May. The 23 players that were chosen threw up no surprises. Rehhagel had already indicated those players that had achieved qualification would have the edge. And there was no late changes to his thinking.

If there were any minor surprises they were perhaps in the form of Papadopoulos and Katsouranis. Papadopoulos was preferred to the likes of Choutos and Amanatidis as the fourth-choice forward behind Charisteas, Vryzas, and Nikolaidis. Rehhagel began choosing Katsouranis just after the halfway point of the qualifying campaign, attracted by the young midfielder's energy and tenacity.

* * * *

Confidence was never a trait that Katsouranis lacked throughout his career. From humble beginnings at Doxa Chalandritsa, the amateur club located just 20 kilometers from Patra where Katsouranis was born and raised, the player made his way through the ranks to become one of the best Greek midfielders of his generation. While he may not have been in the squad for the first half of Greece's Euro 2004 qualifiers, he never worried about his ability to land a spot in the team going to Portugal. "I believed for a while that I would be in the squad for the Euro so I didn't have any anxiety that I would not be amongst the coach's selections," recalls Katsouranis. "I had belief in myself, I had my feet on the ground and was working very hard and thus had every reason to be included. From the time Rehhagel began calling me up until when he left, I was always amongst his choices. I was a player he believed in and I repaid that faith with the way I played on the field."

That self-belief put the player in good stead when making the big switch from hometown club Panachaiki to AEK in 2002. He was close to signing for Panathinaikos and while Olympiacos were also interested, he surprisingly chose AEK instead. He was not expected to step right in and make fans forget about the departing Akis Zikos in the midfield, but he did just that in his first season for the club. It was a transition that the straight-talking Katsouranis did not rate as highly difficult. "My time at Panachaiki was the most important part of my football development in order to obtain the necessary character and ability to progress in my football career," said Katsouranis. "It was not very difficult to move up to AEK to be honest. If you have the talent, the heart, the mental strength, and the spirit to move to a big club like AEK it's not as difficult, especially when you find even better teammates. My four years at AEK were very good, I believe that I offered them a lot just as they offered to me."

Good would be an understatement to describe Katsouranis' impact. With the *Kitrinomavri,* Katsouranis became a leader on and off the pitch as the club faced the prospect of bankruptcy. Despite the financial problems, Katsouranis was a key member of a team that continued to challenge in the league and impress in European competition. He was first called up for the qualifiers against Spain and Ukraine. After debuting as a substitute in a friendly against Sweden in August 2003, Katsouranis became a stalwart in Rehhagel's squads and slowly began to find more playing time.

Katsouranis was as versatile a midfielder as Greece possessed. Strong in the tackle and with bounds of energy, he was also a player that always played with his head up while on the ball. Throughout his career he was adept at providing assists. Even more impressive was his goalscoring record. He scored 17 goals in the two seasons heading into Euro 2004, 13 in the following campaign, and over 100 for his entire career. His fantastic all-around displays for AEK and for Greece in Portugal had caught the eye of major European clubs.

He was transferred to Benfica in 2006 as AEK were in desperate need of funds. In Lisbon, he thrived under Fernando Santos, the man he describes as "the one who helped me most in my career." Even after Santos' departure he retained his place in the team. Across Europe, clubs such as Chelsea, Juventus, Atletico Madrid, and Villarreal were rumored to want the player. Benfica held on to him until he returned to Greece to play for Panathinaikos (2009-2012) and PAOK (2012-2014). Shorter stints followed in India for Pune, Atromitos, and one cup game for Heidelberg United which signaled the final match of his career.

He retired from the national team in 2014, having represented Greece 116 times and being a part of the squads for Euro 2004, Euro 2008, the 2010 World Cup, Euro 2012, and the 2014 World Cup.

* * * *

The other defensive midfielders included in the final 23-man squad were Zagorakis, Basinas, and Kafes. Karagounis and Tsiartas would be the central midfielders. Greece did not possess a natural left-sided attacker. Tsiartas would occasionally play on the left, though he was not a traditional winger. The wingers that made the team, Giannakopoulos, Georgiadis, and Lakis, had played on the right side for most of their careers.

All four players on the bubble of forcing their way in were eventually left off the final selection. Zikos contested a Champions' League final for Monaco against Porto around the time of the squad announcement. There were clamors for his inclusion, but Rehhagel insisted he did not rate the player higher than the ones already in the team. Antzas' move to the third division had seen the end of his chances, while Patsatzoglou's foot problems had forced him to miss out.

Besides the left side of attack, the only area where Greece lacked cover in an otherwise well-balanced side was at right-back. Patsatzoglou's absence meant that the only natural defender on the right side was Seitaridis. If he was injured then either Fyssas or Venetidis, the two left-backs chosen by Rehhagel, would have to play the opposite flank. Rehhagel's preference for a strong, sturdy backline meant there was an emphasis on having plenty of center-backs available. Four made the cut with Dellas, Kapsis, Dabizas, and Goumas, the picks.

Nikopolidis, Chalkias, and Katergiannakis were the three keepers that made the squad in another area with no surprises.

The start of the team's preparations began in Poland with a friendly in the city of Szczecin. The Ethniki suffered a second defeat in a row, going down 1-0 with an own goal from Kapsis. It was not a terrible display, however there was growing angst over recent results. The team was starting to lose matches, something they had become unaccustomed to doing. The problems at AEK were also still being talked about in relation to the team.

Adding to these issues, was a growing number of injury problems as the tournament approached. "Us journalists and photographers who began following the team from the beginning of their preparations encountered a positive environment in the camp. However, there was concern at the recent friendly performances and particularly fear with respect to the mounting injuries," said Triantafyllou.

Dabizas suffered a groin injury against Poland, while there were question marks surrounding the fitness of many other players. Nikolaidis appeared to be struggling mightily to overcome a back ailment. There was real concern over a small knock to Seitaridis and his readiness for the opener against Portugal. A week before that match, Dellas, Lakis, and Karagounis all went down in training.

Fitness was beginning to look like something of a problem. Many players had simply not been playing enough football in the preceding months. Nikolaidis and Giannakopoulos had played sporadically for their foreign clubs. Dabizas had barely featured for Newcastle, so he eventually moved to Leicester where he received more playing time. Even the goalkeepers had question marks. Chalkias was the only one of the three that had games under his belt as Nikopolidis had been frozen out at Panathinaikos and Katergiannakis had lost his starting job at Olympiacos due to injury.

After the Poland match, the team went to Switzerland for the main portion of their Euro 2004 preparations. The time spent in Bad Ragaz seemed to have a rejuvenating effect on the squad. There was a calmness there, an ability to work in peace and focus on the upcoming tournament. The atmosphere could not have been different when compared to the chaotic schedule the Greek team had ahead of the 1994 World Cup, where public events appeared to hold greater importance than on-the-field readiness.

Rehhagel prepared the team mentally and physically at Bad Ragaz. There was great emphasis placed on the opening match of the competition. On many occasions, Rehhagel reiterated how important he deemed that first match to be. It was a message he pounded home, time and time again. The manager often spoke to the players about managing the pressure. Everyone wanted to do well and prove the team's presence at the tournament was not a fluke. At the same time, this was a side with nothing to lose. Outside of Greece, the expectations for the team were non-existent.

In the Ethniki's last warm-up encounter before Euro 2004 started, they defeated Liechtenstein 2-0 on 3 June with goals from strikers Vryzas and Charisteas. It was not a convincing performance. The torrential rain that fell during periods of the match did not help, but it was an average display by Greece who could have won by more after creating a good deal of chances and hitting the woodwork twice. Still, there was a worry at how Liechtenstein managed to threaten on a couple of occasions on counter-attacks. Rehhagel was unhappy with Greece's quality. He was less enamored with the ultra-physical approach taken by the European minnows during the game. A frustrated Rehhagel jumped off the bench several times to complain to the referee about hard challenges from Liechtenstein over the course of the 90 minutes. Avoiding more injuries was key so close to the tournament.

Rehhagel made no changes to his initial 23-man squad as the final deadline passed in early June. Greece headed to Portugal following their final friendly, arriving six days before their first game. There was little fanfare upon the team's landing in Porto, the spotlight firmly affixed on the major nations. The moment of truth was near after 34 months of Rehhagel at the helm. He had succeeded in building a side capable of qualifying for the European Championship, a tournament second in scope only to the World Cup. Now the challenge that remained was to perform when the eyes of Europe and the rest of the world were watching. The most remarkable chapter of Greek sporting history was about to be written.

Chapter 14

Euro 2004 Begins

The injury issues affecting the Ethniki ahead of the tournament would simply not go away. Most of the concerns were minor. It was however the quantity of the problems that made the situation difficult. Katsouranis was battling a bout of flu, Dabizas picked up a hip problem just as he was starting to recover from a groin pull from the Poland friendly. In the two days before the opening game, Dellas, Karagounis, Lakis, and Nikopolidis were all being treated for various ailments.

Nikolaidis was perhaps the biggest concern of all. Rehhagel was continuously answering questions about the striker's readiness and whether he would be fit in time for the competition. There was an assumption that the manager was possibly being too loyal. Other coaches headed into the tournament showing a more cut-throat attitude to players who were struggling for fitness. Even within Greece's own group, Spain coach Saez and his Russian counterpart Yartsev left off defenders Michel Salgado and Victor Onopko, respectively, both deeming it too risky to keep those important individuals in their squads due to late injuries. Rehhagel had stated that Nikolaidis 'deserved' to make the team. There was a worry that Rehhagel was putting loyalty over sporting considerations when it came to Nikolaidis.

The truth was that Nikolaidis was not anywhere near one hundred percent when he arrived to Greece's training camp. Coming off a positive season in Spain, the one sole year he played abroad in his career, Nikolaidis had been missing for Atletico Madrid through injury over the last couple months. At Bad Ragaz, Nikolaidis simply could not run. The national team doctors examined the player and believed a calf muscle was to blame. That diagnosis led to a treatment of massaging his calf in hopes of fixing the problem.

Nikolaidis' personal physical therapist and that of the majority of the Ethniki players was Christos Karvounidis. He was a renowned physio in Greece who had graduated from the Physiotherapy Department of Frankfurt University Clinic in the late 1980s and who afterward was Head of the Physio Department at the Frankfurt Olympics Center. Nikolaidis contacted Karvounidis, however he was not granted access to come assess the player in Switzerland. When Karvounidis told Nikolaidis on the phone that he did not believe the player's issue was his calf, but rather his back, then Nikolaidis trusted the advice of his longtime physio. Rehhagel had given the players a full day break while in Switzerland and they were free until curfew back at the hotel at 10:00pm.

Karvounidis told Nikolaidis he should take a trip to Freiburg, some 250 kilometers away from Bad Ragaz. There his colleague, a doctor for the German Olympic Track and Field Team, would examine him. Nikolaidis and his "little brother" on the team, Kostas Katsouranis, rented a car and travelled to Germany. "We went to Germany from where we were in Switzerland, so that Demis could see a specialist," revealed Katsouranis. Once in Freiburg they found the clinic and Nikolaidis was examined at by the German doctor. He asked Nikolaidis several questions ranging from the pain he was feeling to the way he ran and played. He also asked whether the player planned on continuing his playing career after the tournament. Nikolaidis replied that he was not, having already decided to dedicate his future to becoming AEK's new president.

The doctor told Nikolaidis he could provide him with a cocktail of medicine through injections, beginning from his back down to his calf. He said that after two days he would feel well enough to run. Nikolaidis was inclined to believe the doctor, but called Karvounidis to ask his opinion. The physio's response was to listen to the doctor without hesitation.

Nikolaidis received over 20 injections in less than ten minutes. Katsouranis was in a state of shock seeing his teammate and friend laying on the table with blood pouring out from all the shots. "He gave him a series of shots, so that it would last about a month. The hope was that he could be a part of the squad and play as many minutes as he could," said Katsouranis. The doctor said that Nikolaidis should not drive for a couple hours. It was late in the day by this point as the players made the long journey back. This time though they found themselves searched at the border. The pair failed to bring any identification with them and thus were held up by German officials for more than an hour. After checking back with the Swiss hotel they were staying at, the players were allowed to go on their way. They made it back to Bad Ragaz after midnight, only to see Rehhagel walking around the hotel lobby. They eventually evaded their manager who was completely unaware of the trip they had taken. Katsouranis believes Nikolaidis' great desire to play a part in the tournament saw him take such a giant risk with regard to his health, stating, "The journey was a story of sacrifice. The sacrifice made by a player so that he could play for his country at the Euro."

Within two days, Nikolaidis was back in training. He felt much better and the doctor who had treated him had sent the details of the medicine he administered both to UEFA and the EPO. It was explained by the German doctor that his treatment would only be a temporary fix, probably lasting a few weeks. Nikolaidis was able to play four matches in Portugal, the first three as a substitute. He started the quarter-final against France, a match that would mark the end of his career. His pain eventually returned making him unable to participate in the final two games of the tournament. As he would say years later in an interview with Greek satellite channel NOVA, "How was the German doctor supposed to know he needed to give me a stronger dose? He, like everyone else, thought it was Greece, they probably won't make it through the Group Stage."

As the day of the opener arrived, the excitement for the tournament could be felt throughout Portugal. This was a nation ready to party and there was a fantastic energy present in the host cities. Much of the anticipation was on the host nation's team. There was a real expectation that Luis Felipe Scolari's men could do something special over the next few weeks. "Scolari before the tournament set the target of reaching the semi-finals, and I think that's what most people thought would be required for Portugal to have a successful tournament," recalls Tom Kundert. "We have to remember that although Portugal had done very well at Euro 2000, losing narrowly in the semi-final to eventual winners France, and the team had some terrifically talented players, it had never reached the final of a major tournament and had a disastrous 2002 World Cup."

Portuguese football was on a high. Porto had just shocked the continent a few weeks before in winning the 2003/04 Champions' League. National team members such as Deco, Paolo Ferreira, Costinha, and Maniche were key elements of that Porto side and all were expected to play big roles at Euro 2004. Benfica and Sporting Lisbon, the two other major traditional clubs in the country, contributed other important players such as Nuno Gomes, Simao

Sabrosa, Ricardo Carvalho, Tiago, Ricardo, Rui Jorge, and Beto. Entering the competition, Portugal had an ideal mix of experience and young talent. The golden generation of Luis Figo, Rui Costa, and Fernando Couto were all taking their last shot in a major tournament while the likes of Cristiano Ronaldo, Simao, Tiago, and Helder Postiga were just coming to the fore. Kundert believes that this was a well-balanced team with few weaknesses. "The strengths of this group was a fantastic amount of creativity, a solid and settled defense, and a great understanding amongst most of the players as Scolari took advantage of Porto's 2004 Champions' League winning team. The biggest weakness - as so often has been the case for Portugal - was the lack of a reliable number nine."

Portuguese football commentator Luis Cristovao unequivocally believes that Portuguese side was special. "The expectations were to win. Scolari was world champion with Brazil. Everything was prepared to have a winning side. It was a fantastic team, based largely on that Porto side which had won the Champions' League. It was undoubtedly one of best teams Portugal has ever had," says Cristovao, who has worked for Eleven Sports and Eurosport Portugal.

Perhaps the only bad news for Portugal was that Ricardo Quaresma, an exciting winger playing at Barcelona, was injured before the tournament began. The 21-year-old had broken a metatarsal bone in his right foot and had been ruled out. Otherwise, the only selection issue Scolari had going into the opener was with Beto. The Sporting defender would miss out on that match due to suspension.

On the eve of the opening match, Greece's injury problems seemed to dwindle considerably. Rehhagel could select from a full squad, even if some players, like Dabizas and Nikolaidis, probably could not handle a complete 90 minutes. The good vibes continued when news broke that the man in the middle for the match against Portugal would be Italian referee, Pierluigi Collina. This was to be the final major tournament for Collina as he was closing in on the mandatory retirement age of 45. There was widespread satisfaction amongst Greek supporters that Collina was selected. He was widely considered to be one of the best referees in the history of the modern game and was chosen as the International Federation of Football History and Statistics (IFFHS) Referee of the Year for six straight years beginning in 1998. He was perceived to be an impartial judge on the pitch. With Greece beginning the competition against the hosts, someone with the reputation of Collina was exactly the type of referee they would have wanted.

Euro 2004 began on 12 June 2004, on a perfect sunny afternoon in Porto, Portugal. The Estadio do Dragao was a sea of red and green. The vast majority of the 50,000 in attendance were Portuguese fans, though behind one goal was a section of about 4,000 Greeks. They were outnumbered, but vociferous from the start.

Radio commentator Giorgos Helakis would become well-known for his passionate calling of the matches in the coming weeks. In describing the opening ceremonies for the competition at the Dragao, Helakis said the ship in the midst of countless blue panels was symbolic of a Greek pirate ship ('piratiko') coming into Portugal. The team would later be coined as the *piratiko* for what would occur.

"We have nothing to lose. We just have to show how we qualified, how we deserve to be here in Portugal," said Rehhagel in the press conference the day before the game. He said his side would do its best to get something out of the game as "the outsiders always have a chance." It was the type of thinking that defined much of his coaching career.

Portugal had every reason to be confident. The host country had not lost the opening match of the European Championship since the competition moved to eight nations in 1980 and sixteen teams in 1996. And as Collina whistled the start of the 12th edition of the European Championship, everything pointed to Portugal keeping that streak intact.

10 years earlier in Greece's last appearance at a major finals, the team had given up a goal in just the second minute in the opening match versus Argentina. 45 seconds into their Euro 2004 opener, Greece had a chance to go ahead as Vryzas drove past Jorge Andrade on the left and delivered a low cross only for Charisteas to swing and miss completely from ten yards out. As the first couple minutes passed, the difference between the Greece in Portugal and the one ten years before could not be starker.

Rehhagel did not gamble on Nikolaidis to start, opting for Vryzas to lead the line in what amounted to a 4-5-1 which had Charisteas on the right and Giannakopoulos, reprising his role against Spain in the qualifiers, on the left. At the back, Dabizas was not deemed ready so Kapsis was the center-back with Dellas playing slightly behind him as a libero. The wing-backs were set in stone as Fyssas lined up on the left and Seitaridis on the opposite flank. The biggest surprise was that Tsiartas was left out with Rehhagel going with a midfield trio of Zagorakis, Basinas, and Karagounis. Tsiartas was a creative genius, but the plan was to press Portugal and not allow midfielders such as Rui Costa to be able to get their heads up and play. And in the early stages, it seemed that the hosts were caught off-guard by the aggressive approach Greece employed. Zagorakis set the tone early, going to ground for a few sliding tackles. Six minutes in and Portuguese goalkeeper Ricardo scrambled to clear a long Seitaridis throw-in. That half-chance was a precursor to what would be the first shock of a tournament full of them.

After Charisteas lost the ball on the right, the Ethniki once again showed their willingness to harry Portugal. As the ball went across midfield, Karagounis, Basinas, and Giannakopoulos were all quick to close down on the ball. Portuguese right-back Ferreira looked to be in some panic as he played the ball straight to Karagounis. The Greek midfielder saw acres of space ahead of him as he controlled the ball, took two touches and crushed a low drive from 25 yards out past Ricardo into the Portuguese goal. "I reached a point outside the area where I like to take shots. I tried to hit it hard," says Karagounis. "After it left my foot I believed I had struck it well enough to score. I had the belief that it would fly in."

The Greek crowd behind the goal instantly exploded as Karagounis made his way to them to celebrate. The way Greece had started the game had been extremely encouraging, the early goal capping off a perfect start. According to Karagounis, "It was very important that the first goal came early. That goal gave us wings because our opponents already were tense. The goal basically cut their legs and gave us a more positive feeling, both for that match and beyond."

It seemed more like destiny than anything else that Giorgos Karagounis would become a footballer. Born in the Peloponnesian city of Pyrgos, Karagounis grew up playing football wherever he could. "I never had anything else on my mind other than being a footballer. My family was always close to me so I worked hard and always tried to take something from all the managers and officials I met," says the man commonly known as 'o typaras' (roughly translated as 'the dude').

When former Panathinaikos legend Juan Ramon Rocha decided to try his hand at management as player/manager at Paniliakos in 1989, it was the break Karagounis needed to be discovered. While Rocha remained at the fourth division side for only one season, he succeeded in unearthing one of the greatest Greek players in history. Thanasis Karagounis sought out Rocha and asked if he would consider giving his son a trial. The manager initially was uncertain. He finally agreed to take a look at the 13-year-old. Rocha knew immediately that there was something special about Karagounis. He contacted the Panathinaikos academy, begging them to sign the player. After seeing him play, Panathinaikos officials did not believe he was thirteen, such was Karagounis' dominance over all those around him. As they prepared to pass up on the player, Rocha used his contacts at the club. He went straight to the offices of Vardis Vardinogiannis and asked for help. The chairman of Motor Oil Hellas, Vardinogiannis was a rich and powerful man. He also happened to be the brother of Panathinaikos president Giorgos Vardinogiannis. Vardis heard Rocha's appeal and wasted no time in making a phone call to the club demanding that Karagounis be brought into the academy.

Karagounis flourished in the Panathinaikos youth teams. After two years with the reserve sides, Karagounis made the jump to the Panathinaikos first team in 1998. He featured prominently for the next five seasons. 'Kara' was the team's midfield maestro, his game full of bustling energy. He started to gain attention across Europe as he consistently put forth strong performances in the Champions' League and UEFA Cup. Goals against the likes of Manchester United and Arsenal were just part of the story. Karagounis had become one of the most important players at the club as the team reached the quarter-finals of the Champions' League in 2001/02 and the same stage of the UEFA Cup a year later.

Possessing a high level of technical ability, Karagounis was not averse to also mixing it up. He was a player who had the passing range and dribbling prowess to cause problems for any side. For all his skill, it was his passion that would define him as a player. In the 2001/02 Champions' League quarter-final versus Barcelona, Panathinaikos held a 2-0 aggregate advantage in the second leg at the Nou Camp when Karagounis tore cruciate ligaments and was forced off the pitch. Moments later he was back on the field. He attempted to play through the pain, but even he could not continue on with a serious injury that sidelined him for five months.

It was with the national team where that legendary passion and desire was always on full display. He debuted for Greece in August 1999 against El Salvador. Before that he featured 39 times for the U-21 team, captaining the side to a runners-up finish at the 1998 U-21 European Championship. He would go on to play 139 times for Greece, becoming the country's all-time leader in international caps. The last kick of a ball in his professional career was the 2014 World Cup Round of 16 match versus Costa Rica, where Greece fell on penalty-kicks. In that match, he played the entire 120 minutes, and at 37 years old had ran 13.6 kilometers, good enough for third amongst the 28 players who participated in that match.

He had a storied club career with time at Inter Milan (2003-2005), Benfica (2005-2007), and Fulham (2012-2014) sandwiched around a second spell at Panathinaikos (2007-2012) where he finally won the league title that had eluded him in 2009/10. It was playing for Greece where he will most remembered by Greek supporters. Karagounis' goal against Portugal in the opening match of Euro 2004 has since become one of the iconic moments in Greek football history.

* * * *

Immediately after the goal, Portugal responded with a corner only for Zagorakis to hack it away. It was clear that Scolari's men were rattled. There was virtually no rhythm to their play. Figo tried to dribble his way past Fyssas on several occasions, but was denied either by the Benfica defender or by the covering Giannakopoulos. In fact, it was Greece who looked closer to scoring again as they began to launch swift counter-attacks. Dellas' long-ball was taken down superbly by Vryzas, he split two defenders with a pass to Charisteas who dribbled into the box only to shoot wide. Moments later Kapsis stood up Figo at one end as Greece countered. Vryzas and Giannakopoulos played a give-and-go and the Greek striker crossed for an unmarked Fyssas at the back post. The defender tried to hit a volley at full speed only to blast it well over the goal. It was an exhilarating few minutes for a Greek team that had their opponents up against the ropes.

Figo switched flanks after a quarter of an hour hoping to find some love on the left against Seitaridis. Andrade registered Portugal's first shot on goal, coming close from a layoff from fellow center-back Couto, but seeing his effort fly just past Nikopolidis' post. The Greek backline was showing a high level of tenacity and discipline to start the game. Whether it was clearing balls, covering for each other, or going to ground with well-timed tackles, the back four were not giving an inch to the Portuguese attackers. Portugal were showing some signs of life as the half reached the halfway stage as Pauleta was nearly through on goal only for a poor first touch to let him down.

Portugal were having trouble keeping possession. It took them until the half hour to create their first attack with a sustained build-up. Then Rui Costa headed wide and a couple minutes afterward, another loose touch from Simao, saw Nikopolidis come quickly off his line to smother.

35 minutes into the game and Greece had registered seven shots to Portugal's two. The Greek midfield showed no signs of tiring, offering plenty of energy to continuously disrupt Portugal's time on the ball. Dellas was picking up everything in a sweeper role, while Kapsis was completely shutting down Pauleta. Fyssas and Seitaridis were fantastic in both their defensive duties and getting involved in attack. The Portuguese quality in midfield did at times lead to Greece overcommitting. Karagounis and Basinas both guilty of rash challenges on two occasions.

The halftime whistle probably came at a good time for both teams. Portugal certainly needed to talk things over after a sluggish start. Meanwhile, Rehhagel could remind his players that the job was only half done. Both sides came out of the interval with changes to their line-up. Scolari showed what he thought of his team's first-half display with a double change as Ronaldo came on for the ineffectual Simao and Deco replaced Rui Costa. For Greece, goalscorer Karagounis had picked up a knock late in the half and was substituted off for Katsouranis.

Whatever halftime talk Scolari gave did not seem to change Portugal's approach. And the problems the hosts had were compounded six minutes after the break. Another errant pass, this time by Costinha, caused trouble again. Charisteas broke forward, spotted Seitaridis' overlapping run down the right and played a ball into his path. Ronaldo had followed Seitaridis' run, but was left chasing him. Once the players entered the box, the 19-year-old Portuguese winger barged into Seitaridis and Collina immediately pointed to the spot. Amidst mild protests, Collina smiled and shrugged his shoulders seemingly suggesting 'what else could I call'?

* * * *

Angelos Basinas would not have been overawed when faced with taking a penalty in an important match. In the years preceding Euro 2004, he had converted spot-kicks in the latter rounds of the Champions' League against clubs the stature of Juventus and Barcelona. Like so many others players in the squad, Basinas was playing the best football of his career in 2004. Fresh off of winning a domestic double with Panathinaikos, the midfielder was in fine form heading into Portugal. Basinas was a strong character who struggled in the early stages of his career at Panathinaikos to win over the supporters. He was part of one of the best generations of academy players the club ever had along with fellow Euro 2004 teammates Karagounis and Goumas. Olympiacos' domestic dominance at the end of the 1990s kept Panathinaikos from celebrating any trophies from 1996 until 2004. Players such as Basinas were used as scapegoats for the lack of success. In truth, players like him and teammates Karagounis, Nikopolidis, Seitaridis, and Goumas were the reasons behind the team's success, especially in continental play where the club consistently qualified for the latter stages of the Champions' League and UEFA Cup.

Basinas' influence at Panathinaikos grew as the years passed and by 1999 he had been selected for the Ethniki. He eventually would become a key player in the Panathinaikos sides that heavily impressed in Europe as the new millennium began.

Basinas' all-around game was unique for a Greek footballer at the time. Here was a defensive midfielder who could battle in the physical sense, but who was also technically proficient and able to begin attacks with his passing. A set-piece specialist, Basinas was known as a player who could not only produce an accurate delivery, but who could also score from free-kicks and penalties.

He arrived at Paiania, the location of Panathinaikos' academy, at age 12 and remained at the club until he was 29. In 2005, he was unceremoniously dumped by the club, blamed for having a poor attitude. In truth, he was poorly treated in a time of transition. The way in which such a long-time servant's exit was handled undoubtedly left a blemish on Panathinaikos.

Basinas finished off his career with three strong years in Spain at Mallorca, along with shorter stints for Portsmouth, and Arles-Avignon, sandwiched around six months at AEK. Panathinaikos struggled mightily for years to find his replacement in their midfield. It was the same story with the Ethniki for whom he ended up making 100 appearances for. After his international retirement in 2009, his influence was recognized as the midfield needed reshuffling without an obvious heir apparent.

* * * *

Basinas grabbed the ball, lined up and fired home a perfect penalty, high to the right. Ricardo had gone the other way and never had a chance. There was something incredulous about what was happening in the Dragao. Greece were up 2-0 in the opening match, against the hosts, and playing them off the park. Even the most optimistic Greek supporter would have been hard pressed to write a script like this.

Greece continued to control proceedings and Scolari sent on Nuno Gomes with 25 minutes remaining in a final throw of the dice. Rehhagel countered by installing Nikolaidis on the left for Giannakopoulos. His first order of business was to win a foul deep in his own half from Deco. He did this many times in the final 20 minutes. It was not a part of the pitch Nikolaidis often found himself in, but clearly the player was keen to follow through on Rehhagel's directives. The coach brought off Charisteas in the 73rd minute for Lakis. With Portugal beginning to pour forward, Rehhagel freshened up his wide players in hopes of causing more problems on the break. Portugal were beginning to become more industrious. Dellas and Kapsis always seemed to be properly positioned to cut out any of their promising attacks. Dellas, in particular, looked very assured, both defending and when in possession. After chasing down one loose ball near the corner flag, he audaciously scooped it over the advancing Ferreira effortlessly, finding the open Nikolaidis. It was a play that summed up his performance on the day - cool, calm, and collected.

Deco and Ronaldo's influence grew as the match headed into the final minutes. Deco's control of the ball coupled with Ronaldo's creativity and penetration were increasingly troubling Greece. Ronaldo's deflected shot went inches wide before Gomes' effort in the 85th minute saw Nikopolidis push the ball out at his near post. In between, Greece were themselves offering a threat with counterattacks as Zagorakis and Lakis played a one-two only for the latter to produce a pass just too heavy for Nikolaidis' run.

Rehhagel could see his team retreating too much for his liking and was urging them to come out from their defensive shell. Terrific skill by Figo saw him burst into the box and play a cross, which was deflected out by Dellas for a corner. Figo took it quickly and Ronaldo skied over the entire Greek defense to head past Nikopolidis. Portugal had pulled back to 2-1. The only question would be whether they had enough injury-time to get another chance. They did not.

Collina blew his whistle soon after the restart and Greece had held on to shock Portugal. The Greek players knew their capabilities. Even they seemed shocked though as they celebrated with one another. They had just beaten the hosts and in the process recorded their country's first win at a major international tournament. For Portugal, the defeat would not prove to be disastrous, but it was a wake-up call. "It was a huge shock, for sure. Perhaps Portugal were overconfident, but I think the main problem was they were too nervous and also Scolari made a poor team selection," states Kundert. "He left out several players who had just lifted the Champions' League with Porto. Luckily, he rectified that in the next match and from the second match onwards Portugal stuck to almost the same line-up so you could say the defeat was actually beneficial for Portugal."

It certainly did not feel like that at the time in the Estadio do Dragao. A dejected stadium began to empty with the exception of the contingent of Greek supporters for whom the celebrations were just beginning. The players and the crowd joined as one for a series of 'Oles'. Helakis was right. The voyage of the piratiko had begun and in stunning fashion no less.

Chapter 15

A Point Proven

The opening days of Euro 2004 showcased some high-profile encounters including France coming from behind in the final minutes to defeat England, 2-1. Germany and the Netherlands also faced off, playing to a 1-1 draw as the Czech Republic started with a 2-1 victory over competition debutants Latvia in Group D. Sweden had the score of the opening round, defeating Bulgaria 5-0 in Group C, while Italy were left frustrated by a scoreless draw with Denmark in the same section.

The Ethniki's upset victory over Portugal in the opening match was undoubtedly the biggest talking point of the tournament. It was the sort of result that defined the opening stages of a major finals, similar to the shock factor of Senegal's victory over France at the 2002 World Cup and Cameroon's triumph over Argentina at the 1990 World Cup.

Figo commented to the press that he believed Portugal did not deserve to lose the game, however his view was that of the minority. The Ethniki had received widespread praise from all sides due to their impressive display. The world football media were in agreement about Greece performing significantly better than the hosts. Even Scolari admitted his side "lost control", as he said "Greece were well-organized, they closed up at the back and exploited the counter-attack."

Back in Greece, the front pages of the sports papers were emblazoned with celebratory headlines. 'Historic' was the word that came up most often as the bold print gave praise to a side that had garnered their country's first-ever victory in a major football competition. Rehhagel's post-match comments were as much reflective as they were analytical. "This is the biggest win of any Greek team ever," said the clearly euphoric German. "The tactics we chose over the past week were extremely successful. I hope that Greeks will hang their flags outside their homes."

Rehhagel and the rest of the team had targeted one win as the overarching goal at Euro 2004. Winning one game and proving that their qualification was not a fluke were the main objectives. That victory was seen by many as most likely to come in the group finale against Russia. However, the win over Portugal shifted the narrative. Now with three points under their belts, the team began thinking of a spot in the quarter-finals. Zagorakis, selected as the official UEFA Man of the Match, struck that chord after the victory against the Portuguese. "We do not fear anyone or anything. Our target is now qualification for the next round," said the Greek captain.

The players were given all of Sunday to rest and recover from their exertions against Portugal. From Monday on, the focus shifted completely to the second game against Spain. The atmosphere inside the camp was fantastic, but all involved were committed to avoid getting carried away. At one point Dellas telling the assembled media that he and his teammates had not become a 'Super-team' because of just one result.

The match against Spain suddenly became a battle of the top two sides in Group A. Juan Carlos Valeron's goal in the 60th minute saw Spain prevail 1-0 over Russia in the team's first match. Up until Valeron's goal, which came just 36 seconds after he entered the game, Spain had struggled to find a breakthrough. After an extremely fast start at the Estadio Algarve, Spain found it difficult against a Russian team who had a big chance in the first half to take the lead, Casillas however coming to the rescue and making a fine stop on Dmitry Alenichev. In the end, the important thing was the win, but the match gave Saez plenty to think about. There was a real question over the form and fitness of Raul, Spain's best attacker. He was subbed off late against Russia in favor of a young, energetic Fernando Torres.

Much was expected of Spain in this tournament, especially as they were playing so close to home. Aritz Gabilondo, a journalist who has worked for both El Pais and AS and the author of the book *La Roja: From Children to Legends*, suggests that while Spain had a strong team, they lacked experience and mental toughness to challenge for trophies back during that time. "It was a time when Spain was fragile in mind. We played good football, but we had difficulty responding to adversity. We had a good squad, however some of the most important players were still too young. The clearest case was Xavi Hernandez, who at 24, was still not a permanent fixture in the team," says Gabilondo. Though there were some hints of how good this Spain could become, this was still four years from the beginning of a dominant and historic period where the country won three consecutive international tournaments (Euro 2008, the 2010 World Cup, and Euro 2012), earning widespread praise for their remarkable possession-based style. "The failures of Spain in 2002, 2004, and 2006 served to prove that winning at the highest level is complicated," suggests Gabilondo. "There was a very good team there, but to win you need to familiarize yourself with the latter rounds of a competition and show an ability to overcome difficulties."

Much of the Spanish press called on Saez to make changes to the team for the second match against Greece. Saez took over Spain in July 2002 and had announced his starting eleven on the eve of every match. He decided to forgo this tradition ahead the game against Greece. This fueled rumors that big changes were coming to his side, both in personnel and tactics. Saez was adamant that it made no sense to abandon the team's usual 4-2-3-1 formation. He also clarified his reasons for keeping his cards close and not revealing his team. "Greece are used to adapting to their opponents' way of playing. If we were playing Brazil I would have disclosed the lineup because Brazil would not make changes in light of my selection," the Spain boss explained.

It appeared a peculiar explanation and showed the impact that Rehhagel was already having in a tactical sense on the tournament. Arsene Wenger had tabbed Greece as a team capable of a surprise at Euro 2004, despite not possessing any star players at major European clubs. Wenger indicated that the star was in fact, Rehhagel, a manager he deemed a friend, and whom he described as an 'old fox'. Rehhagel seemed to live up to that name with his tactics against Portugal. His team selection, but more so his bolstering of the midfield and directives to press the Portuguese team so high up the pitch seemed to have an unsettling effect on the hosts and swing the game in favor of Greece. Saez was showing respect to his colleague and upcoming opponent then by not giving him a head-start with his starting eleven.

Dabizas, Karagounis, and Seitaridis sat out at least portions of training sessions throughout the week. Dabizas in particular was a real doubt as he partook in an individual training program to try to get back to full fitness. There was less worry about the other two players as the rest they were afforded was more of a precautionary measure.

At kick-off time at the Estadio do Besa in Porto on 16 June, the thermometer showed a reading of 33⬚. Saez had tried a bluff in not revealing his team ahead of time, picking the same starting eleven as he had against Russia. Rehhagel made one change to his side, taking out first match goalscorer Basinas, and installing Katsouranis, a second-half substitute against Portugal. Spain had no player in their first eleven over the age of 30. They were banking on their quality and youth to take down Greece. In sharp contrast, Rehhagel always valued experience and Greece took to the pitch with five players in their thirties.

The early moments of the game gave a glimpse into the battles that were expected to define the day. Kapsis was the center-back responsible for tracking the movements of Morientes as Dellas reprised his sweeper role once again. Katsouranis was listed as a defensive midfielder, however he played even deeper. It was clear that he had been brought in to man-mark Raul. The flanks were of particular interest as Spanish wingers Vicente and Etxeberria would go up against Seitaridis and Fyssas, respectively. The two Greek full-backs were amongst the top performers against Portugal. Barcelona's Carles Puyol normally played in the center of defense at club level, but Michel Salgado's absence meant Puyol was pushed out to a right-back.

In an even start, both teams tried to pressure the other into early mistakes. It was clear that Rehhagel expected a tougher challenge against Spain as Greece's pressing was not as high as it was against Portugal. Spain's ball movement and sharpness was a concern as Katsouranis saw a yellow just six minutes in. Shortly after Zagorakis was lucky to escape a caution for a rash challenge on Vicente. Nikopolidis was called into action to tip away a corner by Etxeberria as Spain began on top. The quick play of the Spanish side was dictating proceedings, evidenced by Greek forward Charisteas having to make a last-ditch tackle in his own penalty box as Raul Bravo raced onto Raul's inch-perfect diagonal pass.

Greece had a couple promising moments in the opening 20 minutes as runs by Zagorakis and Karagounis had forced Spanish fouls. Otherwise it mostly one-way traffic as the Ethniki could not find any rhythm in possession and were constantly giving up the ball. A challenge on Etxeberria by Karagounis on the right in the 27th minute brought out a yellow card from Slovakian referee Lubos Michel. That was the midfielder's second of the competition and ruled him out of the final group match against Russia. A minute after that, Spain's control of the game was rewarded with the lead.

Raul, who continued to drag Katsouranis higher up the field as he drifted into midfield to find the ball, slipped a nice ball to Baraja. A pass to Morientes was stolen by Kapsis, but his ball to Dellas was poor. Raul picked off the pass and cut toward the middle of the penalty area backheeling for the trailing Morientes. After evading Katsouranis' challenge, Morientes gave Nikopolidis no chance, finishing low and hard from 12 yards out.

The goal opened up the game for the remainder of the half. The tempo became much quicker as Greece attacked with greater conviction. The Ethniki's first chance came on 33 minutes when Vryzas' half-volley was blocked by Marchena. Greece improved in attack just before the interval, but with no clear-cut chances to speak of.

The second half began in much the same way. Vryzas' commitment won a tackle he had no business in winning as Zagorakis pounced on his pass to fire just over with a well-hit drive outside the area. Giannakopoulos limped off just after the restart as Rehhagel sent Nikolaidis on in his place. Unlike against Portugal, Nikolaidis this time moved centrally as Vryzas pushed out to the right. Minutes later, Rehhagel made his second switch as Tsiartas replaced Karagounis. The two teams traded missed chances, Zagorakis stealing the ball and shooting right at Casillas, while substitute winger Joaquin crossed only for Raul to inexplicably fire over with the goal gaping.

Joaquin's influence on the game was immediate after coming on for Etxeberria at the start of the second half. All of Spain's play seemed to naturally gravitate toward the right with the ball ending up at the feet of the pacy and skillful 22-year-old. Fyssas was having trouble containing him and one run saw Kapsis scramble to head away a dangerous cross. Saez then inserted Valeron for Morientes as Raul was pushed up to the main striker role.

Saez's plans for finishing off Greece were put on hold after the hour mark as Charisteas stepped up to occupy Greece's ever-revolving role of hero. Rehhagel had selected other midfielders to play against Portugal and Spain, ahead of Tsiartas. In order to press teams, Rehhagel needed players with a proven ability to win the ball. Tsiartas' strength was his creativity and Greece needed that most down a goal, not necessarily his adeptness at covering ground in midfield. Tsiartas seemed to take a few minutes to get to grips with the pace of the game. As time passed he looked more comfortable in possession, something Greece desperately needed. The playmaker's viciously swerving corner gave Spain a warning about what was to come on 66 minutes. After taking control of the ball inside the Spanish half, Tsiartas spotted Charisteas' run into the area. He delivered a perfect 30-yard ball into his teammate's path. Charisteas still had plenty of work to do as he took down the ball in stride and took a left-footed shot that went through Casillas' legs, hitting the goalkeeper's trailing foot and ending up in the back of the net.

Just as Karagounis' goal had done in the opening game, Charisteas' strike had a stunning effect on the stadium. The predominantly Spanish crowd was left silenced, giving way to the wild celebrations of the 2,500 Greek supporters in attendance. Spain had not dominated as much as they had controlled the game, but they could have led by more than a goal. Now at 1-1, Greece were once again on their way to another surprise result.

Spain responded to Charisteas' goal immediately. Joaquin won a corner as Dellas covered for Fyssas, who had been beaten once again. Helguera's header from the corner-kick was well saved from close range by Nikopolidis. Despite being hampered by a problem with his left quadricep, Dellas looked silky smooth at the back as he came up with key interventions time and time again. He was a player who would never shy away from the physical battles, but so far he had shown an incredible sense of positioning in this tournament, reading the game perfectly from the back.

Spain were still dictating the match as it entered the final fifteen minutes. The goal had given Greece much more energy and there was a real impetus on behalf of Rehhagel's men to get forward. The problem in doing so was leaving space at the back, specifically on the flanks. Vicente came close for Spain as Nikopolidis needed the surest of hands to hold on to his drive. Joaquin looked unplayable and Rehhagel finally sent on Venetidis for Fyssas in a straight swap of left-backs with five minutes remaining. As the final minutes approached, Rehhagel appeared to be trying to physically get his own team out of their area. The coach pacing in and out of his technical box, throwing his hands forward to urge his players to push out. The Spanish pressure was intense and Charisteas and Vryzas both produced crucial headed clearances at the back for the Ethniki. The team were making their own problems with sloppy spells of possession, gifting Spain the ball all too often. Ultimately, the strong defensive play at the back won out and the match finished 1-1.

It was a point that looked unlikely after Greece went down 1-0. This was a team built on scoring first and defending their lead. This time, they had shown the ability to chase a game and come back. It was by no means an all-out attacking effort in the second half, but at the right time Greece pushed forward that little bit extra to find the goal they so desperately needed. They were rewarded as a patented Tsiartas pass was expertly dispatched by Charisteas. They had seized upon the chance that mattered. Nikopolidis had been flawless, while Dellas once again was immense. Zagorakis, Karagounis, and Katsouranis had been mightily challenged by Spain's dynamic midfielders. The Greek trio had done enough, however, to stay competitive and cut off the passing lanes to Raul and Morientes. Gabilondo believes that Spain let the match slip away thinking they were home free, "From the qualifiers we knew Greece were going to be a tough opponent. It was already seen then that defensively they could stop any team. Beating Greece at Euro 2004, coupled with the opening win against Russia would have put us through. We were leading the Greeks 1-0 and the job seemed done. In the end they found a goal and after that everything changed for both teams."

Later on in the day, Portugal secured their first victory of the competition by defeating Russia 2-0. With four points in the bag and an already-eliminated Russia awaiting in their final match of the Group Stage, Greece were on the cusp of a place in the quarter-finals. What had seemed incredibly unlikely just days before was now a reality.

Chapter 16

The Sweetest Defeat

The Spain game was yet another that continued to add to the legend of Rehhagel's 'astro'. This was a Greek term used to describe an aura of sorts having to do with luck or good fortune. Over time, Rehhagel had been seen as a manager who would more often than not have the football gods smile upon him. As the tournament progressed and even later on in his reign with Greece, Rehhagel's 'astro' was pointed to time and time again. This covered events on the pitch, but also extended to such things as draws for qualification or even scheduling.

The prevailing hope was that Greece would need no such fortune against Russia. The Ethniki held the key to their own destiny. A win or a draw would clinch a spot in the quarter-finals, an achievement that would easily go down as the best in the national team's history. The two pieces of bad news to emerge from the match versus Spain was that Karagounis would miss the group finale against Russia through suspension and that Giannakopoulos was ruled out through injury. The Bolton attacker would be missing for ten days due to a calf strain. Many pundits believed that was the end of the tournament for the man the English commonly referred to as 'Stelios'. Rehhagel was also left to contend with the fact that five of his players were on yellow cards. One of those was Giannakopoulos, who would certainly miss the match anyway. The other four were all starters including Zagorakis, Vryzas, Seitaridis, and Katsouranis. One caution would mean they would miss Greece's knockout round game should they advance.

The celebrations in Greece gained great momentum after the point against the Spaniards. There was now widespread expectation that Greece would get the result they needed against Russia to go through. Going into the tournament, this match was already viewed as Greece's easiest of the three. Now, after going unbeaten against Spain and Portugal, the general feeling was that advancing to the last eight was more a formality than anything else. Rehhagel tried to put a lid on qualification being a foregone conclusion. "Everyone seems to think we are through, but nothing has been achieved yet," warned the manager in the days before the game.

Russia had not exactly lit Euro 2004 alight in their first two matches. Still, Yartsev's side deserved more than they received in the losses to Spain and Portugal. In their opening game against Spain, the Russians had succeeded in frustrating their opponents for an hour and had a couple of big chances of their own before conceding the game's lone goal. Against Portugal, Russia gave up an early goal and then were forced to play a half with ten men after goalkeeper Sergei Ovchinnikov was red-carded for handling outside his box. They fought hard with ten men and had chances to equalize in the second half before finally conceding a second goal late on.

To make matters worse for Russia, there were problems in the camp. Much of this focused on 35-year-old playmaker Alexander Mostovoi and his expulsion from the team. The most-capped Russian player in the squad was sent home before the match against Portugal following a massive bust-up between him and Yartsev. Mostovoi had given an interview indicating he believed the team look tired and that too many mistakes had been made against Spain. He was subsequently ordered to leave Portugal with Yartsev saying to the press that "For me, Mostovoi no longer exists."

There were few observers to be found who believed Greece would not win or at least draw this match, considering the trouble in the Russian team and the fact that they had already been eliminated. Russian football expert Artur Petrosyan, former editor-in-chief of the daily newspaper Sport Express, believes that Russia team was a talented one that underachieved. "Russian fans always expected the team to go far. Euro 2004 was no exception. Getting to the knockout stages was the minimum that was expected from Yartsev's team. Russia had a good team, filled with talented and skillful individuals. Take Mostovoi, Izmailov, and Alenichev, three of the best players Russia had in its modern history," said Petrosyan, a frequent contributor to the Guardian, ESPN, and UEFA.com.

Petrosyan points to the fact that for many Russian fans, the match against Greece was seen as "three points already in the pocket." This was similar to the mindset of Greek supporters when looking at the Russia game. Unfortunately for Russia, they were no longer in contention, but Yartsev suggested in press conferences that his team would go out fighting. Pride was now the main motivating factor, something Petroysan confirms. "Yartsev is a man of pride and he managed to motivate the players in the way that the last match was their most important fight. Of course, he didn't want to leave his first, and ultimately, his last major tournament, empty-handed."

If Greece had no idea what sort of fight the Russians would bring on 20 June to the Algarve Stadium, situated between the cities of Faro and Loule, then they were given a glimpse just 67 seconds in. That was how long it took Dmitri Kirichenko to toe-poke past Nikopolidis to give Russia the lead and score the fastest goal in the history of the European Championship in the process. For the first time in the tournament, the Greek defense seemed all over the place. First, Dellas' clearing header rebounded off an opponent and Katsouranis then took a wild swing as Kirichenko nicked the ball past him on the way to scoring.

It was a blistering start for the supposedly indifferent Russian team. Rehhagel had opted to play three forwards in attack with essentially three defensive midfielders in the middle of the park. It seemed an odd choice with no natural player to hold possession or provide service for the front three as Karagounis was suspended and Tsiartas started on the bench.

Greece tried to remain calm after the shock goal and attempted to establish possession as well as play higher up the pitch and take the initiative. It did not work. On 17 minutes a nightmare start was complete as Russia went up 2-0. A Rolan Gusev corner saw the unmarked Dmitri Bulykin produce a low diving header that gave Nikopolidis no chance. Even though Greece responded with their first chances immediately after - a Basinas free-kick beaten away by goalkeeper Vyacheslav Malafeev and a Katsouranis shot deflected out - Russia should have been ahead 3-0 minutes later only for Andrei Karyaka to provide the miss of the tournament as he skied over from ten yards with no one near him.

The confident side that controlled the match against Portugal and who withstood an onslaught by a supremely talented Spain team appeared to be crumbling. Charisteas managed to miss almost as badly as Karyaka on 25 minutes when he shot over an empty net. There was no rhythm to the Greek play. To make matters worse, the Ethniki looked disorganized and unsure at the back. This was further confirmed when a Bulykin header hit the post as the half wore on.

Rehhagel introduced Tsiartas for Basinas on 42 minutes hoping to get a hold of the game. A minute later, the team found a lifeline. Charisteas put in a high cross from the right. Papadopoulos, who had been brought in for his first appearance of the tournament, knocked the ball down for Vryzas. The Greek striker controlled the ball and deftly chipped past the charging Malafeev to get Greece back to 2-1. It was an exquisite finish, a just reward for a selfless worker like Vryzas. The only downside being the player picked up a yellow card just before the break, meaning he would miss the quarter-final should Greece go through.

Despite Russia's dominance, Yartsev made two halftime changes as he brought Igor Shemshov and Dmitri Sychev into the game. Rehhagel countered by throwing on Nikolaidis in favor of Papadopoulos. Vryzas shifted to the left as Nikolaidis began to operate in the central forward position. Russia were playing without pressure, though Greece began the second half with some momentum following Vryzas' goal. The presence of Tsiartas was beginning to change the game. Greece looked much more comfortable playing off of Tsiartas' possession and his accurate passes began to unlock the Russian backline. Greece pushed forward more and more in search of the tying goal, let down only by the quality of the final pass and some bad decision-making near the Russian goal. Pushing players up did allow Russia plenty of space to play on the counter. The match became very tense down the stretch as either side looked capable of scoring the next goal.

Greece came close as Tsiartas' 30-yard free-kick was tipped away by Malafeev at full stretch. Time was winding down and word spread that Portugal had taken the lead against Spain. Greece were still going through, but a goal in either game would have changed that. Four minutes from time, Aleksey Bugayev sent a ball across the face of goal. It might sound cliché to suggest that time slowed down as Kirichenko made contact with the ball just three yards in front of an open goal, but that is exactly what it seemed like for Greek fans as the ball somehow spun wide instead of the logical conclusion of it hitting the back of the net. Katsouranis helped Kirichenko with a cramp moments later, the least he could do for the opposing player as Greece stayed in contention.

Fyssas came on for Venetidis, Rehhagel opting to rest the Panathinaikos left-back for most of the match. The final whistle sounded as the three minutes of injury-time finished. Greece had lost, however, they had advanced. Spain went down to Portugal 1-0, meaning the hosts won the match and Group A in the process. Greece and Spain were both on four points and tied in the second tie-breaker, goal difference, with zero. Kirichenko's miss proved decisive. Rehhagel's men progressed by virtue of the third tie-breaker, goals scored. Greece had scored four goals over the three Group Stage games while Spain had managed only two. Ironically, it was Greece's offensive output that was the difference in progression to the knockout rounds.

Rehhagel looked bewildered and exasperated as he placed his hands on his head at the end. The players initially seemed slow to celebrate, but that changed once news broke around the ground of what had happened. The magnitude of their achievement, slightly dampened by the defeat, still outweighed the result on the night. Greece had made it. The Ethniki had advanced to the knockout round of a major tournament for the first time in its history.

There was mild criticism aimed at Rehhagel and the team the following day when discussing the tactics against Russia. For the most part though it was quickly forgotten and instead widespread acclaim was lavished on the coach and the players. The press labelled the game as 'the sweetest defeat'. The real news not being that the team lost, rather that somehow Greece had found a way, whether it was Rehhagel's 'astro' or not, did not seem to matter.

The players were overcome with happiness and pride, though they did not lose their heads, realizing it could have easily been so different. "The way it developed we felt as though we knocked on the door of Hades and it was not opened. And luckily so, because instead we could have been packing our bags for Athens instead of Lisbon," admitted a relieved Tsiartas to the media after the match.

Praise came from all quarters with politicians predictably taking a lead role in trying to attach themselves to the team's achievements. Many editorials in the days that followed remarked on the ability of Greeks to achieve things when they were united and working together. Rehhagel of course was seen as the architect of making it all happen. He had endeared himself to the country by making this group of players a real team. He had slowly become a well-loved figure, now widely known as 'King Otto' or 'Rehhakles'. Rehhagel was in the eyes of many already considered an honorary Greek thanks to his exploits with the team.

Chapter 17

The Shock Heard Around The World

In Portugal, the success of the host nation in coming back from an opening game defeat to win their next two and qualify for the quarter-finals sent the entire country into party mode. The tournament received a real boost from the feel-good factor of Portugal's increasingly good displays. Undoubtedly, unfancied Greece was the biggest surprise of the Group Stage. The main story to come out of the tournament thus far was the failure of several European heavyweights to advance past the first round. Spain, Italy, and Germany had been eliminated after three matches. Greece had knocked out Spain on goals scored. Italy had to defeat Bulgaria in their final group match to advance, while also needing a winner in the Denmark-Sweden game. Italy scored in the 94th minute through Antonio Cassano to defeat the Bulgarians 2-1. However, Mattias Jonson's last-minute equalizer gave Sweden a 2-2 draw against Denmark ensuring Italy crashed out. The Italians were incensed with many players and officials levying accusations of match-fixing at the Scandinavian countries. Germany's exit was much more subdued. Rudi Voeller's men went down 2-1 to essentially a Czech reserve team and exited the competition winless, just two draws and a defeat over their three matches.

With those three traditional powers gone, the tournament had now opened up for the hosts and for France, Greece's quarter-final opponents. Jacques Santini's men had finished atop Group B, just ahead of an England side led by 18-year-old phenom Wayne Rooney. France had not hit top gear in the Group Stage. They defeated England in their opener 2-1, but only just, needing two injury-time goals from Zidane to snatch victory from the jaws of defeat. There was little momentum to be found after that dramatic win as they drew 2-2 with Croatia. Even a 3-1 win over Switzerland to cap off their Group B campaign was not altogether convincing, with two Thierry Henry goals in the final quarter of an hour needed to beat the Swiss.

France came into the competition as the team to beat. And despite their underwhelming displays in the Group Stage, they remained the tournament favorites. The sheer class of the players in France's squad was enough to convince anyone of the team's chances to defend their title. *Les Bleus* had become the first team in history to win the World Cup and then European Championship back-to-back. In recent years they had faced disappointments, most notably a terrible display at the 2002 World Cup. In a meek defense of their 1998 World Cup victory, the French went winless in three matches, losing to Senegal and Denmark and drawing against Uruguay, as they failed to score a single goal en route to an early exit.

The appointment of manager Jacques Santini in the aftermath of that World Cup debacle seemed to rejuvenate the team. After winning the French First Division title with Lyon in 2002, Santini was given the nod to replace Roger Lemerre as coach of the national team. Santini subsequently led the team to a 2003 FIFA Confederations' Cup victory while also overseeing a perfect qualifying campaign for Euro 2004 where France won all eight of their matches, scoring 29 goals in the process and conceding only twice. The qualifying group was not particularly strong as it featured the likes of Slovenia, Israel, Cyprus, and Malta. That did not change the fact that France was on a 16-match unbeaten run in competitive fixtures as they headed into the knockout round.

Adrien Mathieu is a French football journalist who has covered the national team for such outlets as France Football, RMC Sport, and most recently Goal. com. He explains how good that French side was from top to bottom. "Surely, on paper that French side had unique talent. Probably the best in the world at that time along with Brazil." Mathieu goes on to suggest that while there were issues to be resolved, that side was individually so strong. "The 2002 World Cup represented a first fracture and showcased a tired and worn-out side. Santini's reconstruction had gone well heading into Euro 2004. The championship core of that team remained with Zidane, Henry, Patrick Vieira, Robert Pires, Lillian Thuram, Marcel Desailly, Benoit Lizarazu, and David Trezeguet. Zidane at 32 was still untouchable and was the main engine of that team. Henry and Trezeguet were at the top of their game in attack. The majority of the squad were playing for the biggest clubs in Europe and had experience in major tournaments.

Add to that, the desire for revenge for what occurred in Japan and South Korea in 2002," says Mathieu.

Problems persisted however in Portugal. "One of the major weaknesses of the team was that some of the substitutes were a notch below their predecessors. Louis Saha and Steve Marlet were not bad players, far from it, but what they offered was not enough. Defensively, there were big issues. Some players were at the end of their careers. After his mistake against Croatia, Desailly was benched for the rest of the tournament and his replacements were not up to par," states Mathieu.

Reports suggested that Zidane and Desailly had conversations about changing the tactics ahead of the Switzerland game. Injuries did not help, especially at the back. Willy Sagnol was ruled out of the match against Greece due to a broken hand, defender William Gallas was doubtful, and Vieira, such a key figure in midfield, was also fighting a thigh strain. At 35, Desailly was beginning to show his age. France struggled without his leadership and steadiness at the back. His replacement, Manchester United's Mikael Silvestre, was already guilty of some high-profile mistakes in this tournament.

France still had the aura and the individual skill to beat anyone. And for Greece, this was going to be as difficult a match as could be imagined. Rehhagel reiterated time and time again to the press that France were the clear favorites and they not only possessed phenomenal players who had found success at the highest level, but also that a majority of the squad "were between the peak footballing ages of 24-30."

The French press seemed to collectively agree that this quarter-final against Greece was not as straightforward as some suggested. French players such as Zidane, Pires, and Fabian Barthez all spoke respectfully about their team's upcoming opponents. Barthez indicated that he believed Greece would be as tough an opponent, due to their defensive prowess, as Paraguay was for France at the 1998 World Cup.

Mathieu describes the majority of French supporters having a different view. "Obviously, when the French public found out about our opponent in the quarter-finals, the prevailing belief was the road was open to the semi-finals. With Greece's few international successes and much less impressive individuals, many thought the Bleus would have no trouble."

The official bus for the Greek team in Portugal had the slogan, "Ancient Greece had 12 gods, Modern Greece has 11." Back in Greece, this is exactly how the players had begun to be seen, as modern-day gods. The recognition for the Ethniki's exploits had gone well beyond Greeks. As the words of the French players showed, the respect for the team and these previously unknown players had exploded across Europe. Names such as Charisteas, Zagorakis, Karagounis, and Seitaridis were now recognizable to more than just die-hard European football followers.

The undisputed star of the Greek team was not a player, it was the manager. Otto Rehhagel was the focus of much of the continental media's attention as Euro 2004 progressed to the knockout rounds. The Germans in particular began to cover Greece and Rehhagel much more as the team advanced to the last eight. With their national team out, newspapers provided in-depth coverage of the only German remaining in the competition. Rehhagel would have been surprised with the fact that the German press, whom he generally had such a combative relationship with during his career there, would lavish such praise on him. One layout featured the manager's likeness on the columns of the Acropolis, aptly naming the famous monument, Ottopolis. Rehhagel was portrayed as everyone from Aristotle Onassis to Archimedes, from Zorba to an Evzone. While some may have simply enjoyed the positive coverage, Rehhagel used his success to settle some old scores. During one press conference before the match-up against France, he offered a stinging rebuttal to those critics who had called his tactics and methods outdated years before, saying, "You did not believe I would be with the Greek national team for three years. He who wins is modern."

Rehhagel's handling of the media was just one example of him being in high spirits during that time period. This was a coach in his element. The one thing that Rehhagel needed, he possessed in abundance - control. The players, seeing the transformation they had undergone, hung on his every word. He was already a father figure of sorts to them and they trusted him to no end. This meant that Rehhagel's strategies would be carried out on the pitch to the letter.

Rehhagel possessed a human touch that the Greeks responded to. His instructions would be given in unique ways. Take Dellas for instance. Rehhagel would build him up by calling him the 'Colossus'. In training he would tell the player that he was a lighthouse at the back of defense. That he would see his teammates like a lighthouse would spot nearby ships. He would repeat this with other players. Not only did speaking like that work wonders for an individual player's motivation, sometimes the humour or the special way in which he described something would serve to diminish the anxiety of an upcoming game against a difficult opponent.

In the locker room before the match against France, Rehhagel ended his team talk by shadow boxing with Topalidis. He told his players that they were going up against Muhammad Ali and that if they fought an open match they would lose. Then he began moving around the area, trying to hit Topalidis, who was playing the double role of Ali and France. Rehhagel would punch a couple times then get his guard up, explaining to his players that they would defend well and pick their moments of when to strike against the French. The players were laughing, but it resonated with them. At Bayern Munich he might have been ridiculed for a stunt like that. Not with that Ethniki. That team accepted Rehhagel and his sometimes unconventional style.

Rehhagel was also a master at setting up the narrative. Rehhagel painted his team as the ultimate outsiders. There was no opponent Greece could face, not least a team like France, in which Rehhagel would be wrong by characterizing his side as the massive underdogs. This allowed his team to play with minimal pressure. That tactic did not always work. Sometimes the occasion would be too big, the prize on offer too large, that pressure still played a role. This was clear in the nervy display against Russia. More often than not though, the Greek players looked as if they had nothing to lose. They could play their game without worry of the consequences. Everything after the opening win against Portugal was a bonus. And according to Triantafyllou, the absence of expectation allowed Greek players to be free of the pressure. "The defeat to Russia did not affect the players. After qualifying to the knockout round for the first time in history, Greece had already achieved a big success. There was nothing to lose now and the players felt liberated."

Indeed, the mood could not have been better inside the Greek camp. Dellas produced a diary of his Euro 2004 experience for the newspaper, TA NEA. In it he described how close the team truly was. From backgammon tournaments to PlayStation battles to having coffee together and even massages, Dellas painted the picture of a group that did everything together. Rehhagel had specifically asked for players to have their own rooms for the tournament, believing that everyone would appreciate their own space. Players were constantly in the rooms of others however, some preferring to take naps in teammates' rooms, others just wanting to gather together to analyze potential opponents, still others hanging out and watching movies with fellow players. This was a squad that had developed a close bond off the pitch. They were friends.

The main goal of the Ethniki in coming to Portugal was to give a decent account of themselves. Nikolaidis said during the tournament that the players wanted to give the team a 'varia fanela', translated directly as a 'heavy shirt'. This was a term in Greece given to clubs and countries whose history and tradition would see that particular team hold weight in and of itself, no matter the form or state of that side. Even in bad periods teams such as Argentina or Italy always seemed to be able to grab results. Though they had far from a classic squad at the 2002 World Cup, Germany found a way to advance to the final. Greece possessed nowhere near the history or reputation of countries like that. That was Nikolaidis' point. This tournament would be an opportunity to make some inroads on making the shirt heavier.

6,000 Greeks travelled to Lisbon in hopes of seeing their national side do just that on 25 June. Victory over France would unquestionably be the greatest moment in the country's football history, perhaps the most significant sporting success since the Greek basketball team won the 1987 Eurobasket Championship.

France had some key injury questions heading into the game at the Estadio Jose Alvalade, the home of Sporting Lisbon, and so did Greece. The entire squad had rallied around Vryzas during training that week. Set to miss the match due to an accumulation of yellow cards, his teammates told him to enjoy the rest before the semi-finals hoping to raise his spirits. Besides Vryzas, Rehhagel would also be without Giannakopoulos, who was still recovering from the injury suffered against Spain. The good news was that Karagounis would be back. Greece needed players who could possess the ball and Karagounis would be vital for that.

Lisbon was absolutely rocking on the day of the game, a city still celebrating after seeing Portugal outlast England on penalty-kicks (2-2 after extra-time, 6-5 on penalties) in an epic quarter-final at the Estadio da Luz the night before. The Greek supporters harnessed that energy as they chanted 'Ellas boreis, boreis na prokritheis' (Greece you can, you can advance). And the team promptly responded with a confident start. Zagorakis set the tone early with choice words for Seitaridis after his hospital pass was picked off by Pires on the left. Little chance of winning did not mean much to Zagorakis as he looked to be in the zone from the start. The players appeared ready to live up to what Rehhagel said the day before in the press conference, "if we fall, we will fall like Greeks, we will fall like heroes."

From the start, France looked uncomfortable with Greece's man-marking tactics. The match-ups could be found all over the pitch. Seitaridis shadowed Henry from the kick-off which in turn essentially made Zagorakis a right wing-back who was responsible for Pires on that flank. Kapsis was tasked with marking Trezeguet, Basinas lined up against Claude Makelele, while Karagounis and Fyssas both followed Zidane's roving movements. Dellas slipped back into his now usual free role at the back. From the early minutes, Santini's players appeared to be preoccupied with the man-marking strategy. Thus France attempted to create attacks by beating the Greek team one-on-one rather than through combination play.

A fine cross by Fyssas was just missed by Charisteas' jump as Greece tried to get further up the pitch. A disciplined start in defense was marred only by a silly Karagounis yellow after a tug on Zidane. Fyssas' brilliantly-timed tackle on Gallas after he motored into the box was indicative of a Greek team that was not panicking or in awe of their more illustrious opponents.

Following Euro 2004, Fyssas returned to Portugal to play for Benfica. When he first arrived at the tail end of 2003, he was treated warmly. After his performances in Portugal, specifically against the host nation, there was an element of antipathy directed toward him. Even Benfica fans were lukewarm with regard to the player. Fyssas' goal in the 2003/04 Portuguese Cup final was not enough for the fans to stop referring to him simply as "Greco". While he continued to be applauded following his performances as Benfica claimed the 2004/05 Primeira Liga, a move to Hearts in Scotland followed the next season.

In truth, Portugal supporters would have had reason not to like Fyssas. The left-back was fantastic in both games against the hosts at Euro 2004. His displays in those two matches were top-notch, helping Greece win and convincing the UEFA technical committee to select him in the Team of the Tournament. Against France, Fyssas looked to be completely recovered after a difficult second half trying to chase down Joaquin in the second group game versus Spain. Fyssas famously ensured his wedding should take place after Euro 2004 by setting the date for 9 July. He did not do so because he thought Greece would advance to the final rather that he wanted to "watch the semis and final with my friends with some pizzas and beers", he said in an interview with Sport24.gr in 2017.

Fyssas started his professional career with Panionios. As an academy player,

Fyssas made his first division debut as a 17-year-old when Panionios fielded a team full of youth products to face off against Panathinaikos. He played sparingly in the first team until the 1993/94 season when the club were promoted from the second division. After three full seasons under his belt, Fyssas was beginning to make a name for himself as one of Greece's most promising full-backs. It looked like a step down in his career when Panionios were relegated at the end of the 1995/96 campaign. Fyssas was undeterred as he led the team straight back up the following year, having by that point become a key starter.

After another successful season for the Nea Smryni side in 1996/97, the player had become a main transfer target for all of the country's biggest clubs. He signed for Panathinaikos in January 1999 and was thrust directly into the team's backline, playing 18 matches until the end of the season. Playing for Panathinaikos placed him into the national spotlight and his first call-up to the Ethniki came in 1999 in a friendly against Finland. Less dynamic in some ways than Seitaridis, his partner on the opposite flank, Fyssas was just as effective on both sides of the ball. His defensive work was his strength, that did not mean he was not useful going forward. The Athens-born player had an unbelievable work rate and his forays into attack gave Greece another dimension at Euro 2004 and all through his 60 international caps.

* * * *

Greece's first chance came as Charisteas laid off for Nikolaidis to shoot straight at Barthez. Vieira's replacement, Olivier Dacourt, was looking out of sorts for France and Greece were enjoying more of the ball than they would have expected. Free-kicks were also being won in dangerous areas. The team's most notable chance in the opening stages coming from a dead ball. Karagounis served up from 35 yards and Katsouranis slipped in at the back post. He made contact and his goal-bound effort was eventually smothered by Barthez after the ball came back off the post from his initial save.

France's best opportunity came from Henry's shot in the area that sailed wide after a Lizarazu cross. Dellas looked born for the sweeper role he was playing as time and time again he perfectly read through balls behind the Greek defense. Kapsis looked just as comfortable until a shot to the back by Trezeguet had him wincing. Katsouranis went close again with a well-hit volley.

Greece were controlling the tempo of the game, thanks to their ability to hold possession and their pressure on the ball. Nikolaidis clearly did not look to be one hundred percent, but he was fighting hard up front as Greece's pressing swung back and forth between starting from three-quarters up the pitch to a half-field set-up. Charisteas also looked very mobile as he worked well with Zagorakis on the right while also coming inside often to play as a target forward.

Henry and Pires switched wings hoping for uptick in their fortunes. It proved to be unsuccessful. France looked listless. There was little energy and even less urgency. Zidane was being suffocated by the Greek midfield. Even though he looked sharp when on the ball, the world-class midfielder was constantly hounded by two or three players when in possession.

The half ended with a big chance for the Ethniki. Basinas' superb tackle was followed by a pass to Fyssas on the left. He chested the ball down and half volleyed from 30 yards and Barthez was forced to tip over the viciously dipping effort

France appeared to come out of the interval with renewed purpose. There was increased pressing of the Greek players. It led to some dangerous moments as Kapsis stopped Lizarazu's driving run and then seconds later headed away at the back post at the last instant after Henry tried to pick out Trezeguet. It was a sequence that featured two pieces of magnificent defensive play.

When Rehhagel inserted Lakis for Nikolaidis just five minutes into the second half, it signaled the end of the Greek striker's playing career. He never scored at Euro 2004 or played the role that perhaps he had envisioned, but he battled through injury to make a contribution on the pitch. Rehhagel could see that France were a different proposition after halftime. There appeared to be a concerted push by the favorites to boss the game and find a breakthrough. The early chances that came, such as Henry's shot that forced Nikopolidis low to his left to save, appeared to suggest a goal was in the works. And one was. It incredibly however came from Greece.

In the 65th minute. Zagorakis played a pass to Basinas just ahead of midfield before taking off on a run down the right. Basinas flighted a ball over the top to him. Lizarazu sprinted to intercept, but at the last moment, Zagorakis touched the ball over the defender. After taking another touch and looking into the box, the Greek captain steadied himself before picking out Charisteas in the box. Katsouranis' run pulled Thuram away from the forward and Charisteas' well-executed header whistled past Barthez. It was a sensational goal from start to finish.

* * * *

Charisteas' header was about perfect as could be. The real credit however had to go to Zagorakis' run. His play looked like a magical piece of improvisation by a skilled Brazilian winger. Instead, it was the creation of a player whose main attributes were his hard work and aggressiveness. While playing for Leicester in the late 1990s he was dismissed by some as a simple "up-and-downer", a player who essentially could run around the pitch, but offer up little else. He struggled to assert himself in the English game after opening up his career with time at hometown club Kavala and six years with PAOK. He was not fluent in English and so he found it difficult to make connections to teammates. He preferred to spend his personal time with Greek students at the local university in Leicester. His time there was not all bad, there was a League Cup win to celebrate in 1999/2000. Zagorakis did not make it off the bench for the final versus Tranmere, but he had played in all seven matches leading up to that game.

There were glimpses of the player he could be in England. He made the switch back to Greece and AEK in 2000. He became an influential member of a very fine group at a club suffering from severe economic issues. Zagorakis ensured that the AEK on the pitch was much different to the AEK off the pitch. His work in providing a solid block in front of the backline and linking the defense and the attack was a key component of that side's success. Considering the problems plaguing the club, the fact that AEK were consistently challenging in the league and were able to win the 2001/02 Greek Cup meant they punched well above their weight at the time. Financial issues aside, the talent in the team was vast. Tsiartas was the orchestrator in the midfield that had its energy come from the young Katsouranis and its solidity from the team's leader, Zagorakis.

And that was exactly when Zagorakis thrived, in the teams where he was the leader. Technically good, it was his scrappiness and winning mentality that were his greatest attributes. His style of play set the tone, both for club and country. He was the oldest serving member of the Euro 2004 team, he and Tsiartas both debuting in 1994.

His four years at AEK from 2000 to 2004 saw him playing the best football of his career. He arrived in Portugal full of confidence. Though he very nearly did not make it there at all. A doping test taken in the lead-up to the tournament came back showing a positive test. Zagorakis had previous troubles with doping tests. Both in 2001 and 2002, the player delivered positive tests while playing for

AEK. In both cases, he was cleared of taking any form of banned anabolic steroids. The reason for the positive tests were due to elevated levels of testosterone found in his system. It was subsequently found that Zagorakis' testosterone numbers were from his body naturally producing high levels of the hormone.

The positive pre-Euro 2004 test had EPO President Gagatsis and others scrambling. Several days of document collecting followed so UEFA could be given the proper information. The player himself did not know of the issue until two days before the opening game. The tests were done in-house and the EPO could have just taken the risk that Zagorakis would not be selected for doping tests after matches. However, Gagatsis did not want any complications. He wanted to ensure that things were done right and that there was transparency on the issue. It was a case of the EPO being proactive. The result was the player being cleared by all the official bodies and being allowed to play in Portugal.

Zagorakis went on to star for Greece at the tournament, shockingly earning the nod as UEFA's Player of the Tournament. He made the switch to Bologna the following season and then finished his career with two years at PAOK. He never played for Greece in another tournament, bowing out of the international game in 2007. He led his country in all-time international appearances with 120 until Karagounis surpassed him in 2012.

* * * *

France entered the second half with more fluidity and pace to their game. They looked unshackled to start. Charisteas' goal appeared to chain them up once again. Santini tried to breathe life into a comeback. He took off Trezeguet for the in-form Louis Saha and sacrificed Dacourt for Sylvain Wiltord, another forward. Saha nearly find a way through only for the injured Kapsis to continue his amazing display by crucially stopping him. Finishing continued to let France down as Saha and Henry could not adequately test Nikopolidis when well-placed on two occasions.

Though there was no lack of French effort in the last ten minutes it all amounted to a lot of huffing and puffing. Les Bleus had no rhythm and even less belief it seemed. Zidane tried to take responsibility. His touches at times were magnificent along with his passes and patented pirouettes. Unfortunately, his teammates were usually not on the same page. With five minutes left to play it was nearly 1-1, but Henry yet again flashed a chance wide. There was pressure from the French side as Saha and Lizarazu also came close. It was not to be. It was never going to be. This was a night for Greece. When Anders Frisk blew for full-time, the celebrations inside the Estadio Jose Alvalade were ear-shattering. Greece had won. David had slayed Goliath. Rehhagel and his players were through to the semi-finals of the European Championship.

Chapter 18

The Inevitable Moment

Charisteas' header was the goal heard around the world. In a tournament full of upsets, Greece had just produced the biggest one. Eliminating France meant that the entire globe began to take notice of the Ethniki. The story was nice at the start. An underachieving side pulling off a big victory over the hosts and eventually slipping into the quarter-finals. It was supposed to end there. Now, the story had taken on a different dimension. Knocking out the French was something that reverberated across the football world. Greece had suddenly been thrust into the international football limelight.

The victory brought about absolute pandemonium in Athens with fans spilling into the streets in the tens of thousands to celebrate. Similar scenes unfolded across the country in cities and towns, big and small. Across the Greek diaspora, the same thing had occurred. In Australia, the United States, Canada, and the United Kingdom, Greek immigrant communities partied together no matter if it was afternoon, evening, or even the early morning hours.

Greek celebrities gave interviews with congratulations toward the team. The Archbishop of Greece, Christodoulos, blessed the Ethniki's achievements along with other religious and political leaders. One of the most high-profile names to praise the team was Nikos Galis. The former Greek basketball star, who led the country to a European Championship in 1987, sent a congratulatory letter to the team's hotel. In it he talked about his own pride and joy of winning a continental title. He ended the message by expressing thanks to the team for bringing Greeks out to the streets and said he believed they could do it two more times.

After advancing to the semi-finals, Zagorakis said, "I am afraid to bathe in fear of waking up from this dream." The Greek team was in a state of disbelief. The players, however, managed to stay grounded. Despite being only two wins away from footballing immortality, the focus was always on the next game. "We did not really think like that, in terms of thinking we could win the trophy after beating France," said Dabizas. "All the boys would say before the game is let's go and do what we can so that our countrymen and all Greeks could be proud of their national team. For us, that attitude helped lead us to results."

The final four of Euro 2004 now included Portugal, Greece, the Netherlands, and the Czech Republic. Portugal were through after defeating England on penalties. The Netherlands did the same against Sweden (0-0 after extra-time, 5-4 on penalty-kicks), breaking their hoodoo of going out of the last three European Championships (1992, 1996, and 2000) in shoot-outs.

Two days after the victory over France, Greece found out they would be facing off against the Czech Republic in the semis. Karel Bruckner's team was widely considered to be playing the best football in the tournament even before they swept past Denmark 3-0 in the last quarter-final. After a cagey opening half, Jan Koller's 49th minute goal put the Czechs in front before tournament leading scorer, Milan Baros (five goals in four matches), scored a quick-fire brace to send the Danes home.

What made the Czech Republic such a fierce proposition was the variety in their attack. This was a team that was deadly on the counter. Even more impressive was their build-up play featuring extremely quick ball movement between the midfield and forward lines. The forward duo of Koller and Baros was a fantastic partnership with Koller providing the power and aerial threat and Baros the turn of pace to be able to finish off the team's attacking moves. Midfielder Pavel Nedved was the star with his dribbling and driving runs while Tomas Rosicky provided incisive passing and movement to unlock opposing defenses. Full-backs Marek Jankulovski and Zdenek Grygera also contributed to an offensive machine that was scoring goals for fun.

The Group Stage saw a Czech team go from strength to strength. After sweating a little to defeat Latvia 2-1 with a late winner, Bruckner's men came from 2-0 down in the first 20 minutes to defeat the Netherlands 3-2 in their next game, one of the matches of the tournament. With qualification assured, nine starters were rested, but the reserves did superbly well to defeat Germany 2-1 and knock them out of the tournament after coming from behind yet again. In the quarter-finals, Denmark did well in the first half to keep the Czechs at bay, but it was just a matter of time before the team's offense kicked into high gear.

Michal Petrak is currently the press officer at Czech club FC Hradec Kralove.

Before that career move, Petrak was a well-established football reporter who worked at Czech sports daily Sport. He covered the Czech Republic at Euro 2004 for HATTRICK magazine. Petrak believes that there were muted expectations about Czech prospects in Portugal, but that there was a sense the team could do something special. "On the one hand, we knew we had one of the best teams in Czech and Czechoslovak history, on the other hand several players had fitness problems in the months leading up to the tournament," says Petrak. "When the team lost to Japan in a friendly at the end of April, the feelings amongst fans were mixed. In the lead up to the competition the injury situation improved and everyone hoped for the best. In HATTRICK, we published a special issue before the tournament where we tipped the Czechs to go to the final and lose to France."

The semi-final would then feature the indomitable Greek defense against the slick and explosive Czech attack. Rehhagel and Bruckner were the two oldest managers at the tournament, Rehhagel, 65 and Bruckner just a year younger. They may have had teams with contrasting styles, yet the two managers were also alike. Both were incredibly detail-oriented and were lauded during the competition for the effectiveness of their tactics. Both managers realized the importance of set-pieces and worked quite hard on those. Bruckner was a manager who would stay up well into the night to devise new free-kick schemes and the Czechs had about fifteen plays they ran on dead balls. And like Rehhagel, he was the exact coach his team needed. "Bruckner was the perfect manager for that group," insists Petrak. "He is very charismatic and intelligent, a natural leader. He used to manage many of the younger players with the Czech U-21 national team and mutual knowledge was an important factor."

The Czechs had earned much praise for their free-flowing football. Greece had received plaudits for advancing so far. Their style of play was not to everyone's taste. After beating France, there was significantly more focus on the team's defensive play. Rehhagel had dusted off the how-to-manual of man-marking at the international level. The man-marking and use of a sweeper saw some levy the same accusations at Rehhagel that he had received at times in Germany. Some talked of 'pre-historic' tactics and dour football. The narrative being spun by some journalists and pundits on the continent, that Greece were negative and causing damage to football, may have been extreme, but it was one that eventually took hold. Few Greek supporters would have been bothered by such talk. The manager and players even less so. It may have been more pragmatic than romantic, but the team were unapologetic about their playing style. "In a football sense, we were realists," said Dabizas. "Moreover, from the psychological strength you to have to be a united team, the way you play the game needs to also be realistic. The way we played was perfectly paired to the characteristics we had as a team and we based ourselves on that style and model which gave us results." Entertainment be damned. This group of players trusted in the old-fashioned virtues of organization, discipline, and just plain hard-work. They were steadfast in their belief that winning for themselves and their country meant more than pleasing others. Would it have been smart to attack France from the off? To go into the match versus the Czech Republic abandoning the principles that had got them that far? The answer from Rehhagel and the players was an emphatic no.

The quality of the Czech performances thus far did give Rehhagel and his men headaches. History was not on Greece's side either. In six previous appearances against their semi-final opponents, Greece had failed to record a win, drawing only once and losing the other five games. Petrak describes a mood within the Czech Republic of growing expectations and excitement, "Many Czech fans believed we were playing the best football in Portugal. The excitement in the country was growing. Ahead of the semi-final, I would say the belief was pretty big. The Greeks were widely considered to be the weakest of the four semi-finalists. We believed the strength of our attack would open up their defense."

Confidence for Greek fans could be found in Rehhagel's ability to adapt to opponents. Every game in the tournament was a chess match and Rehhagel was proving himself to be a grandmaster. His formations were very fluid. A 4-4-2 could become a 4-3-3 in attack. A 4-5-1 easily converted to a 3-4-1-2. The ability of the Ethniki to switch formations during a game was admirable. Rehhagel pulled the strings and there was purpose to every move. Above all, Rehhagel's brilliance was probably found in the way he could see his own player's strengths. The manager based so much of his defense on man-marking because he knew he had the personnel to do so. He trusted his players to adequately match-up against world-class stars like Figo, Raul, Morientes, Zidane, Henry, and Pires. He also had faith in the teamwork of the side. There was no better team in the tournament at defensive cover. If one player was beaten, a teammate always seemed to appear to put renewed pressure on an opponent, to make a tackle, or steal the ball.

The semi-final was set for 1 July at the Estadio do Dragao in Porto. After receiving a day off following the France match, Greece arrived at their base for the next game, a hotel situated between the cities of Braga and Guimaraes. The Spanish team had resided in the same facility earlier in the competition. Rehhagel preferred to stay in somewhat secluded and quiet surroundings just as the team had done in Switzerland to prepare for the tournament.

The press conference on the eve of the game showed the mutual respect the two managers had for each other and their respective teams. Rehhagel continued his strategy of playing up the opposition and playing down his own team's chances. "The Czechs have some excellent players who possess a brilliant football education and for that reason we must take advantage of the few chances we will be presented with," said the German. "I hope we can rest so we have plenty of strength and be a good opponent for the Czech Republic. Bruckner did not buy that Greece were only a defensive team, explaining, "Their base is their defensive qualities. They showed good attacking traits in the opening match versus Portugal. They will also have more rest time, that will be significant for the Greeks."

In advance of the match, Rehhagel had held some open training sessions as he allowed his players the freedom to speak to the large media presence at will. Striking a balance between allowing the players to enjoy the experience while also keeping them focused and concentrated was vitally important.

Giannakopoulos' race back to match fitness was good news for the Greek side. The only concerns were with yellow cards. Karagounis and Zagorakis were one away from missing the final should Greece advance. The Czechs would be without defender Martin Jiranek who was suffering from a groin pull. He would be replaced in the center of defense by the returning Rene Bolf.

Advertisements in Greek papers were full of packages available for travel to Portugal either by air or land. More than 11,000 Greek fans made the trip to Porto and that travelling support had easily won the battle in the stands as Collina, refereeing his final international match, blew the opening whistle to start the second Euro 2004 semi-final. Portugal had advanced to the final the day before, outlasting the Netherlands 2-1. The majority of Portuguese fans inside the stadium and throughout the country for that matter were cheering on Greece. Not only did they want to avoid the Czech Republic's fearsome attack, there was also a desire to exact some revenge on the Greeks for the loss instilled on them in the tournament opener.

Rehhagel was banking on his players to once again find success by winning the individual battles. As such, the man-to-man tactics were in full force from the start. Seitaridis was tasked with trying to shut down the dynamic Baros. Kapsis, despite being much shorter, was up against Koller, while Katsouranis was chosen to keep tabs on Nedved.

Koller's height helped create the game's first chance in just the second minute. The big Czech's knockdown set up Rosicky who smashed a volley off the crossbar. It was a massive opportunity and Greece looked very nervy early on. It was a similar start to the Russia game and the Ethniki were guilty of a series of mistakes in possession in the opening stages. In contrast, the Czech Republic looked to be full of confidence. Minutes after Rosicky hit the woodwork, Jankulovski very nearly gave his team the lead. Karagounis tried to use his body to win the ball outside his own area. Jankulovski stole in and fired a stinging effort that Nikopolidis did extremely well to beat away.

Greece were being pinned back. Rehhagel was vehemently urging his players to get forward, the lines too far apart to make inroads on the few counter-attacks his team had. Slowly, the Ethniki found its shape and grew into the game. Karagounis had the team's first shot after ten minutes following some neat build-up play. His ability to penetrate off the dribble was beginning to cause problems with Bolf lucky to escape a yellow after a mis-timed challenge.

The Czechs were such a danger when the pace of their play quickened. Greece wanted to slow the tempo, their opponents the opposite. Seitaridis saw yellow after Baros turned him, a glimpse of the explosiveness of the Liverpool striker. Overall though, the Greek defense had recovered after a shaky start. Dellas was cleaning up the numerous through balls the Czech sent in, while Kapsis was producing a master-class in positioning, beating Koller to headers time and time again.

* * * *

Michalis Kapsis was a late bloomer. While many in the Greek squad began their careers in their teenage years and made the switch to bigger clubs in their early twenties, Kapsis did not sign for AEK until he was nearly 26 years old. He had to wait until he was 29 to earn his first cap for Greece.

After a season each at Aris Nikeas, AO Neapolis, and Anagennisi Artas, Kapsis signed for Ethnikos in the second division in 1993. He played there for six seasons, helping the team into the top-flight early in his spell there. Kapsis had big football boots to fill, his father Anthimos was part of the Panathinaikos side that lost to Ajax in the European Cup final in 1971 and the captain of the Ethniki during Euro 1980. Kapsis' career was nowhere near as spectacular to begin with, but the player showed steady progress. A fierce competitor lay beneath the quiet and humble persona, a defender whose strengths included his quickness and timely tackles. Kapsis was dynamic, but controlled, a center-back whose game was as clean as they come.

Perhaps his low-key personality saw him fly under the radar for a time, however AEK came calling in 1999. The move to one of the country's biggest clubs did not phase Kapsis, as he began well at AEK. Injuries disrupted his first two seasons, but he came back strongly and was one of the star performers in the team's memorable Champions' League run during the 2002/03 campaign. AEK drew all six matches in a group that included Real Madrid, Roma, and Genk.

His fine form for AEK domestically and in European competitions finally saw him earn a call-up to the national team. His gritty performances against Spain and Ukraine in his first two appearances for Greece cemented his place in the team. He was a first-choice center-back for Greece for the next four years when not injured. Kapsis' displays in Portugal earned him a move to Ligue 1 with Bordeaux for one season. He performed very well in France, but opted to move back to Greece for two injury-plagued seasons at Olympiacos, where he did manage to win two league titles. His career ended with another championship in Cyprus with APOEL before a stint at Levadiakos and a final curtain call at Ethnikos.

At just under six feet, his performance against the 6'8 Koller in the semi-final against the Czechs remains the stuff of legend and probably the performance most Greek fans associate with Kapsis' career.

* * * *

The orders from the bench were for Greece to come out of their shell a bit more. The Czechs were on top, there was no doubt about that. There was a growing sense from Rehhagel and his men, however, that they could press forward more. And it was Bruckner's side that were under pressure for a spell as Cech was forced to dive to divert a cross after another impressive build-up by Greece. One of the game's pivotal turning points was the Ethniki establishing some sort of possession. Taking care of the ball allowed a respite from the early onslaught where every attack seemed like a goal in waiting.

The backline was handling things well even if the tempo of the game was fast, something that suited the Czech Republic. As the half wore on, Nedved had become a more influential figure. A long, driving run into the box by the Juventus playmaker was cut out at the last. He just failed to connect with a Rosicky cross late in the half, colliding with Katsouranis in the process. The trailing Jankulovski shot toward goal only to be denied again by Nikopolidis.

Nedved was slow to get up and needed treatment. He tried to run off the knock for the next few minutes. It was to no avail. Nedved was forced to come off as Vladimir Smicer took his place. Smicer was an established international, a quality midfielder who had been at Liverpool for five seasons. Still, Nedved's injury was a cruel blow to the Czech side. He had been playing some of the best football of his career. "I personally do not like the concept of bad luck," says Petrak. "With better finishing, we should have been able to win the game. On the other hand, you can count the injury to the talismanic Nedved, playing in the form of his life, as bad luck, indeed."

Greece emerged from halftime looking much improved. An even opening period saw Dellas engage in a slight tug on Koller that Collina felt was not enough for a penalty while Smicer was forced to take down Seitaridis' surge down the right, earning himself a caution. Kapsis finally fouled Koller after an hour. All in all, the Greek defending was very disciplined. The skill of some of the Czech players had given fits to their opponents, but even when beaten individually, the covering defense of Greece was fantastic. There was always a player to come and help put pressure on the dribbler or shooter. Smicer, Baros, and Koller all had efforts that were put off just enough thanks to a scrambling Greek player.

Vryzas was starved for service up front for Greece. He was doing superbly as a target man, in allowing his team to build attacks with his hold-up play. Midway through the half he tested Cech's handling with a header from a Karagounis free-kick. Charisteas was putting in a real shift as well. The work rate of the two forwards was key in pressing the Czechs and disrupting their flow.

Increased Czechs pressure in the final twenty minutes had Greek players struggling to cope. Loose possession saw the Czech Republic produce two massive chances. First, Koller and Rosicky played a slick give-and-go as Koller entered the area. The striker shot inches wide with more time to shoot than perhaps he thought. It was a chance he would have loved to have back. The

Czechs were finishing the 90 minutes the stronger side. Six minutes from the end, another error by Greece saw Baros pick up the ball and dribble at Kapsis outside the box. Baros' cut sharply inside and effort also narrowly missed to the left of the goal. It was nearly in the same spot as Koller's shot.

By that point, Giannakopoulos had been brought into the fray, replacing Basinas. Karagounis fouled Smicer and was not spared by Collina. The Greek midfielder's pleas were futile. The brandished yellow card meant he would miss the final. "I did not think at all about how I would not play in the final. I only focused on ensuring how I could help my team advance. Only later on did it hit me that I would not be able to play. There was so much tension in the match that I didn't think about it then," recalls Karagounis. Indeed, Greece had to get there first and just barely scraped into extra-time after Kapsis' crucial late headed clearance from a ball into the box.

Vryzas had given all he could and thus Rehhagel took him off in favor of Tsiartas. Charisteas moved centrally to start the first period of extra-time. Either side could win the game by the end of the first period of extra-time if they scored during that fifteen minute spell. This was the Silver Goal rule which had been adopted by UEFA in the 2002/03 season. A team would not lose automatically when the opponent scored, but would have the remainder of the first extra-time period to be able to tie the match. Having never been in any sort of position like this ever, there was a question as to how Greece would fare. "The national team never had any experience in such situations, some players did at club level, but not with the Ethniki. The key I believe was that the team's psychology was positive and they were so united. Against the Czechs, Greece survived the entire game. Only in overtime, did things change and there was less pressure," says Triantafyllou.

Rehhagel's two substitutes, Giannakopoulos and Tsiartas, had given Greece new life to start overtime. Giannakopoulos gave the team a fresh burst of energy with his dribbling. Tsiartas' inclusion meant that the Ethniki had a player who was comfortable in possession and able to play penetrative passes.

The first chance of extra-time came from Greece. Charisteas won a header and Giannakopoulos broke into the box all alone. He tried to head over Cech, but the goalkeeper was alert off his line and made the save, deflecting the ball away. The momentum had suddenly changed. With their fans in full voice, it felt as if Greece were for the first time in the game, playing on their terms. As they began to attack more consistently, the Greek side could sense the vulnerability of the Czech backline. Rehhagel's men had created more chances in extra-time then they had over the whole of regulation. Katsouranis' long ball to Charisteas saw the Ethniki win a corner. There appeared to be just enough of the first fifteen minute period for the corner to be taken.

Tsiartas went to grab the ball. Giannakopoulos came in for the short corner option. Tsiartas dismissed the notion. He waved his teammate off. Twice before in overtime, Tsiartas had targeted Dellas with a dead-ball. The defender forced a save from Petr Cech just minutes before with a glancing header.

Sport is known for its ability to surprise. Not least in football. And yet, there are times when there is an inevitability of what is about to happen. The two most well-known Greek commentators of Euro 2004 were Kostas Vernikos and Giorgos Helakis. Vernikos covered the televised broadcasts of the tournament for Greek state broadcaster ERT. Helakis was the voice behind SPOR FM's radio coverage. They differed in their styles. Vernikos was more of the straight man. His polished style full of well-researched material of Greece's own players and their opponents. Vernikos' passion came through clearly, perhaps just not as loudly as his colleague. Helakis' match calls were more chaotic. There was not as much background as Vernikos brought to the table, however, Helakis attempted to bring listeners into the stadium with him. His was a more frantic play-by-play, perhaps more suitable for radio, and he often referred to the Greek players by their first names. Both commentators had tried to capture the Ethniki's magical run in their own way. They were each very experienced and the disbelief of what they were seeing along with their pride was clear every time they announced a match.

As Tsiartas prepared to take the corner, Vernikos said on-air, "If a goal was scored right now..." Helakis, at the same time, in the same stadium as Vernikos, told radio listeners, "Goal and we leave for the Final."

Both had essentially called it. The inevitability of the moment was not confined to just those two. As Dellas made the move to attack Tsiartas' near-post delivery, one wonders whether all Greek supporters had already started to yell before the ball had hit the net. Either way, it did. "It was a spontaneous moment," admits Vernikos, "I said it and it happened, just like when you want something very, very much. It was a beautiful moment. I did not even believe afterward that I asked for a goal and the wish came true."

The players on the pitch were too busy with matters at hand to concern themselves with the plausibility of predetermined events. "I don't believe us who were playing could say anything like that. We were thinking about the next play and the game. If the goal came great, if not, we would have continued. We had a great corner-kick taker in Tsiartas. We had plays we worked on in training for those situations and where players would go such as the near post and far post. We did what we laid out in training and that is how the goal came," says Katsouranis.

With Bolf still holding on to him as he wriggled away to celebrate, Dellas' header had beaten Cech at the near post. Vernikos, Helakis and millions of other Greeks across the world started screaming goal at the top of their lungs. Dellas headed to the technical area where the entire Greek bench cleared and celebrated as one. Katsouranis was stood right next to Dellas as he scored. He was ecstatic and had forgotten about the silver goal rule. "I was very, very happy. I had no idea the match was going to end soon after. That didn't come into my head at the moment. I was thinking that we had another half of extra-time to play. But, my joy was such that I believed we would keep that 1-0 lead regardless. Then the referee whistled and I remembered about the silver goal," admitted Katsouranis. "The joy we felt was incredible and what can I say, we were through to the final and it was an amazing feeling for all of us."

Greece had indeed won, beating the favored Czech Republic 1-0 thanks to Dellas' header. It would be the only time in international football history that a match was decided by a silver goal. It was the first time in three years that Bruckner's team had conceded a goal from a corner.

Petrak strongly believes that Nedved's injury and the Czechs' profligacy in front of goal were the key factors in Greece prevailing. "We played well. Rosicky hit the woodwork, Koller had a wonderful chance, but missed by inches. Baros was also close in the final minutes of the game. The Greeks man marked and allowed us fewer chances, but we were still the better side. Things very probably might have been different had Nedved not been injured. He was a threat to the Greek defense and his injury was a big blow to our game plan. Who knows what would have happened if he had remained and if Bruckner brought on Heinz, who had a brilliant tournament, into the match."

Sadness reigned in the Czech Republic following the defeat, a similar feeling to the loss against Germany in the Euro 1996 final, then on a golden goal. "We were proud having been recognized for playing the most beautiful football, but the lost semi-final felt like a chance wasted for a very strong generation," admits Petrak. "The players were treated as sad heroes. They brought a sense of pride to the nation for the way they played, but there was strong disappointment about the fact they lost in the semi-final to those pragmatic underdogs."

Greece had beaten a more talented side, not for the first time in Portugal. And as crazy as it sounded they would now play the hosts in the Euro 2004 Final for a chance to lift the Henri Delaunay trophy and become European champions.

Chapter 19

Sikose To (Lift It Up)

Greece was a country that was marching to the beat of its football team. It was quickly becoming a regular occurrence for the streets to flood with wildly cheering fans after the Ethniki would win. Following the dramatic semi-final victory, over 100,000 Greeks filled Omonia Square in Athens to celebrate. This was a scene reproduced across the country. Greek communities the world over did the same. 4,000 fans gathered in Berlin's city center. New York, Chicago, Toronto, and Montreal all featured sizable gatherings for matches and the celebrations that inevitably followed. In Australia, celebrating fans in Sydney brought morning traffic to a halt while in Melbourne, the massive Greek community there produced epic scenes complete with chants and flares in a sea of blue and white.

News reports suggested that not since the liberation of Greece from German occupation in World War II had so many flags been hung outside of Greek homes. Television coverage featured interviews with citizens, many of whom did not even follow football, suddenly captured by the moment and relaying their stories of having watched the matches. It was a sign of how deeply this team's journey had touched the average Greek.

The television ratings for the semi-final versus the Czech Republic were astonishing. Three million households had tuned in to watch Dellas' goal. The number was only for actual households and did not account for how many people watched together in addition to the huge crowds that gathered in cities across the nation in cafes and squares to watch on big screens. In a country of just eleven million people, one would have been hard pressed to find too many who had not watched.

And what those viewers saw in the moments after Dellas scored were images that would likely live on in their minds forever. Rehhagel running around the pitch, arms outstretched, celebrating like a child. The tears of joy of Greeks fans in the stadium, many overcome by the moment. Giannakopoulos bringing his young son onto the pitch, explaining to him the reason for the scenes of jubilation. Players celebrating, some hoisting teammates on their backs, others hugging and laughing together, all appearing to not fully believe in what they had just done. Except by that stage the group's expectations had grown considerably. Karagounis explains that the Ethniki were not in awe of the Czech Republic. "The Czechs were an extremely good side as they had shown up until the semi-final. Since we had defeated a team like France though we had huge belief in ourselves. Without trying to underestimate the Czech Republic, because we knew they had played really well and won four matches in a row, we believed one way or another we could beat them and make the final."

The front pages of the country's newspapers the following day were all emblazoned with pictures of the team's unbelievable achievement. The newspaper, TA NEA, led the celebrations with the headline, "GOOOAL! And now the Cup." Eleftherotypia ran with "Hail, O Hail", drawing their inspiration from the words of the national anthem.

By this point, the most well-known chant of the Greek fans in Portugal had caught on everywhere. The words, "Sikose to, to timimeno, den boro, den boro, na perimeno (Lift it up, the honored [cup], I cannot, I cannot, wait)", reverberated throughout the stadiums of Greece's matches, especially after the win over France. The word timimeno (honored) was commonly substituted for "gamimeno" (f***ing) in the stands or on the streets. In the press, barring a few exceptions, the less vulgar option was used. Though many believe this chant was born out of the Greek side's run at Euro 2004, there are suggestions that it was invented earlier. Video footage from the 2003 Greek Cup Final clearly shows PAOK fans singing the same words as their side played city rivals Aris. Nevertheless, by the time Greece made the final, Ethniki fans around the globe had adopted it as their battle cry.

Greece's win meant that the Euro 2004 final would be played between the host nation, Portugal, and the tournament's surprise package. It would be the first time in the history of the European Championship or the World Cup that the final would feature the same teams who contested the opening match of the competition.

And Portugal were, undoubtedly, the overwhelming favorites. Scolari's side had gone from strength to strength after the defeat in their first game. Defensively, the host nation was looking solid and in attack the options were numerous. The proper chord had finally been struck between veteran stars and the exciting young talent in the team. Deco was pulling the strings in midfield, Figo had found better form and a 19-year-old Ronaldo was beginning to show signs of the world-class player he would become. The hosts responded after losing to Greece in that first match, improving their level with each passing game. "There is no doubt it was a case of building momentum," analyzes Kundert. "Portugal improved their performance level in every match. Also, outside the pitch, the atmosphere surrounding the team grew match-by-match, with the country almost reaching a state of collective euphoria by the time the final arrived."

While Scolari and the players would not talk about payback, revenge was on the mind of most Portuguese fans. Greece had nearly spoiled the party at the start of the tournament. Now, there was a chance for the perfect ending to the story. The national team had not lost a match in Lisbon in 30 years. Everything pointed to a Portugal win. Kundert relays how great the belief of the country's fans and observers was ahead of the final, "It was absolute. I don't think you could find one Portuguese person who did not think Portugal would win." Cristovao agrees that virtually everyone in the country believed their team would lift the trophy. "The England match was an epic. Facing Holland seemed even easy, after all that. Portugal was sure to beat Greece in the final, no question about it. The belief amongst fans and observers was very, very big," reiterated Cristovao.

One high-profile Portuguese supporter did have doubts though. Greek journalist Triantafyllou, working for sports newspaper GOAL News at the time, tells the story of speaking with Eusebio. "One story stands out. I was able to interview the dearly departed Eusebio on the eve of the final. After the interview was done and I turned my recording device off, he came closer and said 'I am very afraid that Portugal will not be able to do it tomorrow.'"

If there was one area of discontent from the host nation it centered around Markus Merk. The German referee had been selected to oversee the final. That story was sensationalized in the Portuguese press, the suggestion being that Merk would in some way be partial to his compatriot, Rehhagel. The Greek coach attempted to squash those theories saying Merk was always strict with him back in Germany, once even sending him off. The conspiracy theories did not stop until the final kicked off.

Portugal was trying to become the first host country to win the competition since France did so in 1984. Scolari was also trying to make history. If he led Portugal to the trophy he would have become the first coach in history to follow up a World Cup win with success in the Euro two years later. Scolari was experienced enough to know this would not be as straightforward as many people had been saying. In the pre-match press conference, Scolari was effusive in his praise of Greece and Rehhagel. He branded his upcoming opponents as the "real winners" of Euro 2004, going on to say that "Greece had been a perfect example of how collective strength can overcome individual talent." The Brazilian coach also called on Greece to be treated well in the final just as he hoped Athens would warmly welcome Portuguese athletes at the upcoming Olympic Games.

Rehhagel's mantra in the press conference remained consistent. Greece had nothing to lose at this stage. That did not mean they would be lacking in effort and motivation. "I promise that our players will be passionate and very motivated," said a proud manager who proceeded to praise Portugal for their play. "The tournament has been a success for Portugal, who after losing to us, still came back to make the final."

Both managers had big decisions to make ahead of the final. There was a case to be made for Nuno Gomes to start over Pauleta for Portugal. Scolari insisted that he would keep the faith with the same starting eleven. Rehhagel could not do the same. Karagounis' absence would be a big blow. The player had paid the price with his yellow in the semi-final. His game was always about passion and intensity. Occasionally, that led to needless bookings. Greece would miss Karagounis' energy, but mainly his ability to hold the ball and penetrate, either with his passing or dribbling. Nikolaidis would also miss out, however the good news was that Kapsis was set to start. The central defender had overcome a knee problem in training to be declared fit.

What would one have heard if they were embedded in that Greek team in the days leading up to the final? According to Katsouranis, he and his teammates remained grounded, ready to take their shot at history. "If people would have been in the hotel, training pitch, or anywhere else they would have seen a team that was humble, however one with spirit, with heart, and with bravery. We had a passion that since we made it so far, we had to win the final no matter what," reveals Katsouranis. He describes a team that was not content with merely advancing to the final. "We never thought that it was a game we should just be glad to be competing in and that we were already successful. We never said that we were already accomplished having reached the final. At the same time, we had nothing to lose if we didn't win. We wanted however to go down in history, forever."

As the Greek bus headed toward the stadium, Katsouranis paints a picture of a team in no way overawed by the magnitude of the occasion. "Everyone was focused and concentrated. We were discussing the match and what each of us could do in order to be successful," explains Katsouranis. "I did not see much nervousness. We were going to play the final of the Euro, but it appeared as though we were about to play a typical match. I believe the way we approached it helped us greatly. It was a beautiful day in a beautiful stadium and we knew there would be many Greeks in the stands. We had already made history, but that didn't matter as much. We reached the final and were prepared to give everything to win the final and lift the cup."

The entire world tuned in on Sunday, 4 July 2004 as Nelly Furtado finished singing FORCA, the tournament's official anthem, and hundreds of balloons were released from the center circle as part of the closing ceremonies of Euro 2004. Other highlights of the pre-game festivities included dancers performing the Pauliteiras de Miranda, a dance from Portugal's Minha region. To finish everything off, a model of a futuristic caravel made its way across the pitch with the flags of all the countries that participated in the tournament. The flags of the two finalists were placed in the middle of the pitch.

The colors in the stands mirrored those on the flags. The majority of the 62,865 capacity crowd was decked in red and green as the host fans vastly outnumbered their blue and white-clad counterparts. Some reports had the number of Greeks in Lisbon at close to 25,000. Inside the Estadio da Luz there were roughly 12,000. Fewer than half who had travelled to Portugal were lucky enough to get their hands on, to what amounted to, a golden ticket.

This was Portugal's third time playing in the stadium having defeated Russia and England in their previous matches. They appeared comfortable as good work by Figo earned them an early corner as the game began. The match took the shape of how many had predicted it would, a cagey opening with Portugal on the ball and Greece looking to play quick counter-attacks. Portugal lined up with the same eleven that began against the Netherlands in the semis. Greece saw Rehhagel prefer Giannakopoulos over Tsiartas as the way to replace the missing Karagounis.

Costinha was forced to haul down Seitaridis earning himself a yellow. The play had started with some slick possession by Greece. Once again, it was clear that this team was not overawed by the occasion. The game's first real chance came 13 minutes in when Miguel ran down the right and fired a blistering shot which was tipped away by Nikopolidis' low dive. Greece replied with a big chance of their own three minutes later. Katsouranis' played Seitaridis out wide as the right-back picked out Vryzas. The striker one-touched a ball to Katsouranis who had continued his run into the area. His pass for Charisteas was claimed at the last moment by Ricardo who saved at the feet of the Greek player. Pauleta then tested Nikopolidis with a shot the other way. It was held by the goalkeeper after a slight bobble. Space began to open up as the half progressed.

Both sides were having their attacking players switch positions. The front three of Vryzas, Charisteas, and Giannakopoulos interchanged often, especially the latter two on the flanks. Figo and Ronaldo did the same in the wide positions for Portugal. Greece were mostly employing zonal marking the midfield. There were individual battles to be found as Kapsis marked Pauleta and Katsouranis followed Deco's movements. Pauleta was the sole Portuguese striker leaving Dellas to roam around freely in the Greek backfield. He made a crucial intervention in a one-on-one duel with Ronaldo in the box, stealing the ball away before winning a foul.

Clear-cut chances were at a premium. Halfway through the first 45 minutes, Maniche let loose from distance with a shot that sailed wide. The Portuguese midfielder was full of confidence after his wonderful strike against the Netherlands in the semi-finals, one of the goals of the tournament. Long-range shots were what Portugal were being reduced to as the Greeks kept things remarkably tight at the back. Even a Fyssas mistake was atoned for by the player himself, recovering to win the ball back off Ronaldo in a wide area. As Ronaldo swung to the opposite side, a brilliant piece of defensive play by Seitaridis saw him win a foul from Portugal's bright young star. Around the half-hour mark, the first chants of "Ellas, Ellas" could be heard as the Portuguese fans began to enter a more subdued state after a strong start.

The half ended at 0-0. Portugal had been frustrated once again by their opponents. The Greeks would have been happier with the scoreline. It was another game which was being played to their tempo. Scolari had swapped

Paolo Ferreira for Miguel just before the break, otherwise, Portugal, like Greece, made no changes at the interval.

Figo was cutting a frustrated figure after he engaged in a foul throw a short while after the second half commenced. The teams traded chances in the opening moments. Charisteas' exceptional work on the right side saw him swing in a cross for Vryzas that just failed to hit the mark. Ronaldo's diagonal ball up the other end found Pauleta, but his shot was blocked away. Portugal were visibly more energetic to start the second half. Scolari had directed his players to press the Greeks higher up the pitch and Pauleta looking increasingly more willing to make diagonal runs to drag Kapsis and create space.

It was all working well as the hosts controlled the first ten minutes after the break. Regardless, time and time again the Portuguese players seemed to be rushing, either playing hurried final balls or snatching at shots. Greece were not immune to their own mistakes, ceding possession on many occasions, mostly through loose passes in the midfield.

In one instance, Dellas and Zagorakis made two errors in quick succession. The ball landed at the feet of Maniche. Just as the midfielder was about to strike from 25 yards out, a backtracking Giannakopoulos snuck in to steal the ball away. It was most likely an intervention that few would remember. The plays that generally stick in the memory from big matches are the goals or saves that usually define them. Giannakopoulos' play was one that had become second nature to all the Greek players. When a teammate was beat, someone else was supposed to cover. It sounds simple, yet it takes an immense amount of work to get every individual on board.

Maybe Giannakopoulos' excellent covering was lost in the shuffle because seconds later, the play that would become the defining moment of the match, the tournament, and Greek football history occurred. Fyssas dispossessed Figo and passed to Giannakopoulos. He dribbled forward and cut back for Basinas, who was waiting just behind midfield. Superb awareness from the Greek midfielder saw him switch the attack to the streaking Seitaridis, all alone on the right. Seitaridis' magnificent control kept the ball in play. He reached the byline and attempted a cross that was blocked out by Ronaldo for a corner.

Basinas trudged toward the ball. The match had reached the 57th minute. Basinas struck his corner well. Vryzas was occupying Carvalho in the box. Charisteas beat Costinha to Basinas' ball and headed downward toward the goal. Ricardo had come halfway, realizing too late that he was in a goalkeeper's no man's land. Charisteas' header landed into the empty net. Greece had scored to take the lead against Portugal, again.

Charisteas ran back up the pitch to celebrate, revealing an undershirt that many viewers assumed featured a picture of his son. It was actually a photo of his two-year-old nephew. Charisteas had asked his sister to send a shirt with her son's image on it. It was delivered to Portugal and Charisteas had said it would be his lucky shirt. And so it proved.

The celebrations inside the stadium and for Greeks the world over had not yet been quelled when Ronaldo shot wildly wide after the restart. It was a reminder that there was lots of time remaining in the game. Greece threatened again as Zagorakis' accurate diagonal ball for Giannakopoulos saw him head across the goalmouth. Ricardo grabbed the ball at the last second in front of an expecting Katsouranis.

Greece's goal immediately saw Scolari send on Rui Costa for Costinha. Portugal began to throw everything forward. Ronaldo found space to shoot again, this team unleashing a blistering drive that Nikopolidis did well to push away. Portugal, forced to reshuffle their formation and send players up the pitch, left bigger gaps at the back. Greece found space to counter and Zagorakis released Vryzas into a dangerous area, but his cross was cleared away.

It was Portugal though who were threatening in a more consistent manner. Rui Costa nearly made an instant impact, dribbling into the area and sending in a teasing cross that had no recipient. Deco fired over a free-kick before an uncharacteristic error from Kapsis saw his clearance land at the feet of Figo. His low, hard shot was smothered by Nikopolidis. Zagorakis' delightful scoop pass for Katsouranis was crossed into the box where Giannakopoulos arrived just a fraction of a second late to pounce on.

The action continued at breakneck pace. Fyssas slid through on Figo late earning a yellow. Portugal's pressure showed no signs of stopping. Kapsis came through with two clutch clearances. Then came three successive Portuguese corners. The hosts were turning the screw by this point, a goal looking possible at any instant. Kapsis and Dellas were first to every ball into the box. Another corner was given up as Charisteas had come all the way back to clear a ball at the back post.

As much as Greece were playing with their backs to the wall, it was if they relished the situation. While they struggled to keep possession and relieve some of the tension they faced by holding the ball, there was never a sign of panic.

"One problem was that Portugal thought that everything would be solved sooner or later. It was clearly a bad move," analyzes Cristovao. "Portugal may have focused too much on the way they wanted to play and in the process forgot to look at Greece and how they could exploit their weaknesses."

Scolari made his final substitution by inserting Nuno Gomes for Pauleta in the 74th minute. In the twenty minutes following the goal, Portugal played their best football of the night. They were creating opportunities from the flanks and with fast ball movement through the midfield. The hosts were also using their individual skill to cause problems for the Greek backline. Failure to score in that period of the game saw the belief in an equalizer slowly seep out of the team. The evidence of this was in the way Portugal attacked as the match entered its final stages. Speculative crosses were sent into the box as the ideas ran out. It was more hit and hope rather than organized moves from Scolari's men.

Ronaldo broke the offside trap in one promising attack, however, the onrushing Nikopolidis forced him to hurry his shot and he blazed over. On the next play, Figo won a series of challenges and crossed, but Nikopolidis, 'the Greek George Clooney' as he had been nicknamed for his striking resemblance to the Hollywood actor, showed safe hands. Nikopolidis continued his fine goalkeeping performance with a difficult stop in traffic to hold on to a Nuno Valente cross.

Rehhagel had taken off Giannakopoulos in the 76th minute and put Venetidis into the game. Rui Costa's entrance had pushed Deco to the right for Portugal. Venetidis was trying to offer help to fellow left-back Fyssas on that flank as he tried to deal with Deco and Figo.

Papadopoulos replaced the tireless Vryzas with nine minutes to go as Greece wanted a fresh striker to be able to hit on the counter-attack. Portugal came close when Carvalho took a thunderous shot from outside the box. Nikopolidis saw it late through a great deal of traffic, but made the save. With four minutes to go, the match was interrupted by a pitch invader. Jimmy Jump would become notorious for interfering in high-profile sporting and entertainment events. He ran onto the field, threw a Barcelona flag at Figo and proceeded to jump into the Greek goal before being tackled by security.

Portugal picked up where they left before the interruption. Katsouranis did well to break up Nuno Gomes' intended pass for Figo. The latter then received the ball, turned quickly, and shot agonizingly wide. Not long after, Andrade headed over after the Greek defense had blocked the initial shot.

The game was well into injury-time as the Greek national anthem was being belted out in the stadium. The Portuguese players, probably sensing that time was now their biggest enemy, began to commit a series of needless fouls, many in their offensive end. By the time Valente had earned a yellow for a foul on Zagorakis, there was what amounted to an air of acceptance that permeated the stadium. Greece were going to win. That was confirmed moments later as Merk blew his whistle three times to signal the end.

At first, the once-divided underachievers had morphed into a decent side. Coming to Portugal they were still considered no-hopers by anyone who had bothered to take a look at them. Now, they had transformed into European champions. Greece had achieved the impossible.

For commentator Kostas Vernikos, the victory capped off a surreal few weeks. "At one point, I stopped taking notes and I commentated standing up. Cameras from other foreign channels were taping us during the broadcast to record our reactions during the game. Everything during the game went beautifully. I understood at the moment that I carried the joy and pride of an entire ethnicity and I tried to respond as best as I could. I tried to say the things I would want to hear if I was watching the game back home, with of course the intensity that every Greek felt, but not forgetting that football was still just a beautiful game," a reminiscing Vernikos recalls.

To say the celebrations after the final whistle were epic would be an understatement. Players simply did not know where to go or what to do. There was a beautiful chaos as some hugged each other, some celebrated with the Greeks in the stands, while others sat alone accompanied by their own smiles and tears. "After the whistle there was indescribable river of joy and happiness. The scenes were unbelievable. Rolling around the field like little children. Players carrying teammates on their backs. The feelings were incredible and overwhelming. If you are not able to live it like we did, it is very difficult to describe it," remember Dabizas. The Prime Minister of Greece, Kostas Karamanlis, and the EPO President Gagatsis, both clearly emotional, celebrated from the VIP seats. The crowd cheered, switching between the "Sikose To" chant and "Natoi, Natoi, oi Protathlites (Here are, Here are, the Champions)."

Ronaldo's tears became an iconic image as did those of Eusebio as he prepared to present Zagorakis with the Henri Delaunay trophy. The Portuguese side honorably accepted their runners-up medals on the podium. They were saluted by their disappointed, but appreciative countrymen. "There was huge sadness obviously following the final," says Kundert. "There was a feeling that it was probably Portugal's best chance to win a major trophy and having missed this opportunity the Selecao would probably never win a tournament. That said, there was pride in how the tournament had been organized and in Portugal's performance on a more general level."

After Scolari and Rehhagel shared an embrace, the Greek players took to the stage. In the midst of their happiness must have been a feeling of disbelief that undoubtedly all Greeks felt. Zagorakis went last and when handed the cup turned lifted it toward the perfect Lisbon sky. Then he turned and faced his teammates and hoisted it up it once again. This was a moment that belonged to these coaches and players.

Epilogue

The distance between Athens Airport and the Panathenaic Stadium, or Kallimarmaro as it is known, is 30 kilometers. Roughly, it's a 35 minute drive. When the Greek national team arrived back home on 5 July, a day after the final, the plan was to go from the airport by bus to a celebration at the historic stadium, which was first constructed in 144 AD. The trip took nearly three hours. Ecstatic Greeks lined the entire route, the bus needing to stop completely as it reached deeper into Athens as the crowds were so thick there was no way through. 110,000 people squeezed into the 45,000 capacity stadium to celebrate the most unlikeliest of sporting successes. As the music bounced between famous Queen hits, *We Will Rock You* and *We Are The Champions*, to Mikis Theodorakis' compositions, his famous *Zorba* and the song he specifically composed for the Ethniki, there was absolute delirium as Zagorakis, Rehhagel and other members of the team spoke to the crowd. When Zagorakis lifted the trophy, there might have been a real worry about whether the stadium, made entirely of marble, could withstand the earth-shaking roar let out by those reveling in an achievement they would have never dreamt of.

On 14 November 2014, Joan Edmundsson's goal gave the Faroe Islands an improbable win away to Greece in a Euro 2016 qualifier. The defeat was cited by the Guardian as quite possibly the greatest upset in the history of the FIFA Rankings, Greece at the time were 18th and the Faroes figured toward the bottom at 187th.

A few months before, Greece had advanced to the Round of 16 at the 2014 World Cup in Brazil. A last-gasp Georgios Samaras penalty in the final Group

Stage match against the Ivory Coast saw Greece win 2-1, leap-frogging the African side into second place and earning a knockout round berth. Against Costa Rica in the following match, the Ethniki went down 1-0, but fought back to level the score in injury-time with a dramatic goal from Sokratis Papastathopoulos. After missing several chances to put away the 10-man Ticos in extra-time, Greece went to penalties for the first time in team history. Theofanis Gekas' miss from the spot proved decisive as the team went out, while the surprising Costa Rica side moved on.

That defeat marked the end of an era that began with Otto Rehhagel's appointment in August 2001. From then until 2014, the Ethniki consistently participated in major tournaments in what became the golden age of the national team. While Rehhagel failed to lead his team to the 2006 World Cup, Greece participated in the 2005 Confederations Cup and qualified for Euro 2008 and the 2010 World Cup under his watchful eye. During the 2010 World Cup, the team were knocked out in the first round, but a 2-1 win over Nigeria gave Greece its first ever victory in the competition. At the end of that World Cup, Rehhagel stepped down as manager of the national team. It seemed like the end of an era.

Rehhagel's successor was Fernando Santos, a Portuguese coach who like Rehhagel, had tons of experience managing at club level. Also like Rehhagel, Santos was a pragmatist. Keeping the disciplined system that he inherited from the German, Santos also kept Greece playing a more defensive game and placed his faith with a core group. That familiarity saw Greece continue to find success at the international level. Santos was the man who led Greece to the last sixteen in 2014 and two years earlier he oversaw the Ethniki's trip to the quarter-finals of Euro 2012, before they lost to Germany 4-2.

The end of the Rehhagel period and all throughout the time of Santos had Greece consistently hovering around the top 10 of the FIFA Rankings, rising as high as eighth on a couple of occasions. For all the fault of the rankings over the years, the fact that Rehhagel took a team that was ranked 57th when he arrived and brought them into the top 10 puts into context what he was able to achieve. And Santos, building upon the foundations laid down by Rehhagel, deserves great credit for succeeding in keeping Greece amongst the top teams in Europe and the world for that matter until he left in July 2014.

For 13 years, the Greek national team experienced an era of unparalleled achievement. Claudio Ranieri's appointment following Santos' departure was supposed to continue that run. It did not. The Italian boss surely had a hand in the blame for that. There was more to the story however. Changes at the top of the EPO ushered in a new group of individuals running the Greek game. Suddenly, there were whispers of power plays, and of officials attempting to influence squad selections. An early defeat against Romania in the Euro 2016 qualifiers was a blow. An uncertain side began to emerge in the following matches and the off-the-pitch problems began to manifest. The loss to the Faroes was an example of how easily something that took so long to build can be dismantled so quickly. The return to the issues that plagued the team in the past had a disastrous effect on the Ethniki. Further embarrassments followed. A second defeat to the Faroes in the reverse fixture along with a friendly loss to Luxembourg. Ranieri had long since been sacked. It did not matter. These were historical issues that could not be fixed solely by changing the manager. The meddling in team affairs by outsiders, infighting, and questions of player commitment had all returned. Without Rehhagel, without Santos, and with the retirement of the last of the "2004ers" in Karagounis and Katsouranis after the 2014 World Cup, the ties to a different era had been cut. The Ethniki morphed back into what it had historically been.

One explanation for the return to below par results and team dynamics of the past is certainly that as time wore on, all of the players and coaches in that Euro 2004 team began ending their careers. Another reason why a new dawn of Greek football was never seen after the Euro victory was the lack of strategic planning and resources that were put into the game. The opportunity to build the sport after winning Euro 2004, to effect real change and create a healthy environment in which it could prosper was squandered. There was no focus on building the game so that the amazing success of 2004 could someday be repeated. "For Greece to win a championship like this again is very difficult. It will not be easy to replicate what we did in 2004. We have gone back to the point where we are not even qualifying for big tournaments. In order for it to happen or for us to even dream about it happening the foundations of our game need to be improved," says Karagounis. Greece's all-time leader in international appearances began his career with the youth national teams as a teenager. His experience offers a unique insight of someone who has gone through the whole Greek national team system, one that he believes needs lots of support and investment to help the country develop players. "The foundations for developing players to begin with and then the ways in which we bring them along needs improvement, as does the entire infrastructure of Greek football. We still lack a serious national league where young players can be developed properly. Unfortunately, in Greece we are beginning at zero with such things. We may be the worst in Europe with regard to these matters. We had a difficult economic crisis, where little investment was made in football. Even so, others who want to have no idea how to invest in Greek football in order to make a difference. The political establishments have also offered little help. All of this together creates an environment where we cannot expect much from the national team unless big changes are made."

* * * *

At club level, major shocks and underdogs winning titles in football leagues across the world are relatively commonplace. Even at the highest level. Leicester winning the 2015/16 English Premier League is possibly the biggest surprise in the history of the modern game. Unfancied teams achieving similar feats are well documented.

In international football, smaller sides winning major competitions are a rarity. Before 2004, the first example that most would point to was Denmark winning Euro 1992. It was a spectacular achievement by a team that were officially included in the competition just ten days before their opening match. The breakout of civil war in Yugoslavia meant the country was barred from competing in the tournament. Denmark were installed as replacements. With barely a week to prepare and most players literally coming off the beach from their summer holidays, Denmark finished second to hosts Sweden in Group A, ahead of France and England. A semi-final date with the defending champions Netherlands followed and the Danes emerged victorious on penalty-kicks. In the final against Germany, the momentum of Richard Moller Nielsen's men was too much and after a 2-0 victory, Denmark were champions.

While Denmark's win was unexpected, it did not exactly come out of nowhere. This was a team with fantastic individual talent such as Peter Schmeichel and Brian Laudrup. Denmark also had a previous history of success at major tournaments. 1992 was their fourth European Championship, and there were fine tournament performances in 1964 (fourth place) and 1984 (semi-finals). Six years earlier, Denmark had reached the Round of 16 at the 1986 World Cup. The country had also succeeded in producing big-name European players. Besides Schmeichel and the Laudrup brothers (Michael and Brian), Denmark could also point to top-class players such as Preben Elkjaer, Morten

Olsen, Jesper Olsen, and Jan Molby amongst others.

Greece never possessed the history or football pedigree of a nation like Denmark. Their victory truly was one no one could have ever logically predicted. It was the result of a perfect storm. The right manager came in at the right time with the right group of players. You work with what you have in international football. What did Rehhagel realize he had? A group of talented players, amongst the best Greece ever had, who had underachieved for their country. Rehhagel could then use his strengths of instilling discipline, organization, and motivation to create a battling team.

Accusations of anti-football were levied against Rehhagel and his players as they progressed through the tournament and ultimately won it. This had a tendency to annoy Greek supporters, but those comprising the Ethniki would not have been bothered in the least. "Without being incredibly entertaining, we instead showed determination, fighting spirit, and intelligence. We possessed a footballing intelligence you must have to play and defeat opponents who have more quality and are theoretically better than you," reasons Dabizas. Katergiannakis points to an instance when Rehhagel laid matters out plainly. "I remember Mr. Rehhagel answering a reporter's question back then about how we played. These are the weapons I have he said, that's the way I play. If I had Germany or England I would play differently. The funny thing is that so many top, modern sides have played that style of football over time."

What then was the secret to this miracle on the pitch? Again Dabizas, the unlucky center-back, who never made the pitch during Euro 2004, perfectly sums up how Greece managed to accomplish what they did. "It was a group of 23 lads, together with the coaches, that were one. A team in the proper sense of the word. There was never a "me", but only "us". And that was hugely important. We were a very tight and united group, which is difficult for 23 different personalities. As I said before, we put the "I" way, way down and it was the "us" that we focused on."

Dabizas' teammates agreed. "We were a team with capital letters. There was no one, absolutely no one, no matter the name, and there were a lot of big names in that team, who considered themselves above the team," states Giannakopoulos. Unity, teamwork, and selflessness were undoubtedly big factors, but so was the presence of quality. "It was not only that we had a good team, the individuals we had were also very good. We possessed quality players, many at a very good footballing age, who all had big personalities. Everything altogether combined to make it happen," believes Karagounis. His assertion is that it all started with a golden generation of players. "Simply, sometimes we do not rate how good the individual players in that side were. People talk about luck or everything gets put down to being united and our teamwork. Teamwork was exceptionally important, but it also had to do with the high level of the players and coaches and their characters too."

Accusations of anti-football be damned, for millions of Greek fans, Euro 2004 was a beautiful dream. It was a magical time when footballing logic was defied. Karagounis described the celebrations following the victory over Portugal as like "being in a different world." This held true for all the Ethniki supporters around the globe. Celebrating on that day was a surreal feeling. It proved that occasionally in sport and in life that not only can the unexpected occur, but in rare instances the impossible can too. Otto Rehhagel, Ioannis Topalidis, and a special group of Greek footballers proved that at the 2004 European Championship in Portugal. Regardless of whether another national side will ever be able to achieve a similar feat, that 2004 Greek side will always be remembered for pulling off a sporting miracle, the likes of which there are few in history to rival it.

Acknowledgements

If you find this book in your hands or on your device it's mainly down to the work of the good people at Fair Play Publishing and publisher Bonita Mersiades. Her initial interest in this idea and her corresponding guidance and advice was crucial in allowing this project to come to fruition. Thank you Bonita!

In researching this book, several colleagues have been instrumental in providing information and views on the Greek national team and their opponents. My sincerest thanks to Aritz Gabilondo, Artur Petrosyan, Adrien Mathieu, Jean-Julien Beer, Luis Cristovao, Michal Petrak, Tom Kundert, Sotiris Triantafyllou, and Kostas Vernikos.

The likes of Athanasios Demetrakopoulos, Pantelis Tigas, Kevin Hatchard, Alex Politis, Ellie Melachroinidou, Alexey Spectre, Abdellah Boulma, and Graham Wood were essential in providing additional information and helping to track down important contacts. Thank you so much to all.

My deep gratitude to Sarantos Kaperonis and the crew at AGONAsport. com. Sarantos and his wonderful site have been instrumental in helping to support this book from its inception.

I have been so fortunate to speak to several members of the Euro 2004 winning side, including players, coaches, and officials. Thank you Giorgos Karagounis, Stelios Giannakopoulos, Kostas Katsouranis, Nikos Dabizas, Fanis Katergiannakis, Ioannis Topalidis, and Vasilis Gagatsis for the time that you gave and the experiences you relayed. Their stories provided an incredible first-hand account of a remarkable sporting tale and this book is greatly enhanced by their contributions.

On a more personal level there are many others I would like to acknowledge. My love of the game of football comes from my dad. That love became a passion thanks to the experiences shared with those I have played, coached, or analyzed the game with. Many thanks to my dear friends, the Matchfield crew from Walpole, New Hampshire and my family members and friends from Pefkofyto, Greece, where we played the game on the church square during many endless summers.

Many thanks to the editors and writers who gave me the incredible opportunity to write about football over the years, especially Stewart Coggin, Graham Lister, John Iannantuono, Engel Schmidl, Angela Asante, Phillip Buckley, Paul Hendren, and Alfons Rubbens. Two teachers who have had a great influence on me are Robert Grenier and Bill Ranuaro. I thank you both very much.

Special thanks to my in-laws, Charles and Janyce St. Pierre. You not only raised an amazing daughter and family, but you show your goodness every day and that has had a profound effect on how I live my life.

All my love and thanks for the support offered to me throughout my life by the St. Pierre, Lakin, Putnam, Diamantis, Ioannou, Demetrakopoulos, and Tsitsonis families.

In the beginning, you have your own family. Luckily, I was blessed with a wonderful one. As Greek immigrants to the United States, my parents, like so many others, did not have it easy. Elias and Lambrini Tsitsonis carved out a life for themselves in a foreign land, having a family and eventually starting their own business. There were times when days off, were not weeks, but months, apart. They showed me the worth of hard work and the importance of family. If I have done anything remotely decent with my life it is because of the path they worked so tirelessly to open for me. I am indebted for all you have given us. Sas agapo.

Thanks to my sister and best friend, Athanasia (Soula). We've been inseparable since day one. She has often been my editor, not only in writing, but in life. I have often been the subject of some world-class sarcasm from her over the years, but mostly she has been an unbelievable, lifelong source of support, advice, and love. I love you Chim.

Finally, to my wife Sheila and children, Mariella and Elias. Thank you for your patience, understanding, and support throughout the entire process of writing this book. I love you three more than you could ever know. Mariella and Elias, my heart bursts with pride seeing the people you have become, you are my greatest joys. Sheila, you are the most perfect travel partner in this journey of life. Your love motivates me to look forward to every single day. Gia panta.

Bibliography

Books

Ahlstrom, Frits. FANBOOK - UEFA EURO 2004 Official Programme. UEFA and EURO 2004 S.A., 2004.

Asimakopoulos, Nikos. Zito to Elliniko Podosfairo. Taksideftis, 2014.

Bomis, Andreas. Afti einai i istoria tis Ethnikis Elladas. Ekdoseis Erechtheias, 2009

Chrysochoidis, Thomas. 29 meres ston Paradeiso. Action Images, 2004.

Gagatsis, Vasilis. EURO 2004 - I alithini istoria opos tin ezisa, Ekdoseis Topos, 2010

Glanville, Brian. The Story of the World Cup. Faber and Faber, 2014.

Georgakopoulos, G., Giannatos, S., Gougas, G., Dimitroulas, L., Ladopoulos, M., Liggris, G., and Triantafyllou, S. Gia Panta Protathlites - Ethniki Omada Podosfairou. Skai Biblio, 2009.

Goldblatt, David. The Ball Is Round - A Global History of Soccer. Riverhead Books, 2006.

Goldblatt, David. Soccer Yearbook 2004/5. Dorling Kindersley, 2004.

Mamouzelos, Giannis and Thodoros Davelos. 100 Hronia Ethniki Elladas. AGYRA, 2007.

Koutos, Christos. Ethniki Elladas, geia sou: I poreia pros tin kataktisi tou EURO 2004. Ekdoseis Iliotropio, 2004.

Kuntze, Norbert. Otto Rehhagel: To protreto enos idiofuous proponiti. Trans. Stefan Mitman. Empiria Publications, 2004.

Radnedge, Keir. The Ultimate Encylopedia of Soccer. Carlton Publishing Group, 2006.

Tsakiris, Dimitris, et al. Elliniko Podosfairo 2002-2003. Ekdoseis Athlotypo, 2003.

Tsakiris, Dimitris, Pallis, Kostas, and Sahtouris, Pavlos. Elliniko Podosfairo 2003-2004. Ekdoseis Athlotypo.

Wilson, Jonathan. Inverting The Pyramid. Orion Books, 2009.

Xenidis, Giorgos. Stadia.gr Ellinika Gipeda Podosfairou. Athlotypo, 2006.

Magazines/Newspapers

FourFourTwo	The Irish Times	To Vima
World Soccer	Evening Standard	Goal News
Soccer International	The Telegraph	Sportime
Der Tagesspiegel	The Times	Sport Day
Inside SOCCER	The New York Times	TA NEA
FIFA magazine	The Daily Mail	Active
The Guardian	Greek Press	
The Independent	I Kathemerini	

Websites

Agonasport.com	Onsports.gr	NovaSports.gr
BBC.com	Sport-retro.gr	Zonalmarking.com
CNN.gr	Sport24.gr	Ekathermerini.com
EPO.gr	Contra.gr	Uefa.com
ESPNFC.com	Gazzetta.gr	
in.gr	Skai.gr	

Other really good football books from Fair Play Publishing

The Time of
My Football Life
by David Picken

Surfing for England
Our Lost Socceroos
by Jason Goldsmith

Encyclopedia of Matildas
by Andrew Howe
and Greg Werner

Encyclopedia of Socceroos
by Andrew Howe

'If I Started to Cry,
I Wouldn't Stop'
by Matthew Hall

The A-Z of Socceroos -
World Cup Edition 2018
by Andrew Howe (with Ray
Gatt and Bonita Mersiades)

Playing for Australia
The First Socceroos,
Asia and the World Game
by Trevor Thompson

The World Cup Chronicles
31 Days that Rocked Brazil
by Jorge Knijnik

Chronicles of Soccer
in Australia - The
Foundation Years 1859 to
1949 by Peter Kunz

Support Your Local League,
A South-East Asian
Football Odyssey by
Antony Sutton

The Aboriginal Soccer Tribe
by John Maynard

Whatever It Takes - The
Inside Story of the FIFA
Way by Bonita Mersiades
(Powderhouse Press)

The Australian Youth
Footballer Regulatory Guide
by Peter Paleologos
(Popcorn Press)

Introducing
Jarrod Black
by Texi Smith
(Popcorn Press)

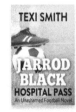

Jarrod Black
Hospital Pass
by Texi Smith
(Popcorn Press)

Jarrod Black
Guilty Party
by Texi Smith
(Popcorn Press)

www.fairplaypublishing.com.au/shop

FAIRPLAY

PUBLISHING